Exploring World Englishes

'This is an insightful and multilayered volume which provides a clear and concise introduction to world Englishes' approaches to both research and pedagogy.'

Kingsley Bolton, *City University of Hong Kong*

Routledge Introductions to Applied Linguistics is a series of introductory level textbooks covering the core topics in Applied Linguistics, primarily designed for those beginning postgraduate studies or taking an introductory MA course, as well as advanced undergraduates. Titles in the series are also ideal for language professionals returning to academic study.

The books take an innovative 'practice-to-theory' approach, with a 'back-to-front' structure. This leads the reader from real-world problems and issues, through a discussion of intervention and how to engage with these concerns, before finally relating these practical issues to theoretical foundations. Additional features include tasks with commentaries, a glossary of key terms, and an annotated further reading section.

In this book Philip Seargeant surveys varieties of English existing within the world today, and the debates and controversies surrounding its present forms, functions and status in diverse world contexts. It examines how English has evolved to become a 'global language' and looks at the political and cultural history that has influenced this evolution.

Beginning with a discussion of real-life challenges relating to world Englishes that are faced by language professionals – particularly in the contexts of language education and language planning – the book explores and illustrates the ways in which the actual use and management of English, as well as the beliefs and ideologies associated with it, play an increasingly important role in contemporary globalized society.

Philip Seargeant is Lecturer in Applied Linguistics at The Open University, UK. He is the author of *The Idea of English in Japan*, editor of *English in Japan in the Era of Globalization* and co-editor of *English in the World: History, Diversity, Change* (with Joan Swann, Routledge and The Open University, 2012).

Routledge Introductions to Applied Linguistics

Series editors:

Ronald Carter, *Professor of Modern English Language, University of Nottingham, UK*

Guy Cook, *King's College London*

Routledge Introductions to Applied Linguistics is a series of introductory level textbooks covering the core topics in Applied Linguistics, primarily designed for those entering postgraduate studies and language professionals returning to academic study. The books take an innovative 'practice-to-theory' approach, with a 'back-to-front' structure. This leads the reader from real-world problems and issues, through a discussion of intervention and how to engage with these concerns, before finally relating these practical issues to theoretical foundations. Additional features include tasks with commentaries, a glossary of key terms and an annotated further reading section.

Exploring English Language Teaching
Language in Action
Graham Hall

Exploring Classroom Discourse
Language in Action
Steve Walsh

Exploring Corpus Linguistics
Language in Action
Winnie Cheng

'The innovative approach devised by the series editors will make this series very attractive to students, teacher educators, and even to a general readership, wanting to explore and understand the field of applied linguistics. The volumes in this series take as their starting point the everyday professional problems and issues that applied linguists seek to illuminate. The volumes are authoritatively written, using an engaging 'back-to-front' structure that moves from practical interests to the conceptual bases and theories that underpin applications of practice.'

Anne Burns, *Aston University, UK,*
University of New South Wales, Australia

Exploring World Englishes

Language in a Global Context

Philip Seargeant

 Routledge
Taylor & Francis Group

LONDON AND NEW YORK

First published 2012
by Routledge
2 Park Square, Milton Park, Abingdon, Oxon OX14 4RN

Simultaneously published in the USA and Canada
by Routledge
711 Third Avenue, New York, NY 10017

Routledge is an imprint of the Taylor & Francis Group, an informa business

British Library Cataloguing in Publication Data
A catalogue record for this book is available from the British Library

Library of Congress Cataloging in Publication Data
A catalog record for this book has been requested

ISBN: 978–0-415–57209–5 (hbk)
ISBN: 978–0-415–57210–1 (pbk)
ISBN: 978–0-203- 11551–0 (ebk)

Typeset in Sabon
by Saxon Graphics Ltd, Derby

Printed and bound in Great Britain by the MPG Books Group

Contents

Figures

Series editors' introduction

The Introducing Applied Linguistics series

This series provides clear, authoritative, up-to-date overviews of the major areas of applied linguistics. The books are designed particularly for students embarking on masters-level or teacher-education courses, as well as students in the closing stages of undergraduate study. The practical focus will make the books particularly useful and relevant to those returning to academic study after a period of professional practice, and also to those about to leave the academic world for the challenges of language-related work. For students who have not previously studied applied linguistics, including those who are unfamiliar with current academic study in English speaking universities, the books can act as one-step introductions. For those with more academic experience, they can also provide a way of surveying, updating and organising existing knowledge.

The view of applied linguistics in this series follows a famous definition of the field by Christopher Brumfit as:

> The theoretical and empirical investigation of real-world problems in which language is a central issue.
>
> (Brumfit 1995: 27)

In keeping with this broad problem-oriented view, the series will cover a range of topics of relevance to a variety of language related professions. While language teaching and learning rightly remain prominent and will be the central preoccupation of many readers, our conception of the discipline is by no means limited to these areas. Our view is that while each reader of the series will have their own needs, specialities and interests, there is also much to be gained from a broader view of the discipline as a whole. We believe there is much in common between all enquiries into language related problems in the real world, and much to be gained from a comparison of the insights from one area of applied linguistics with another. Our hope therefore is that readers and course designers will not choose only those volumes relating to their own particular interests, but use this series to construct a wider knowledge and understanding of the field, and the many cross-overs and resonances between its various areas. Thus the topics to be covered are wide in range, embracing an exciting mixture of established and new areas of applied linguistic enquiry.

The perspective on applied linguistics in this series

In line with this problem-oriented definition of the field, and to address the concerns of readers who are interested in how academic study can inform their own professional practice, each book follows a structure in marked contrast to the usual movement from theory to practice. In this series, this usual progression is presented back to front. The argument moves from Problems, through Intervention, and only finally to Theory. Thus each topic begins with a survey of everyday professional problems in the area under consideration, ones which the reader is likely to have encountered. From there it proceeds to a discussion of intervention and engagement with these problems. Only in a final section (either of the chapter or the book as a whole) does the author reflect upon the implications of this engagement for a general understanding of language, drawing out the theoretical implications. We believe this to be a truly applied linguistics perspective, in line with definition given above, and one in which engagement with real-world problems is the distinctive feature, and in which professional practice can both inform and draw upon academic understanding.

Support to the reader

Although it is not the intention that the text should be in anyway activity-driven, the pedagogic process is supported by measured guidance to the reader in the form of suggested activities and tasks that raise questions, prompt reflection and seek to integrate theory and practice. Each book also contains a helpful glossary of key terms.

The series complements and reflects the Routledge Handbook of Applied Linguistics edited by James Simpson, which conceives and categorises the scope of applied linguistics in a broadly similar way.

Ronald Carter
Guy Cook

Reference

Brumfit, C.J. (1995) Teacher professionalism and research. In G. Cook and B. Seidlhofer (eds) *Principle and Practice in Applied Linguistics*. Oxford: Oxford University Press, pp. 27–42.

Note

There is a section of commentaries on a number of the tasks, at the back of the book from p. 180. The (TC) symbol in the margin indicates that there is a commentary on that task.

Acknowledgements

I would like to gratefully acknowledge the assistance and support of the following people in the preparation of this book: Guy Cook, Ron Carter, Barbara Mayor, Kieran O'Halloran, Lionel Wee, as well as Louisa Semlyen and Sophic Jaqucs from Routledge. Earlier versions of certain sections of the book have appeared in the following articles: 'Naming and defining in World Englishes' (2010) *World Englishes*, 29:1, pp. 99–115 (with kind permission of Blackwell Publishing); 'Lexicography as a philosophy of language' (2011) *Language Sciences*, 33:1, pp. 1–10 (with kind permission of Elsevier); and 'Disciplinarity and the study of world Englishes' (2012) *World Englishes*, 31:1, pp. 113–29 (with kind permission of Blackwell Publishing).

Poem by Aig-Imoukhuede, F. (1982) *Pidgin Stew and Sufferhead*. Ibadan: Heinemann Educational Books. Reproduced with permission from Heinemann Educational Books.

Poem by Nissim Ezekiel (1989) *Latter-day Psalms*, Oxford University Press, pp. 22–5. Reproduced by permission of Oxford University Press India, New Delhi.

Every effort has been made to seek permission to reproduce copyright material before the book went to press. If any proper acknowledgement has not been made, we would invite the copyright holders to inform us of the oversight.

General introduction

English as an object of study

This book is about English in the world today. It is about the nature and character of English around the world, but also about the debates and controversies surrounding the language: debates and controversies concerning the forms, functions and status the language has in diverse world contexts. For although it is a seemingly straightforward statement to say that the book will survey the existence of English around the world, such a statement presupposes that we know what we mean when we talk of 'English'. It presupposes that English, as an object of study, is a clearly definable entity that exists out there in the world, and that people (speakers, learners, teachers, academics) have a mostly solid and mutually compatible understanding of what constitutes this entity.

This is far from being the case, however. Disputes about what counts as English – what constitutes proper English, what role the language does or should play in various contexts, and how it should be evaluated and regulated – are legion. A key intention of this book, therefore, is to provide clarification of what exactly is meant by the concept of English, as it is understood both by the millions of people who use or work with the language and by the large body of scholars who study it. The book is about English in the world today and the roles it plays, as both code and concept, in the lives of a global population.

Concerns about how exactly the object of study (i.e. 'English') should be conceptualised can be seen in the proliferation of names used to refer to the language (e.g. American English, Singaporean English, Nigerian English, etc). This book, following a tradition that has emerged in the last two or three decades, opts for the plural noun *Englishes*, thereby suggesting that in the modern world, the language needs to be viewed not as a single, monolithic entity, but as something that has multiple varieties and forms. The use of this term is motivated by an attitude which argues that it is no longer accurate to say that there is just one 'English' in existence around the world – but that instead we need to begin our investigation from the perspective that diversity is the norm, and that the multiple forms the language takes are, each and every one, both linguistically and sociologically interesting. As Braj Kachru writes: "The result of [the language's global] spread is that, formally and functionally, English now has multicultural identities. The term 'English' does not capture this sociolinguistic reality; the term 'Englishes' does" (Kachru, 1992b, p. 357).

Some scholars suggest that an even more radical re-baptising is necessary; that the language previously known as 'English' should be renamed completely, and be called, for example, something such as 'Global' (Toolan, 1997), 'Englic' (Suzuki, 1975) or 'Globish' (Nerrière, 2006; McCrum, 2010). By suggesting such alternatives, these scholars are arguing that the language as it is used at a global level is now significantly different from the one which developed on the British mainland and came to have the status of national language in England and the United Kingdom. They are arguing that this difference is such that the language needs to be rebranded; that its history should no longer play a determining role in its current or future existence, and so the ties with the past need to be symbolically severed.

These and related issues will be discussed in greater detail later in the book. For the time being, the relevant point is that in studying the English language today we need to pay attention not solely to the forms it takes in different geographical, cultural and social settings, but also to the beliefs that adhere to these different forms, and to the concepts of the language which result from these beliefs.

Why, though, is the issue of what is understood as 'English' – and the nature of the various beliefs which coalesce to produce this understanding – of any particular importance? Why should debate about the language matter for a study of the existence and nature of the language? The simple answer is that these beliefs have serious and far-reaching consequences for its use and perception in society. Language operates as a vital resource in society, both in terms of its communicative affordances (what we are able to do through the use of it) and as a marker of identity and a means of social distinction. It is beliefs about the language that play a large part in the way that the value of this resource is determined, and that it is distributed amongst the population. In other words, beliefs about the language have a causal relationship with the way that people are able to effectively use the language. The study of English in the world today is thus both a linguistic issue and a political one.

Disciplinary approaches and linguistic globalisation

Issues concerning what is understood as 'English' are also of central importance for the disciplines that study the language. Today, English is in an unprecedented linguistic position in that it is more widely used, and in more domains, than any other language across the globe. And this pervasiveness – and the diversity that accompanies it – is forcing a recalibration of basic notions of the relationship of language to everyday lived experience. In other words, the way the language is used, the way it is perceived, and the way it is regulated, is so qualitatively different from the circumstances of other languages that it is forcing a rethink about some of the fundamental axioms of modern linguistics. The nature of contemporary English is obliging the discipline to take into consideration issues and dynamics – particularly of a social nature – to which it has previously been mostly oblivious. And so, over the last two decades, the discipline of English language studies has increasingly had to adopt an approach which, by default, takes account of the language's increasingly global character. In short, globalisation has become the point of orientation for all discussions of the language: English today exhibits the trace of globalisation in all aspects of its identity – from the varieties and forms it takes, through the functions it is put to, to the attitudes people have towards it. For this reason *linguistic globalisation* becomes a key theoretical framework within which to view practically all social issues related to the use of the language.

English in the world today is thus a fertile area for the theoretical investigation of the use and nature of natural language, and the research and theoretical investigations being pursued in this field are having implications for the discipline of linguistics in general. In addition, the unprecedented position that English now occupies brings with it new *practical* challenges – challenges both for those who use the language as part of their everyday life, and for language professionals whose job revolves around English. It is within this context that this book initially approaches its subject. The book examines how English has evolved to become a 'global language' and looks at the political and cultural history that has influenced this evolution. Beginning with a discussion of real-life challenges relating to World Englishes that are faced by language professionals, this book explores and illustrates the ways in which the actual use and management of English, as well as the beliefs and ideologies associated with it, play an increasingly important role in contemporary globalised society. In taking this approach, the book both surveys the formal nature and functional existence of English in the world, while also looking at how an examination of World Englishes provides insights about the interplay between the language and everyday social existence.

Beginning with the evidence

The structure of this book is one which begins with the evidence and works outwards to arrive at a body of theory which is capable of explaining the nature and significance of this evidence. In other words, we start, in Section A, with the actual phenomenon of English in the world today and the various 'problems' related to its worldwide spread, along with the contexts which give rise to these problems. In Sections B and C, we then plot how people have aimed to regulate this phenomenon (i.e. how language professionals have, through the pursuit of their profession, dealt with the language and the problems associated with it), and how this practical knowledge can then be abstracted into theoretical knowledge – which results in the disciplinary knowledge which constitutes 'World Englishes studies'. In certain respects, this approach is an unconventional one: as the series editors explain in their introduction, it has a 'back-to-front' structure when compared to traditional introductions which begin with the theory (which constitutes the core knowledge of the discipline), and turn to the phenomena for the purposes of illustration and exemplification.

Yet there are sound philosophical reasons for employing the present structure. Although theories are often promoted as having a general and a historical validity (Nagel, 1989), they always begin life as responses to particular problems. They are developed at a particular time and a particular place as a means of explaining certain observed phenomena that have been perplexing a particular scientific community. In other words, theories are the result of historical events. It is within this context that the pragmatist philosopher William James contends that truth can be understood as being *that which works*, and that "our beliefs are really rules for action" (1997 [1907], p. 94). For James, what we take as established theoretical knowledge (i.e. truth) is the retrospective interpretation of the process of problem solving. However much we may abstract and generalise theories, they exist for the solving of particular problems – and though the details of these problems may get erased from the retelling of the solution (i.e. from the formula which gains the status of a theory) – they are, in fact, its inevitable starting point. Thus it makes sense to start with the problems themselves – as it is these which will determine the truth value (or usefulness) of our theories.

The need for theory

If theories are tools to assist with the solving of problems, the question then arises: what is the nature of the problem we wish to solve here? One answer would be that it concerns successful communication. Languages are, among other things, instruments for communicating, and as English spreads across the globe the communication afforded by it can, presumably, operate on a global level. In other words, a global English can presumably function as a language that operates across traditional linguistic and cultural borders, and become an international *lingua franca*. 'Problems' related to this aspect of the language's role would concern intelligibility – the extent to which the spread of the language and the diversity in linguistic form that results from this spread produce difficulties in understanding across the different varieties which develop. And certainly, issues relating to the mechanics of successful communication are touched upon by much of the debate about and research into World Englishes.

But possibly the most pervasive issue – the issue which exists as a context for all the other concrete issues and problems we shall be looking at – relates to the role played by the language in power relations around the world. This is an issue directly related to *beliefs about* the language rather than simply the use of the language. It relates to the way the language's development in different contexts is perceived by different communities, to the impact of the history that is responsible for the spread of the language, and to the way that English language resources are differentially distributed across the globe. The theory we will work towards in Section C will therefore seek to explain the role played by English in the organisation of various societies around the world, and the inequalities which can arise as a consequence of this organisation.

It is for this reason I suggested at the beginning that English in the world today is a political issue. English in the world today operates as a means of communication – and many of the English language-related problems people struggle with concern how to ensure that it acts efficiently in this capacity. But it is also implicated in practices and debates relating to cultural identity, and in this capacity can play a crucial role in the most fundamental aspects of people's everyday lives. The languages people speak – or aspire to speak – relate to who they are, and thus prejudices towards the language become prejudices towards people themselves. The relationship between language and culture has to do with the ideas, histories and belief systems that adhere to the language. In looking at English today, the questions we need to ask are not simply what the nature of the language around the world is, but what the consequences of its variegated nature are; not simply how it is that people around the globe use English, but also what it means for them to use it. The theory we will work towards will thus attempt to help explain the implications – both linguistic and social – of English as a global language.

Another brief word about names

One of the consequences of postponing the theoretical overview until Section C is that certain issues that are often presented as central to a discussion of the topic are not covered in detail until later in the book. As has been suggested, there are philosophical advantages to this strategy; namely, that empirical foundations can be securely laid in the earlier sections of the book, and then built upon in the final section. On occasions, however, it is necessary to disrupt this structure in order to introduce aspects of the conceptual vocabulary and background context that are needed to provide an accurate and insightful description of the spread of English worldwide. This is particularly the case in the early parts of the book, where the conceptual and contextual foundations are laid for the introduction to the issues which preoccupy World Englishes studies. In such circumstances, therefore, I will succinctly gloss the concepts that are required for this initial explanation, and then return to the full discussion of them in the later section, where they can be related to the wider theoretical concerns of the discipline as a whole.

One such need to jump ahead occurs here at the very outset of the project, and concerns the choice of name for the book. In using the title *Exploring World Englishes*, I am, as noted above, following a recent tradition which stresses the multiplex nature of the language today and the need to take account of this multiplicity when studying the subject. This term 'World Englishes' is often used to refer to the general discipline that examines the nature and use of English worldwide or of English in globalised contexts, and it is this meaning which is being invoked in the title. But the term can also be used to refer to a specific school within the discipline (the approach associated most closely with Braj Kachru), and is sometimes taken to indicate an allegiance to this school's particular approach to the subject. The ambiguity over the use of this term and the significance it has for rival theoretical approaches is just one of the many points of debate which animate the discipline – and all of these will be covered in detail in Section C. In an attempt to avoid too much in the way of terminological confusion, however, throughout the book I will use the phrase 'World Englishes studies' to refer to the discipline as it is most broadly conceived (and which constitutes the subject of the book), and will highlight in the text whenever I am referring to particular schools or approaches within the broader academic field.

In summary then, this book presents an investigation of the nature of English in the world today, of how this nature presents 'problems' for those who use or work with the language, and of how we can understand the linguistic and social dynamics which produce these 'problems'. The contention that the book begins with is that worldwide English is as much a political as a linguistic issue, and for this reason we need to pay attention not only to what people do with the language but also what they think about it. And finally, while the subject of the book is English in the world today, English would not exist without its speakers; thus perhaps it would be more accurate to say that the subject of the book is the role of English in the lived experience of a global population for whom English is a vital part of everyday existence.

A note about the organisation of the book

The book is divided into two parts: *Part I: English in the world today*, which deals predominantly with practical issues; and *Part II: World Englishes as an academic discipline*, which deals with theoretical issues. Part I comprises two sections – the first (Section A) exploring the 'Problems and Contexts' of World Englishes studies (and including an overview of the history of the development and spread of English, and the scope of its current distribution across the globe), and the second (Section B) focusing on the 'Interventions' made by practitioners in the field. Part II of the book consists of only one section (Section C), which looks at the body of 'Theory' which comprises the core knowledge base of World Englishes studies.

The text is punctuated throughout by a number of 'Tasks', which are located at the end of each chapter. These take the form of study questions asking you to reflect on particular issues addressed in the text, and they can be used either as a reflective tactic for self-study purposes or as a prompt for classroom activities. At the end of the book there is a 'Commentary on tasks' section which provides feedback on these questions, and offers concise summaries of the key issues that each of the chapters contribute to the overall picture of what, how and why the topic of World Englishes is studied today.

At the end of the book there is also an annotated section on 'Further reading', which highlights some of the important and foundational texts associated with the topics discussed in the chapters. Finally, there is a 'Glossary' which provides short definitions of the key technical terms introduced in the text. When these terms are first introduced in the text (or when they are first dealt with in a significant way), they are highlighted in bold.

Part I

English in the world today

Section A

Problems and contexts

1 Introduction: defining and identifying problems

As I wrote in the general introduction, we begin by looking at the phenomenon of English in the world and considering the ways in which the language presents challenges for those who use or work with it as part of their everyday routine. The heading for this first section is 'Problems and contexts', and by formulating the topic in this way we immediately begin with presuppositions both about the relations people can have to the language, and the approach we are going to take towards its study. It is taken for granted in the use of this subheading that English in the world *is*, in certain circumstances, a problem. Indeed, the book as a whole is devoted to identifying the nature of these reputed problems, and reporting on theoretically informed practical solutions to them. Before stepping directly into this task, though, it is worth considering what constitutes a 'problem' in this context. Why should English present challenges for those who use or engage with it around the world? And what do these challenges consist of?

To jump straight to the punch line, the short answer is this: in the ordinary day-to-day activities of life, the use of English as a means of communication may not be – or at least not seem – in any way problematic. For an increasingly large number of people across the globe, the use of English is a normal and everyday occurrence, and one they will likely not reflect upon in any explicit way. Instead, it is something they simply do. To borrow a metaphor that has recently become popular in parts of the sociolinguistics literature (e.g. Shohamy, 2006; García, 2009), 'English' can be thought of not as a noun but as a verb. That is, English is an activity rather than an object; it is something people do rather than something they acquire, possess, or use.

The point here is that it is impossible to fully abstract the entity away from its actual use. And indeed, when all is going well it is not necessary to abstract it away from its use. We do not need to have a general or theoretical concept of English to be able to communicate in English. To borrow Mikhail Bakhtin's observation about the way we instinctively and unreflectively use different speech genres whenever we speak, we can say of all our commonplace communicative habits that "[w]e use them confidently and skilfully *in practice*, and it is quite possible for us not even to suspect their existence *in theory*. Like Molière's Monsieur Jourdain who, when speaking in prose, had no idea that was what he was doing, we speak in diverse genres without suspecting that they exist" (Bakhtin, 1986, p. 78). For the proficient English speaker, the majority of communication in English will be conducted without any need to know about such things as the typological character, the grammatical structure or the philological history of the language they are using. I was able to communicate perfectly adequately in English long before I knew the first thing about linguistics; just as I am able to watch the world going by outside my window without knowing the slightest thing about optics.

It is when the user of the language comes up against difficulties of some sort, or is presented with particular challenges, that a shift takes place: the shift from *procedural* knowledge to *propositional* knowledge. In other words, it is when a user of the language runs into a problem that strategies which draw upon an analytic understanding of language become useful. This is when it is necessary to know not simply *how* to do something, but how to understand *what* it is you are doing. By understanding what it is you are doing, it is then possible to see how you might be able to change it: to modify, improve or repair it.

The problems that produce the need for this shift of perspective can be of various types. They can relate to communication and intelligibility, to identity and cultural politics, or to professional concerns such as education. In each case, use of the language will not simply be a matter of intuitive communication but will involve issues which are causing a ruction of some sort in other social interactions. And although such problems can and do occur with respect to any language, the extensive reach and global profile of English means that it especially is the site for a great many such problems, and is thus worth dedicated investigation.

As one of the key precepts of this book is going to be that the exact nature of these language-related problems rely for their scope of meaning on the contexts in which they occur, it is important to examine real-life instances. For this, we need to begin with some representative examples of the nature of English use around the world today. It is to this, therefore, that we turn in the first chapter.

2 English in the world today

English and variety: examples

Varieties and functions

Let us begin by looking at a selection of examples of English usage from various global contexts. For each example I have provided a basic explanation of the context, followed by the data and then a commentary summarising some notable features. In the sections that follow, as we map out the areas in which applied linguistics problems relating to the global use of English most often occur, I will refer back to these examples and offer further analysis, drawing out the significance of the features on display here for World Englishes studies.

Example 2.1

The first extract is from a conversation between three people: M, S and H. M is an American and speaks English as his mother tongue; S is a German speaker; and H is a Chinese speaker. They are discussing the price for some decorating work. In this, and subsequent transcripts, each of the **turns** in the conversation (i.e. each instance that the conversation switches from one speaker to another) have been numbered so they can be easily referred to in the discussion that follows.

```
1 M:    Let's say we need decorations and we need it cleaned up.
        What's your bottom line?
2 S:    What's my what?
3 M:    What is the bottom line. What, what's the-⎤
4 H:             bottom line, yes
5 M:                        least you can do it for? The least it
                            can be done for?
6 S:    The lowest, uh-⎤
7 M:            Yeah
8 S:             price? Four thousand.
9 M:    Four thousand.
        (Roberts, 2005, p. 151, cited in Seidlhofer, 2009, p. 201)
```

Comment

In this short extract, English is being used as a means of communication by a small group who do not share a common first language. As such, they are using it as a *lingua franca*. They are engaged in a task – negotiating the price of some decorating work – which involves the need for mutual understanding and agreement. By the end of the exchange they appear to have reached this common understanding, but for a short while in the middle (turns 2–7) they have trouble fully understanding each other, and the flow of communication stumbles over the meaning of the phrase "the bottom line" (turn 1). This is an **idiom** which the *Oxford English Dictionary* records as being of US origin, and is not an expression with which S and H, the **non-native speakers** in the dialogue, appear to be familiar. By rephrasing his question though, M eventually makes himself understood, and the interaction has a successful outcome.

Example 2.2

The next two passages are both excepts from poems. The first is by the Nigerian writer Frank Aig-Imoukhuede (1932–2007), and the second (Example 2.3) by the Indian writer Nissim Ezekiel (1924–2004).

> My fader before my fader get him wife borku
> E no' get equality palaver; he live well
> For he be oga for im own house.
> But dat time done pass before white man come
> Wit 'im
> One wife for one man.
>
> (Aig-Imoukhuede, 1982, p. 46)

Example 2.3

> I am standing for peace and non-violence
> Why world is fighting fighting
> Why all people of world
> Are not following Mahatma Gandhi,
> I am simply not understanding.
> Ancient Indian Wisdom is 100% correct.
> I should say even 200% correct.
> But modern generation is neglecting –
> Too much going for fashion and foreign thing.
>
> (Ezekiel, 1989, p. 237)

Comment

Both these poems are early examples of writers using a style of English which reflects or draws upon the ways in which the language is used in their native communities. As such both display linguistic features which are divergent from a standard British or American English, and instead represent an 'indigenised' use of the language. Frank Aig-Imoukhuede's poem 'One Wife for One Man' (Example 2.2) is written in Nigerian Pidgin English. Among the many features which mark this as different from standard English is the spelling (which reflects the pronunciation; so 'fader' instead of 'father') and the distinct vocabulary of words such as *oga* meaning 'master' and *borku* meaning 'plenty'.

Nissim Ezekiel's 'The Patriot' (Example 2.3) is also imitative of local patterns of speech, in this case a form of Indian English. Again there are several features which differ from standard British or American English. These include the use of the present progressive (e.g. "I am standing for peace") instead of the simple present tense (standard British or American English would have "I stand for peace"); the reduplication of words such as "fighting fighting", which is used to intensify the meaning (Gargesh, 2006); and missing out the object after a transitive verb, as in the phrase "modern generation is neglecting" (where standard British or American English would normally be "the modern generation is neglecting it"). Many of these grammatical patterns are to be found in Indian languages and have been transferred onto the way English is spoken in this context. In the poem they are used specifically to indicate a local voice for the opinions that are being expressed, and when the poem was published in the anthology *Contemporary Indian Poetry in English* (Peeradina, 1972) it was given the title 'A very Indian poem in Indian English', to highlight the deliberate use of this local style of the language.

It should be noted that both these poems are *representations* of these types of English. That is, they are not transcriptions of real-life spoken data in the way that the speech in Example 2.1 is. Instead, they are creative imitations of typical local speech patterns which are being used as part of the creative repertoire of the two poets. The Nissim Ezekiel poem, for example, uses these patterns of speech as part of the characterisation of what is a slightly comic central character, while Aig-Imoukhuede's poem is about the clash of cultures that resulted when the "white man come", and the use of Pidgin helps to illustrate this on a textual as well as thematic level.

Both poems also mark early attempts by writers to develop a distinctive use of English in literature which is authentic to their own experiences of the language. A critic writing in 1971, for example, commented that Aig-Imoukhuede "is one more example of an African poet who is eager to use English as his medium and yet find a voice which is at once African and genuinely his own" (Roscoe, 1971, p. 42). Likewise with Ezekiel, this attempt to represent an 'Indian English', although viewed in some quarters as verging on caricature (Parthasarathy, 1976, p. 8), has also been described as "break[ing] the stranglehold exercised on poetic style by the notion of a standard language … [by] allowing poetry to explore parts of the human structure it had not earlier known it could accommodate or inhabit" (Patke, 2009, p. 281).

Example 2.4

This next extract – which is again real-life data – comes from a conversation between two young women, Dream and Cherry, who are originally from Thailand but at the time of this exchange were living in London. They are conversing via an instant messenger service on their mobile phones, and the topic of the conversation is the state of Dream's love life. Again the individual turns in the conversation are numbered, and phrases which are not in English are translated below the original **utterance** in square brackets.

1 Cherry:	oh
2 Cherry:	Ken-noi ngai
	[How about Ken-Noi? (Ken and Noi are popular TV personalities in Thailand)]
3 Dream:	Mai wai la
	[No way]
4 Dream:	Too young
5 Dream:	They are the same age as my students loei
6 Cherry:	shouldnt b phd...
7 Cherry:	should b undergrad...
8 Cherry:	but everything too late now
9 Cherry:	herr
	[<sigh>]
10 Dream:	Why don't u have a bf?
11 Cherry:	i have
12 Cherry:	hahaha
13 Cherry:	but i want exciting thing banggg
14 Dream:	I can't believe. U r cute mak mak na
	[You are cute!]
15 Dream:	Gu wa laeww
	[This is what I think]
16 Dream:	Dee mak I will tell ur bf dee gua lol
	[Great. I'd better tell your boyfriend about your plan]
17 Cherry:	oh

18 Cherry:	no la no laaa
	[No]
19 Cherry:	jai rai
	[You are mean]
20 Dream:	Eeh eeeh
	[Ha ha ha]

(Example from Seargeant and Tagg, 2011, p. 10)

Comment

What is particularly interesting in this extract is that although both participants have Thai as their mother tongue, they regularly switch into English as well. English is not being used as a *lingua franca* as it is in Example 2.1, therefore, because the two women share a common language. Instead, it is part of their everyday repertoire of linguistic resources, and they are shifting between different languages (what is technically known as **codeswitching**) as part of the natural flow of the conversation. This switching happens extensively, both between turns (e.g. between 3 and 4), and in the middle of utterances (e.g. turn 16).

As well as the codeswitching, this extract is also notable for the way that the English they use is influenced in many places by their native language, and so again displays features which are not found in standard British or American English. For example, there is the frequent use of **discourse particles** (words added to an utterance – often at the end – for the purpose of emphasis) such as 'loei' (turn 5), 'banggg' (turn 13) and 'laaa' (turn 18). These particles are frequently used in Thai (Smyth, 2002), and when they get transferred over to English they create what could be described as a specifically 'Thai English'. Another distinctive feature is the use of particular grammatical patterns such as "everything too late now" (turn 8) where the copular verb "is" is dropped (standard British or American English would have "everything is too late now").

This conversation also includes several linguistic features which are often found in the informal use of language online. For example there are instances of contractions such as 'b' for 'be', 'u' for 'you' and 'bf' for 'boyfriend' in turns 6 and 10. There is also some non-standard punctuation, such as the lack of capitalisation and apostrophes in turn 6 ("shouldnt b phd"). The result is a use of English which again is far from standard, but which, in this instance, is related not to the geographical or cultural backgrounds of the people using it, but to the medium of communication they are using. It is thus known as **computer-mediated discourse**, and the combination of this, the codeswitching and the 'Thai English' illustrates the diverse and creative forms English can take in the era of globalisation.

One final point of note in this example is the way that the Thai language is rendered in the Roman alphabet. Thai has its own alphabet, but here – due to the fact that the mobile phones the two women were using did not have the correct software for them to write in this alphabet – they transliterate everything into Roman script. The need to do this (i.e. the fact that the technology they are using favours the Roman alphabet rather than the Thai) may well be a motivating factor for why they chose to switch into English so frequently – and points to the way that language choice can be related to a range of social, cultural and material factors.

The visual display of English

The last two examples are slightly different from those above. These are illustrations of the visual display of English in public spaces. For both, the context in which they are displayed and the material form they take are very important, and illustrate something about the influence of English on cultural landscapes around the world.

Examples 2.5 and 2.6

The photo in Figure 2.1 is of the hoarding for a flower shop in Kuwait. Figure 2.2 is an artwork by the American-based Chinese artist Xu Bing, from a series called 'Introduction to Square-Word Calligraphy'.

Figure 2.1 FLY Flowers, Kuwait (Photograph courtesy of Hossein Zand, with thanks to Barbara Mayor)

Figure 2.2 Square Word Calligraphy: 'Art for the People' (2002), ink on paper (Xu Bing, 2004, p. 338)

Comment

As with the conversation between Dream and Cherry, both these examples involve English mixing with or rubbing up against other languages. In both instances, words in English are written in a manner which also incorporates elements associated with another language. And in both this illustrates ways in which Anglophone forms – that is, 'bits' of English, such as words, expressions, writing styles (Blommaert, 2010) – spread around the globe and are picked up or have an influence on other cultures, even when the English language itself is not being used in its totality as a system of communication within the society.

In the first of these examples, the shop is using two English words for its name: 'FLY Flowers'. Using a little 'bit' of English in this way is maybe not that unusual – in global cities such as London or New York, for example, shop signs can be found in hundreds of different languages, and restaurant names especially, all around the world, are often in the language of the cuisine they are serving rather than the community in which they are located. Yet this example does illustrate an important feature about the use of English in non-Anglophone contexts – namely, that it can have a *symbolic* value in different contexts due to its association with particular cultures such as those of the US or the UK. In other words, even in places where people do not normally use English as a means of everyday communication (and where the majority of the community may therefore not understand the language), it can still signify a certain 'cultural meaning' or set of connotations.

In this case, both the words 'fly' and 'flowers' are foreign as far as the Arabic language is concerned (i.e. they have not been systematically 'borrowed' into the Arabic lexicon and thus become a regular part of contemporary Arabic), and their denotational meaning (the fact that they denote to the concepts of 'flight' and 'flowers') would not be understood by a monolingual Arabic speaker. But the name of the shop is written in both the Roman and the Arabic alphabets, the one above the other, with the Arabic version being a simple transliteration of the sounds of the English words. A non-English speaker is therefore still able to pronounce the two words, and thus, in a sense, the top version is still 'English', despite it being written in an alphabet usually associated with another language. The result is that the name can be phonetically read by both English and Arabic readers, and it gives the shop a sense of 'exoticism' by drawing on linguistic forms which are not native to the local environment.

The second example (Figure 2.2) is, as noted, a work of art by the American-based Chinese artist Xu Bing. At first glance this may not look like English at all. It appears – at least to a non-Chinese reader – to be a text written in Chinese. This is not the case, however, and it is in fact entirely English: within what appear to be Chinese characters Xu has spelt out the English words 'Art for the people'. For example, the middle character is composed of a shape which approximates to the letter T in the centre, with an H and E on either side, thus spelling 'the'.

This work was part of an exhibition in 1997 which marked the return of Hong Kong to China. The relationship between Chinese and English-language culture is thus a central theme, and Xu has chosen to explore this by actually merging the forms of the two languages. In many ways, this is an extension of what the two poets in Examples 2.2 and 2.3 were doing, but whereas they were attempting to imitate the actual speech patterns resulting from the coming-together of different linguistic practices, Xu is re-imagining the language as it is reshaped by its global trajectories.

The reason for including these last two examples – which would not normally feature in a mainstream account of World Englishes studies – is to indicate some of the more diverse social and cultural phenomena which result from the global spread of English. The study of World Englishes predominantly examines the different varieties of English around the world (such as those illustrated in Examples 2.2, 2.3 and 2.4), along with issues related to its status and use as an international language (as illustrated in Example 2.1) – and this book will itself concentrate for the most part on these. But the existence of English around the globe is not solely about how the language is used as a means of international communication or what different forms it takes and how and why these develop. An equally important aspect of its spread is the way it becomes part of what we might call the **semiotic** repertoire of global communities, the way it in some sense penetrates the lives of people all across the globe and how they draw on this influence as part of the expression of their own identities and concerns. And this also will be a focus of our investigation in this book.

∗∗∗

To summarise, then, in these examples we have English being used by people from America, China, Germany, India, Nigeria, Thailand and Kuwait; we have the language being used for casual conversations, for business and commercial purposes, for literary venture and as both a subject and a resource for fine art. We have it used by people to communicate with those with whom they do not share a common language, but also by non-native speakers who speak the same language yet still choose to switch occasionally into English. It is being written in the Roman and non-Roman alphabets, is being mixed with other languages, and is being used in a variety of different styles such as the elliptical forms of online communication. The overall picture then is of diverse uses and diverse forms: some of which would likely not be understood by a monolingual native speaker, others of which might barely be considered to qualify as 'English' at all, and others which are predicated on the idea that they should be as widely understood as possible.

But how might these various examples constitute 'problems' for people working with the language? An initial observation is that they all differ in some way or another from standard English usage. Examples 2.2, 2.3 and 2.4, for instance, all include linguistic features which are not to be found in the form of the language which is described in mainstream dictionaries or grammar books. The words *borku* and *loei*, for example, are not recorded in the *Oxford English Dictionary*, and a phrase such as 'But modern generation is neglecting' would be marked incorrect if used in an exam such as the Test of English for International Communication (TOEIC). But these various differences are not, in themselves, a 'problem' – they only become problematic when they occur within social situations which make them a problem.

Before we go on to discuss the specifics of such social situations, however, let us first consider how it is that these various uses of English differ from each other, and how we can describe this difference. Being able to do this is important for giving us the tools to discuss English around the world, and it involves two levels of sociolinguistic analysis: a focus on form (the sounds, features, and structures of language), and a focus on function (the uses to which language is put). Form first.

Variation in form

When looking at differences of form there are three central notions to take account of. The first is that **language variation** – the way in which the features and structures of a language vary according to the people who use it and the situations in which they do so – is ubiquitous. No two people speak or write a language in exactly the same manner. The way an individual pronounces the language, or organises the words and phrases he or she uses, is in some sense distinct, and everyone does it slightly differently. Yet it is also the case that people use language in a broadly similar way to those around them, and so patterns of usage exist which correlate to the contexts in which speakers live and interact. Taken together, these patterns constitute the linguistic identity of different **speech communities**.

The second point is that most modern societies have the concept of a **standard language** which plays an important role in the way people relate to linguistic practices within their community. This is the notion that for any named language (e.g. Japanese, Latvian) there is a core set of rules about its look and use; and that these rules govern what is thought of as the 'correct' or 'proper' form of the language. It is this form that is consequently used in key social institutions such as education, politics and the media.

Finally, we need a conceptual vocabulary for describing the types of variation found in language – for dissecting the stream of sound or ribbon of marks on paper and screen into something which can be analysed to explain how it operates as a communicative and meaning-making system. To do this it is necessary to break the features of language up into different 'levels', each of which itself operates in a systematic way.

In this section of the chapter, we shall introduce these three notions in turn, and look at how they assist in describing the diverse and variegated nature of World Englishes. To do so we may occasionally need to step back and consider some further fundamental issues about the use of language in society, as an understanding of these is essential for a lucid analysis of the debates around English in a global context. And to begin with we need to give some thought to the basic notion of what constitutes human language.

Language variation

A very straightforward, layperson's understanding of language is that it consists fundamentally of words. In this conception, each different language is a large storehouse of words which denote things out there in the real world, and the meaning of each word is simply the object or phenomenon to which it refers. This is a view that the philosopher W. V. Quine mockingly characterised as the "the myth of a museum in which the exhibits are meanings and the words are labels" (Quine, 1969, p. 27). The purpose of language, according to this view, is to itemise the exhibits in the museum of shared human experience and provide a label for all the aspects of material and social reality. To learn a new language, then, is just a matter of memorising as many of these new words and their definitions as possible.

As anyone who has struggled with learning a foreign language knows, things are actually a lot more complicated than this. First, words do not always correspond simply and directly to things out there in the world. Instead, words appear to be at least partially complicit in the way that we, as social groups, mediate our knowledge of the world. Different languages use their vocabulary to divide the world up into different conceptual configurations (e.g. English has two separate words for the 'leg' and the 'foot'; Japanese has one 足 [*ashi*]); words can refer to things that do not exist ('manticore'), to imaginary concepts and constructs; or they can fail entirely in the face of the ineffable ("I love you more than words can express"). And even if it were the case that words corresponded symmetrically to all the distinct parts of nature, there is a great deal more to language than just a depository of words. There is the issue of how the words are combined, of how they are voiced and articulated, and how they are used in specific contexts to do specific things: to apologise to people, to order cups of coffee, to prevaricate and dissemble. All these actions require much more than the mobilisation of a fixed set of sounds-standing-for-things.

Part of the complexity of real language is that it always conveys a great variety of different types of meaning with every utterance. Even the simplest phrases, when uttered, can mean several things depending on the participants (who they are, where they come from, etc) and circumstances (the context and dynamic of the conversation). In fact, much of the meaning of what is expressed when we speak does not come from the content of the word itself – but from the circumstances of its utterance. If we take the example of a basic and commonplace word such as 'yes', we can see how its everyday use goes far beyond a straightforward correspondence between single form and single idea. The core meaning of 'yes' is usually thought of as an expression of affirmation. But consider the ways in which it can be spoken, and the additional information conveyed by this. From simply hearing someone speak the word you are likely to get – along with the expression of affirmation – an indication of what area of the country or the world the speaker comes from, as well as intuitions about their social and educational background. If you are speaking over the phone, you will probably be able to tell their gender and possibly their age (certainly whether they are a child or an adult), despite not being able to see them. In addition, tone of voice and manner of expression will colour the meaning (which is something we will return to a little later). This is all conveyed via the use of language but is not, in a strict sense, to do with the 'meaning' of the word.

Variety of this sort also exists in the way the same concept (in this case, an affirmative response) can have markedly different forms. Rather than use the word 'yes', for example, people may use the words 'aye' or 'yeah', 'yep' or 'yup'. In fact the range of alternatives for signalling something as simple as agreement is very extensive: 'sure', 'okay', 'right you are', 'agreed', 'fine by me', 'you bet' and so on. And again, each of these alternatives is likely to convey a measure of information about the speaker's identity or personality.

So even in the case of a simple and commonplace word, variation is a constant. Add to this the fact that language does not consist of a staccato succession of single words, but that crucially it is about both the choice of words and the order in which they are put, and the opportunity for variety multiplies exponentially.

As noted above, variation of this sort can occur on anything between an individual to a national (and possibly even transnational) level. This can be seen most markedly in the way that literary writers such as Henry James, William Burroughs or James Joyce have very distinctive, individual **styles** of writing which are manifested on a textual level in the choices they routinely make about the way they organise their language into sentences and paragraphs. Yet the same principle is true in more everyday scenarios as well, and all individuals in their casual conversations, or in the way they write emails, will favour certain turns of phrase or habitually use certain words more than others. For the purposes of this book, though, we are interested in the way specific patterns of variation emerge on a broader scale – in groups or communities. Any distinctive and systematic usage of this sort – usually consisting of a complex of different variables – is described as a **variety**. And this concept is at the very heart of World Englishes studies.

Varieties, dialects and languages

A variety is defined as a recognisable system of linguistic features which are associated with a community of speakers or with a particular social context. There are a number of broad parameters of variation: geography, social class, and type of activity or context. In other words, a language can take slightly different forms depending on where it is spoken, who is speaking it, and what is being spoken about. A number of distinctions are traditionally made in the technical vocabulary to cover these different uses. Forms of a language influenced by the people who speak it are referred to as **dialects**. These can in turn be divided into those influenced by the geographical background of their speakers (regional dialects) and those influenced by the educational or class background of their speakers (social dialects). For example, the distinctive patterns of English used by communities in Liverpool constitute a Liverpudlian or Scouse dialect. Forms of a language which are influenced by the purposes for and contexts in which it is used are referred to as **registers**. These are often characterised by the use of a specialist vocabulary or jargon which is suited to the specific tasks for which the language is being used. The distinct types of English needed to write an academic essay, for example, constitute an 'academic register'.

These conceptual terms are well established in linguistics, but there is an area of controversy associated with one aspect of them which has particular significance for World Englishes studies. This is the issue of what gets categorised as a 'language' and what as a 'dialect'. On linguistic grounds it is difficult to make a hard-and-fast distinction here. Attempts have been made to formalise the categorial boundaries, but to do so it is necessary to draw upon both scientific and social factors. For example, the German linguist Heinz Kloss (1967) identified two ways in which named languages are distinguished in society (and which thus provide essential criteria for the definition of a 'language'). The first is when they are linguistically distinct from other languages and so are likely to be mutually unintelligible. French and Portuguese, for example, may have had a common root in Latin several centuries ago, but today they are linguistically quite separate and their respective speakers are not able to fully understand each other. Kloss refers to these as **Abstand** languages (*Abstand* meaning 'distance') in that there is a clear linguistic gulf separating one from another. But there also exist pairs or groups of languages which are linguistically extremely close to the extent that they are mostly mutually intelligible, yet which nevertheless get promoted as separate entities by governments or community authorities. Kloss describes these as **Ausbau** ('building away' or 'building out') languages, in that they involve specific acts of policy or planning which highlight or augment the ways in which their linguistic features differ from those of their close siblings. Examples include pairs such as Serbian and Croatian or Urdu and Hindi, which can both be mostly understood by their respective speakers but for which there is a political desire to mark them as distinct.

What is apparent from this analysis is that the category 'language' can be as much about politics (and the status of the variety) as about linguistic issues. Conversely, the term 'dialect', at least as it is used outside the academic linguistics community, suggests a lower status. To refer to something as a dialect rather than a language is usually thought to afford it less respect (Lippi-Green, 1997). For this reason, the term 'variety' is often used in place of 'dialect' or 'language', as it is considered less politically loaded. So we could talk of both the Indian English and the Nigerian Pidgin in Examples 2.2 and 2.3 as being varieties of English (they are both habitual and systematic patterns of linguistic features used by particular speech communities), and in this way avoid entering into the arguments about their linguistic and socio-political status that would inevitably follow were we to categorise them as 'languages' or 'dialects'.

As we shall see, though, these issues of categorisation and status are central to many of the debates about World Englishes, and using a 'neutral' term is not always the aim of the discipline. In fact, one could suggest that the spread of English around the globe has had a significant influence on how the entire debate about the categorisation of linguistic systems has developed in recent years. For this reason we shall explore these issues in greater detail in later sections of this book. For the moment, though, we need to look in more detail at how language varies, and then begin to consider the consequences of this variation.

Standard English

The idea of a standard language – in this instance standard English – refers to the variety that is considered the norm for a given society or nation. This variety is uniform in that it is not localised and so does not vary from region to region. It is the variety described in mainstream dictionaries and grammars, accepted as the appropriate model of the language in educational contexts (and thus associated with the 'educated classes'), and the one that is predominantly – or at least traditionally – used in the media and all administrative contexts.

In terms of the way it is viewed, the standard language has the highest status in society – in part due to its association with the contexts in which it is used – and is thus considered a **prestige variety**. Indeed, in social terms it is often seen as the 'correct' form of the language: for some people, 'standard English' is synonymous with 'good' or 'proper' English. Within this social context, 'non-standard' then has two meanings. First, it refers to whatever differs from the standard (i.e. most regional and social dialects). Second, it has the evaluative meaning of 'incorrect' or 'bad' usage, of language which is not merely non-standard but sub-standard. In linguistic terms, however, there is nothing intrinsically better or worse about a standard language – it simply plays a different role in society from other varieties.

In one tradition of linguistic description, the term 'standard English' is used to refer only to the grammar and vocabulary of the variety, and to exclude issues of pronunciation. In this conception, standard English can be spoken with any type of accent. Other traditions, however – especially popular ones – also include accent in the definition. In the British context, a standard English accent is most commonly associated with **Received Pronunciation** (**RP**). This is a social rather than a regional accent, traditionally associated with the educated middle and upper classes in the UK, and conventionally considered the most prestigious accent of British English. It is colloquially known as the Queen's English or BBC English, reflecting its institutional status.

As well as being used as a yardstick within certain sectors of society for deciding what counts as appropriate or correct usage, the concept of the standard is also used as a fundamental point of reference in the study of linguistics. As noted, though, in linguistics evaluative approaches are mostly avoided, and instead the notion of the standard acts as a benchmark or point of contrast against which other varieties are defined. In this respect, standard English is what Randolph Quirk describes as the 'unmarked' variety of the language (Quirk, 1990b), and by extension, all other varieties are marked – and their distinctive features can be highlighted in relation to the unmarked variety. This is precisely what we shall be doing when describing levels of variation in World Englishes in the next section.

It should be noted that a standard language is always to some extent an idealisation. This is because, as we have discussed above, variation is ubiquitous, and there are as many subtly different varieties of the language as there are speakers. Some people suggest that rather than being absolute, therefore, it should refer to a set of core features which govern the basic rules of the language. But even here, discerning what actually constitutes standard English is difficult to determine with any precision – this despite the fact that many people use the term as if its meaning were widely accepted and unproblematically self-evident. But the question that always arises is who sets the standard. Where does the authority that the standard language commands actually come from?

Some societies have specific institutional bodies, known as language academies, whose primary purpose is regulation and maintenance of the national standard. The earliest of these was the *Accademia della Crusca* of Florence, founded in 1572. Sixty years later the French set up the *Académie française*, and in the following century Spain established the *Real Academia Española* in 1713. The motto of the Spanish academy – "Limpia, fija y da esplendor" ("Purify, fix and glorify") – indicates the functions that it and its counterparts elsewhere in the world are intended to fulfil: to 'purify' the language (i.e. establish and uphold the 'standard'), and to elaborate its forms and functions so that it is fit for use in a range of different domains, including the arts and sciences (Ferguson, 2006). In the seventeenth and eighteenth centuries, inspired by continental examples, there were motions to establish an academy for the English language. The writers Daniel Defoe and Jonathan Swift both proposed one for Britain, and at the end of the eighteenth century, John Adams proposed one for the newly independent America, suggesting that "[a]n academy instituted by the authority of Congress for correcting, improving, and fixing the English language would strike all the world with admiration and Great Britain with envy" (cited in Milroy and Milroy, 1999, p. 158). Nothing ever came of these proposals however, and English in the UK and USA has remained unregulated at this central institutional level.

Despite the absence of an academy, English does have certain institutions – such as the *Oxford English Dictionary* – which are viewed as authorities on the standard language. But another problematising issue is that the case of English complicates the ideal even further precisely because of its extensive global spread. The language is, in effect, polycentric, with different authoritative models vying for status as the standard. Indeed, there does now exist one language academy for English, set up in South Africa (the English Academy of Southern Africa or EASA), where English is an official language alongside ten others. In recent years, therefore, there have been moves in academia and policy to reframe the discussion in terms of a multiplicity of different standards: a standard British English, a standard American English, a standard South African English and so forth. Again, this is an issue that exercises much debate in World Englishes studies and is one we shall be returning to later in the book.

Levels of description

Using the (idealised) notion of the standard language as a benchmark, linguists dissect the flow of speech or writing into different 'levels' of language, so as to be able to describe its different aspects and features.

There are three main levels of language variation, which match the three levels at which language is analysed in terms of its structure as a meaning-making system. At the most basic level there are the sounds people make to produce speech. Each variety has a set number of these which are distinguishable from each other (Received Pronunciation, for example, has 44 distinct sounds in all: 24 consonants and 20 vowels). These sounds are then combined to make words, which in turn are combined to make sentences. The way these different elements can combine up through these three levels means that, from the limited sounds we have at our disposal, we are able to make an infinite number of sentences. As the eighteenth-century German philosopher Wilhelm von Humboldt wrote, human language is a system which "makes infinite use of finite means" (quoted in Chomsky, 1965, p. v).

The three structural levels are referred to technically as **phonology** (sounds), **lexis** (words), and **grammar** (sentences). Variation can occur at each of these. In addition, the written language also has **orthography** or spelling, which can also exhibit variation. Let us look at each of these in turn, and highlight a few examples of the variables to be found in varieties of English around the world.

Phonology

The first level of description is the phonology or sound system of a variety. Habitual patterns here constitute different **accents** of English – that is, the different features of pronunciation that indicate a person's geographical or social background. This is one of the most noticeable ways in which English usage both within a country and from country to country varies. Specific features which are salient in different accents of English around the world include things such as:

- the way that in varieties such as Ghanaian English, certain long and short vowels, such as /iː/ and /i/, and /uː/ and /u/ are not distinguished, resulting in words such as 'sleep' and 'slip', and 'pool' and 'pull' having identical pronunciations (Kachru and Smith, 2008, p. 81);
- the way that many accents, for example those of many Asian speakers (e.g. Japanese), do not distinguish between the /r/ and /l/ sounds, resulting in pronunciations such as "If we get good *glades* we will continue our education" (Sebba, 2009, p. 414).

Although all but Example 2.1 (the conversation about the decorating costs) from the first section of this chapter are instances of written rather than spoken English, we did see in Aig-Imoukhuede's poem that the spelling of Nigerian Pidgin broadly reflects the way the words are pronounced. So, for example, 'father' is written 'fader', and "with him" is "wit 'im".

Before moving to the next level of description it is worth highlighting a rather paradoxical situation that occurs with the composition of a book such as this. Although phonology is a very important part of variation, a book about World Englishes is necessarily a *written* description and so does not lend itself easily to an account of the full range of phonological variation. For instance, the majority of the examples given at the beginning of this chapter are from the written rather than the spoken language. Describing the spoken language is often an involved and technical process (it requires specialised systems of transcription and annotations such as the International Phonetic Alphabet), and it is obviously far easier to record features that occur in the written form of the language. However, several of the features that mark different varieties are not found in the written language, and it should be remembered as we discuss the diversity of English around the world that spoken language and written language are in many ways separate things: the former is usually ephemeral and mostly spontaneous, the latter, more considered, and often more formal. The fact that the two often are conceptually elided or treated as identical is yet one more complicating dynamic in the way that debates about the diversity of English proceed.

Lexis

The next level of description is lexical variation, which refers to differences in vocabulary. This can include both the way the same word can have different meanings in different varieties and the way that different varieties can use different words for the same concept. Examples of the latter include the South African word *veld* being equivalent to what the Australians call the 'outback' (Schneider, 2011, p. 21); or the use of 'mobile phone' in British or Indian English compared to the use of 'cell phone' in American or South African English (Mesthrie and Bhatt, 2008, p. 116).

This type of lexical variation also results from varieties of English adopting words from other local languages – a process known as **borrowing**. For example, the East African English spoken in countries such as Kenya, Tanzania and Uganda uses the words *daka* for 'shop', *kibanda* for 'black market', and *matutu* for a 'taxi bus' (Trudgill and Hannah, 2008, p. 131). And in the Aig-Imoukhuede poem in Example 2.2 we saw the use of **loanwords** such as *oga*, which has been adopted into Nigerian Pidgin from Yorùbá, an indigenous language of West Africa. Other differences in vocabulary are due to extension or alteration of the meaning of words. For example, in Indian English the word 'backside' means 'behind' or 'in the back of', while the compound word 'eve-teasing' refers to the teasing of girls (Trudgill and Hannah, 2008, p. 139).

Different varieties also have terms which are specific to the culture in which they are used. Examples include *kaross*, a cloak worn by the Bushmen in South Africa, *hangi*, a Maori earth oven, and *ugali*, a type of porridge eaten in eastern and central Africa (Schneider, 2011, pp. 198–9). As English spreads around the world, it often assimilates lexical items in this way, especially to refer to traditional cultural practices or the local fauna and flora. In some instances, these words can then get taken up by other varieties as the local culture spreads internationally. Examples here include the word *kiwi*, originally a borrowing from Maori; and *koala*, a borrowing from Dharug, an Australian Aboriginal language used in the area around Sydney. Both of these were first recorded in English in the early nineteenth century, and are now part of the lexicon of all standard Englishes. Just as words were needed for the cultural landscape encountered by the European colonisers, so they were also needed for the landscape created by the colonisers. This included names for the colonisers themselves. So Hong Kong English has the colloquial word *Ang mo* for a foreigner, borrowed from the Cantonese (紅毛) where it literally means 'red hair' (Kirkpatrick, 2011). Similarly, Aboriginal English has the word *balanda*, used, often derogatorily, for a non-Aboriginal person of European descent, and deriving from the earliest European name for the Australian territory, *Nova Hollandia* or New Holland (Moore, 2011).

An important related category is **idioms**, that is, set expressions whose meaning cannot be deduced from the sense of the individual words. Idioms are often, at least in origin, quite culturally specific, and many of those found in new varieties of English are expressions transferred over from local languages. Examples include:

- from Hong Kong English: "laziness is my largest enemy", derived from the Cantonese expression 最大嘅敵人 (Li, 2000, pp. 52–3, cited in Kirkpatrick, 2007, p. 143);
- from Ghanaian English: "I met your absence" meaning "you weren't there" (Sebba, 2009, p. 415);
- from Indian South African English: "to want mutton curry and rice every day" meaning "to have unrealistic expectations" (Mesthrie and Bhatt, 2008, p. 116);
- from Caribbean English: "your tongue flies" meaning "you cannot be trusted not to repeat what you hear" (Kachru and Smith, 2008, p. 75).

Grammar

The third level of description is grammar. This is conventionally broken down into two further categories: **syntax**, the order in which words are arranged in a sentence; and **morphology**, the structure of words. For instance, in standard English the plural of a noun is often morphologically indicated by adding the **inflection** '–s' at the end of the word. So, for example, singular 'monkey' becomes plural 'monkeys'. There are several mass nouns in standard British and American English, however, which are 'non countable', and so do not take an '–s' despite referring to multiple objects. Many of the new varieties of English treat uncountable nouns in the same way as countable ones. For example, pluralisation of non-count nouns in certain varieties results in sentences such as:

- "I lost all my furnitures" (West African English)
- "Do not throw litters on the street" (Indian English)
                        (Trudgill and Hannah, 2008, pp. 130, 134).

Examples of syntactical variation include the use in Indian English of the present tense for durational phases indicating a period from past to present, where standard British English conventionally uses the present perfect. So Indian English will have "I am here since two o'clock" where British English would have "I have been here since two o'clock". Similarly, Indian English uses the progressive aspect with habitual action, resulting in phrases such as "I am doing it often", where standard British English would be "I do it often" (Trudgill and Hannah, 2008, pp. 136–7). A similar feature was apparent in the Ezekial poem in the phrases "I am standing for peace and non-violence" and "I am simply not understanding".

Another common feature in some new varieties is the omission of articles. This happens, for example, in West African English in sentences such as "I am going to cinema" (Trudgill and Hannah, 2008, p. 130), and similarly we saw it in both the Ezekial poem ("But modern generation is neglecting") and in the Thai English in Example 2.4: "but i want exciting thing".

A related feature is the use of discourse particles. As explained above, these are words or short phrases which are used, most often in spoken conversation, to help organise the flow of what one is saying or to indicate something about the how the meaning is to be interpreted. Examples in standard British or American English include 'ah', 'well' and 'you know'. In varieties such as colloquial Singapore English, the use of particles is very common. Many of these are derived from Chinese and are used to convey senses which in other varieties would be indicated by intonation or turn of phrase. For example, the particle *lah* can signal a range of meanings, including solidarity, heightened emotional engagement or emphasis, as in the phrase "Please lah come to the party", which in standard British or American English would approximate to: "Please *do* come to the party" (Trudgill and Hannah, 2008, p. 141). The Thai English of Example 2.4 similarly uses several discourse particles, such as "They are the same age as my students loei", again adding an additional emotional stamp to the declaration – what in other forms of written English might be signalled by an exclamation mark.

Orthography

Finally, for the written language, variation also occurs at the level of orthography or use of the writing system. Orthographic variation occurs most notably in different spelling conventions. There are two main reasons for varietal discrepancies in spelling. It can either be the result of an authoritative body within a speech community purposefully setting out to make reforms, or because the variety does not have established spelling conventions and operates on a mostly *ad hoc* basis. The paradigmatic example of the former is the different conventions between British and American English; for example, 'colour'/'color'; 'centre'/'center'. The divergence here is the result of specific historical interventions – which we shall look at in detail in Section B, Chapter 7 – and was motivated by both political and practical goals, including the perennial desire to make English spelling reflect pronunciation in a more consistent manner.

In some varieties – especially those which do not have a long-standing written tradition – the spelling system is not fixed in the way that it is in contemporary standard British or American English. As we noted, the word *fader* in Aig-Imoukhuede's poem represents the local pronunciation of 'father'; in other records of the language it can also be spelt *fadar*, and *borku* likewise has an alternative version of *boku* (Naija Lingo, 2011). Here, then, orthographic variation occurs both between varieties ('father' in standard British English versus *fada* in Nigerian Pidgin), and within the same variety (*fader* versus *fada/fadar*).

✳✳✳

The above is a very brief and indicative selection of some of the variables that distinguish different varieties of World Englishes. An in-depth sociolinguistic study of the subject would map the features in far greater detail, and correlate their occurrence against the speech communities who use them – and the 'Further Reading' section at the end of the book gives details of some such studies. As this book is primarily an applied linguistics treatment of the topic, however, our focus is on the issues, challenges and debates to which variation of this sort leads, and on how variety in the worldwide use of the language affects the social practices of its users. The point to register here is that variation occurs at all levels of linguistic description, that variables such as these combine together in patterns which are habitual and systematic, and that such patterns develop their own idiosyncrasies and native identity wherever the language takes root.

From basilect to acrolect

Before leaving the topic of variation of form, it is worth stressing that the different varieties we have been referring to should not be thought of as entirely distinct systems with set stores of features. In talking of Indian English, East African English, or Nigerian Pidgin, we are talking of the aggregate of features which are habitually used by speech communities within those regions, and which are therefore described by linguists or cultural commentators as constituting a named variety. But there will also always be variation *within* those broad speech communities: both because they are large and diverse groups (West African Pidgin, for example, is the umbrella term used to describe the broad shape of the variety used in that part of the continent, but different communities within that area will have their own particular patterns of use, such as Nigerian Pidgin, Ghanaian Pidgin, and so on), and because people will be exposed to different forms of the language in different contexts of their life, and will therefore have a 'repertoire' of different styles to draw on. This is the case in practically all communities where there is a standard version of the language. In the UK, for example, a majority of people initially learn the local variety used in the neighbourhood in which they grow up, and then also learn standard English when they go to school. They will then shift between these different varieties depending on the contexts in which they are using them. In work situations, for example, they may tend towards a more formal standard variety, but when at home with family and friends they revert to a more localised variety.

One way of conceptualising this is to see all varieties existing along a cline of variation, ranging from a standard version at one end, to a localised version at the other. Stages along this cline are described as an **acrolect** (the prestige variety, which shows no significant difference from standard English), through a **mesolect** (an intermediate variety in terms of its distance to the standard), to a **basilect** (the variety most removed from the standard). This set of terms was first used by Derek Bickerton (1975) to describe variation within **Creoles** (a particular type of language that results from contact between a number of other languages), but are now also used to describe other varieties. If we take the example of the Englishes used in Singapore, for instance, it is possible to see a cline between a variety modelled on British standard English norms (the acrolect), through usages which constitute an emergent 'standard Singapore English' (the mesolect), to what is known as 'Singlish' (the basilect), a local 'hybrid' or mixed variety which diverges acutely from standard British English to the extent that the two are mutually unintelligible (Platt and Weber, 1980).

As a standard language is closely associated with the educated classes, this hierarchy of varieties is sometimes considered to reflect different educational backgrounds – that is, the acrolect is predominantly spoken by educated people and the basilect by those without much experience of formal schooling. But cultural identity is also an important element in their use, and people will often switch between the different levels depending on the social context. For example, Andy Kirkpatrick suggests that in the case of Australian English, it is in situations where people wish to purposefully exhibit their Australian identity that they are more likely to use an informal, 'non-standard' variety (Kirkpatrick, 2007, p. 78). Richards and Tay give the example of two shop assistants in Singapore speaking a standard English when talking to customers, but switching to Singlish, marked by frequent discourse particles, when they are alone and chatting between themselves: "Why do you wear your hair like that *la*? Better you lift a bit at the back *la*" (Richards and Tay, 1977, cited in Mesthrie and Bhatt, 2008, p. 136).

***

In summary, then, variation exists at all levels of sociolinguistic description, and in correlating different features or variables with different speech communities we can talk in terms of different varieties of the language. But both the categories we use – whether we describe something as a separate language, a variety, or a dialect – plus the names we give the varieties – for example, West African English, Nigerian Pidgin, Singlish – are not set or pre-determined terms. They are constructs, used for analytic purposes by sociolinguists, and for identification purposes by society at large. Furthermore, speakers often have a range of resources at their disposal. They can orient more to a standard variety, or to a more informal one, or they can mix different languages, styles and registers in the same conversation, as in the case of Example 2.4 where the two women use Thai along with bits of standard English, bits of 'Thai English' and bits of a **discourse** associated with online communication. Thus although we use something akin to a structuralist framework for describing variation – dividing by difference and categorising in relation to other varieties, and often a centrally positioned standard – it is worth remembering that actual usage is more nebulous than this, as well as being dynamic and constantly evolving.

Variation in function

It is also the case that simply showing diversity of formal variation does not yet constitute a set of 'problems'. It is a truism of **descriptive sociolinguistics** that all varieties, and indeed all languages, are linguistically equal – they are all complex and adaptable systems of meaning-making and expression. From a purely linguistic perspective, therefore, there is nothing about this range of variation which is exceptional or challenging. It is only when these forms are located in particular contexts and used as acts of real communication that problems can arise. To examine this we need to look at a further type of variation.

As well as shape and structure, variation also occurs in how the language is used to make meaning in different contexts. If we return to the example of the use of the word 'yes', we can see that not only is there variety related to the identity of the speaker (different accents, dialects and registers), but there are also a range of different possible meanings related to the circumstances of its use and the intentions of its user. A dictionary such as the *Concise Oxford* gives the simple definition of 'yes' as 'an affirmative answer'. And when written down the word does look like a single concept, non-complex and without ambiguity. But when it is loosed from the pages of the reference book and actually used – when it relates to a specific context and is part of a specific conversation – it can convey a range of different meanings. It could indeed be a simple affirmative: *Would you like a cup of coffee? – Yes, please.* It could, however, mean the exact opposite – the tone of voice and the context could indicate a sense of irony, or perhaps sarcasm: *Are you some sort of idiot?? – Yes, that's exactly what I am!*

It could mean that the person is not really listening at all, that they are entirely non-committal but just responding out of reflex: *Do you think this is a suitable present for a 17 year old? – Yes, yes, whatever*. In each of these cases, meaning is generated from the combination of the language, the speakers, and the context in which and about which they are conversing. And *successful* communication requires that the meaning generated produces the conversational or social effect that is being intended by the speaker.

This is an approach to the analysis of language that was developed in the first half of the twentieth century, and is particularly associated with the philosopher J. L. Austin. Language is seen not simply as something which refers to an external reality but as an action in its own right – an action which has effects and gets things done. And it is here that we begin to encounter how the diversity in World Englishes can produce problems for users around the world. This brings us on to our second level of analysis – the communicative function of the use of English in global contexts.

Exchange of information and 'intelligibility'

In Example 2.1 at the beginning of the chapter, three people are negotiating the price of some decorating work. We could characterise this conversation as being primarily an attempt by the participants to exchange information. The function of their use of language is to convey a particular thought or proposition to their interlocutors, and in doing so reach agreement about an issue.

The conveying or exchange of information is one of the principal functions of human language. Indeed, some people consider it the primary function and, as we shall see in Section B, Chapter 6, there is a long history of attempts to regulate, tighten or even engineer languages so that they might better fulfil this purpose. A key and necessary component of communication in these terms is **intelligibility**. The participants in a conversation need to be able to understand the meanings of those with whom they are speaking, and to respond in such a way that their interactions have a successful outcome. The immediate 'problem' that could therefore arise in the case of the conversation about the decorating – and that in fact almost does happen – is that the three people are unable to understand each other. Each of them, after all, has a different mother tongue, all three of which are mutually unintelligible, and this is why they have settled on English as a means to overcome these linguistic barriers. In this context, then, English as a global language means English as a means for communicating internationally.

It may sound as if I am labouring the point here, but this is one of the key issues related to World Englishes studies, yet one which can and does attract a great deal of confusion. Much of the discussion of English around the world relates to how variation can produce problems of miscomprehension or troubled communication, and many of the interventions proposed are concerned with how best to ensure intelligibility for English speakers across the world.

Given the pivotal position of this issue for the discipline, it is worth considering what exactly is meant by intelligibility, especially within contexts where communication is taking place across linguistic borders. Larry Smith has proposed a useful set of distinctions of what it means to have knowledge of a language (Smith, 1992). He distinguishes between three levels of knowledge:

1 **Intelligibility**, which refers simply to the ability to recognise an utterance or expression as being in a particular language – for example, to know that めんどくさい (*mendokusai*) is in Japanese.
2 **Comprehensibility**, which refers to knowing the basic meaning of an expression – for example, that *mendokusai* means something along the lines of 'troublesome to do'.
3 **Interpretability**, which refers to knowing what an expression actually does in a particular social or cultural context – that is, when it is appropriate to use it, how it is likely to be received, and so on.

It is somewhat unfortunate that Smith gives the first level of this taxonomy the same name as the general issue. But it is Levels 2 and 3 which are of particular relevance for World Englishes, as miscommunication can occur at both.

Miscommunication arises when the meaning of the utterance is not understood. This can be a product of the variation in form of different Englishes (i.e. at the level of what Smith calls 'comprehensibility'). For example, the pronunciation of different varieties can prove a particular challenge in some contexts. Jeff Siegel recounts an anecdote about a Japanese tourist whose difficulty in comprehending the local accent resulted in a rather abrupt shock after she had had to spend the night in a Sydney hospital. When the nurse came in the following morning and said "You're going today", what she heard, due to the Australian accent, was, "You're going to die" (Siegel, 2010, p. 148). While this example may well be apocryphal, it is certainly the case that the range of pronunciations for English around the world can result in challenges to smooth communication, if not perhaps to complete misconstruals such as this.

Similar examples of miscommunication due to formal variation are often used in books or classes on intercultural communication as warnings of the type of solecisms one can commit if one does not have full command of the language as it is used by the community one is dealing with. Ricks, for example, records what he describes as "an interesting but misleading translation [that] showed up on a sign in a Japanese garden. The posted sign read, 'Japanese garden is the mental home of the Japanese'" (Ricks, 1999, p. 81). And a website for a consultant on cross-cultural communication lists a similar selection, including:

- In a Bangkok dry cleaners: Drop your trousers here for best results.
- Tailor in Jordan: Order your summer suit. Because if big rush we will execute customers in strict rotation.
- Tokyo hotel posted this sign: You are respectfully requested to take advantage of the chambermaids.
- Outside a Hong Kong tailor shop: Ladies may have a fit upstairs.

(Examples from Swallow, 2011)

In all these cases, single instances of lexical or idiomatic variation are promoted as illustrations of unintended meanings that can, apparently, mislead or cause some form of communicative disjuncture. Whether examples such as these actually cause real miscommunication is a moot point. In each of the above cases, the intended meaning seems mostly clear from the overall context (or at least it does to me), despite the fact that the slight mis-phrasing of an idiom produces an alternative literal meaning. For example, while a 'mental home' may indeed be a synonym for an asylum in standard English usage, I have no difficulty in interpreting its use here as referring to the idea of a 'spiritual home'. After all, miscommunication requires not simply that the listener notices a solecism in an utterance, but that that solecism causes confusion and misunderstanding. And usually the wider context of the conversation or the circumstances in which the utterance is used will supply clues to the intended meaning. Having said this, different usages of English can undoubtedly produce communicative challenges, as we saw in Example 2.1, and thus variation of form is, at least on some level, a problem for intelligibility. But it is not the only – nor indeed the most likely – aspect of variation which can lead to intelligibility difficulties.

Another important aspect about communication is knowing what a particular expression means in a particular context – what Smith refers to as 'interpretability'. In the 1970s, the linguistic anthropologist Dell Hymes (1974) coined the term **communicative competence** to refer to this aspect of a person's linguistic abilities. His contention was that not only does one need to be able to understand the literal meaning of a given phrase, but that for real-life communication one also needs knowledge about how to use language appropriately depending on the social situation.

The reason there is a difference between simply knowing the literal meaning of a phrase and the functional meaning it has in an actual conversation is that the way we interpret an utterance is always informed by the circumstances in which it is used. Another way of saying this is that the words and structure of a phrase do not in themselves determine the meaning of the phrase. The meaning is understood from the **context** – which includes such things as knowledge of the world, of society and of cultural norms. Take, for example, the phrase "What's wrong with you?" in the following two short exchanges. In each case it means a different thing, despite the fact that it is word-for-word the same phrase in both:

Sam: Coming for a drink?
Andy: Sorry, I can't. My doctor won't let me.
Sam: What's wrong with you?

Sam: Coming for a drink?
Andy: Sorry, I can't. My mother-in-law won't let me.
Sam: What's wrong with you?
                     (Examples from Kecskes, 2010, p. 2895)

The only difference in these two snippets of conversation is that "My doctor" is changed to "My mother-in-law" in the second. Yet in the first, the implied meaning of "What's wrong with you?" is "What physical ailment do you have which prohibits you from drinking?" while in the second it is something along the lines of "That's absurd that you should be so in thrall to your wife's mother!" These different meanings are understood because of a complex of social norms and world knowledge which is not explicitly expressed linguistically, but is nevertheless triggered by the content and structure of the conversation.

If both participants in a conversation share the contextual background upon which these meanings are built, there is no communicative problem. But this sort of contextual background can be very culturally specific (in the case above, it revolves around social relations between mother-in-law and son-in-law, which are often the subject of stereotypical humour in many Western societies), and so miscommunication can take place even when all the individual words in an utterance are fully comprehensible. This is why the issue is of such importance for World Englishes studies.

Take, for example, the following short exchange between a wife (W) and her husband (H). The wife is British-born, the husband of Iranian origin; they have been married for several years, and both are expert English speakers.

W: Do you want a cup of tea?
H: Thank-you.
W: Is that a yes or a no?

Explaining her confusion, the woman noted afterwards that "My [follow-up] question was prompted by many occasions when I've got this wrong!" This is because, for many monolingual English speakers, 'thank-you' is likely to indicate assent; but in other cultures – such as the Persian-language norms within which the husband has been socialised – it means 'no'. Thus, as we saw with the example of the word 'yes', so the equally commonplace 'thank-you' can mean different things depending on the context – and the context here includes the cultural and communicative norms in which speakers have been socialised. For English, which is spoken in different cultural contexts all across the globe, this aspect of communication becomes an important issue when the language is used to converse with people who have different cultural experiences of it. And as Schneider suggests, in cross-cultural encounters these misunderstanding can cause not simply intelligibility problems, but also interpersonal problems (Schneider, 2011). That is, different cultural conventions of language use can result in accidental breaches of etiquette or politeness, which can also unsettle smooth communicative interaction.

A related issue is that in certain contexts the very act of using English rather than another language is itself meaningful. In other words, the use of English can have a *symbolic* significance. It may, for example, indicate exoticism, modernity, or prestige – though the exact nature of the symbolism will differ from place to place according to beliefs people have about the language in different societies. We saw one such example in the name for the flower shop in Kuwait (Example 2.1), where the very fact that this was written in English was as significant as what the words themselves meant. In this way, the cultural associations of the language, as well as the local cultural norms which govern its use, are an important aspect of the communicative process. And for a language with multiple incarnations and identities in diverse locations across the globe, this aspect of its variety can present significant challenges for those working with and using it.

Variation and the analogy of Latin

Another issue about English and intelligibility which is often raised – at least in popular discussion – is whether the spread of the language will lead, eventually, to the emergence of a range of mutually unintelligible varieties. The analogy here is with the fate of Latin after the fall of the Roman Empire, which resulted in the present-day existence of distinct languages such as French, Spanish, and Italian. A number of people have posed this question. Robert Burchfield, for example – editor of the *Supplement to the Oxford English Dictionary* and known for his "championing [of] the 'varieties' of world English" in his work on the dictionary (Simpson, 2010) – suggested in the early

1980s that in a century's time British and American English would be as different from each other as French and Italian are now. A few years later the linguist Randolph Quirk likewise asked whether we were heading for the "diaspora of English into several mutually incomprehensible languages" (Quirk, 1985, p. 3).

There are a number of responses that can be made to this. The first is that in many ways this has already happened. Varieties such as Tok Pisin (spoken in Papua New Guinea) or Singlish (in Singapore) have already diverged from standard British or American English to the extent that they are far from mutually intelligible. Take, for example, the following passage from a Tok Pisin version of the New Testament story of the loaves and the fishes, which diverges significantly from standard British or American English (a translation into standard English is given below):

> Jisas i askim ol, "yupela i gat hamas bret?" Na ol i tok, "7-pela." Na cm i tokim ol manmeri, na ol i sindaun long graun. Na, em i kisim dispela 7-pela bret, na em it tenkyu long God, na i brukim, na i givim long ol disaipel, bilong ol i tilim. Na ol i tilim long ol manmeri.

> Jesus asked them, "how much bread do you have?" And they said, "seven". And he spoke to the people and they sat on the ground. And he took these seven loaves of bread and thanked God, broke them and gave them to the disciples so that they could distribute them. And they distributed them to the people.
> (*Nupela Testamen*, 1967, cited in Mühlhäusler et al., 2003, pp. 177–8)

At the same time, however, English does still act as an international language and, as we shall see in the case study of Singapore in Chapter 8, both an international standard and distinct localised varieties can co-exist, with people switching between the two as and when they wish. In other words, the development of linguistically distinct varieties does not necessarily entail wholesale fragmentation of the language.

It is also worth remembering that mutual intelligibility – or the lack of it – was an issue prior to the recent global expansion of the language. Larry Smith and Cecil Nelson point out that for at least the last two centuries there have been mother-tongue English speakers in various parts of the world who have not been understandable to other mother-tongue English speakers elsewhere in the world. So this phenomenon "is not something that is 'going to happen' but something that has happened already and will continue to occur" (Smith and Nelson, 2006, pp. 428–9). Furthermore, it is not by any means necessary that all varieties of English should be intelligible to everyone – only that they are understood by those with whom we wish to communicate.

And as has been suggested above, there are several other elements involved in successful communication; simply speaking the same 'language' is not in itself sufficient.

We shall return to these issues in Section B when we look at the interventions people have proposed for dealing with the problem of international communication. Intelligibility and the exchange of information is not the only function that a language has in society, however, despite the way the issue often dominates debates. Another equally important issue is the role that languages play in the politics of cultural identity.

Cultural identity

The subject matter of the poems in Examples 2.2 and 2.3 is, in both cases, about cultural values in the local community. Aig-Imoukhuede's poem is concerned with the way that indigenous marriage practices were altered following the arrival of European colonisers and the values they brought with them; and Ezekial's poem offers (and perhaps lightly mocks) the personal views of an Indian patriot comparing his own traditional values with the disorder of modern global society. As such it is apt that the poets are able to complement this local subject matter with localised forms of the language. In being used in this way, the language itself acts as a marker of cultural identity.

The ways in which patterns of variation are associated with different communities, combined with the fact that varieties are constantly evaluated and that people form judgements about speakers based on their use of language, means that variation plays an important role in cultural identity politics. In other words, precisely because linguistic variation is ubiquitous it acts as a means of distinction between different groups, and so becomes an integral part of people's identity. For this reason, debates about different varieties of English around the world have a marked political aspect to them as they concern the way that groups are perceived and perceive themselves, and the actions people take on the basis of these perceptions.

It is this link between language and cultural identity, and the complex dynamics produced by the global influence of English, that lies behind the art work by Xu Bing that we looked at in Figure 2.2. Xu writes that his work "exists on the borderline between two completely different cultures" (cited in Xu Bing, 2004, p. 338). In other words, it is a disquisition on the coming together of two separate worldviews and their distinct traditions and practices of coding experience. He continues:

> To viewers from these two cultures, the characters [in the artwork] present equal points of familiarity and of strangeness. A Chinese

person recognizes the characters as familiar faces but cannot figure out exactly who they are. To a Westerner, they first appear as mysterious glyphs from Asian culture, yet ultimately they can be read and understood ... This total disconnection between outer appearance and inner substance places people in a kind of shifting cultural position, an uncertain transitional state.

(cited in Xu Bing, 2004, pp. 338–9)

The close link between a language and a culture, when brought into contact with the vast and diverse spread of English in a globalised world, produces new frames for the understanding of national and cultural identity. And although Xu Bing's work is not an 'everyday' example of the use of English, the ideas he plays with are ones which also exist for more mundane English utterances as the language gets drawn into the cultural practices of groups dispersed all across the globe.

✳ ✳ ✳

These, then, are examples of some of the problems that exist for English around the world today. But to understand them properly, and to consider the implications they have for language professionals, we need to look in further detail at the specific contexts in which they arise. We shall do this in Chapter 4; but first it will help if we block in some of the more general background to the spread of English, in terms of both its historical roots and its current global profile, as this also has an important bearing on many of the key questions we are going to explore.

Tasks

In light of what we have discussed in this chapter, consider the following study questions:

- In what ways does the global spread of English complicate the notion of a single standard of the language?
- Why is intelligibility considered such a key issue in debates about English in the world today?
- How does cultural context play a part in communication, and what implications does this have for World Englishes?

Feedback for these questions is given in the 'Commentary on tasks' section at the end of the book.

3 The context and history of World Englishes

The significance that language variation has in different contexts is a product of the history that has produced this variation. To understand the many issues related to the nature and use of English around the world, therefore, it is helpful to have an understanding of the provenance and complexion of its current global profile; to know how many people speak the language, who these people are, why and for what purposes they use English, and how it developed to become the global linguistic force it is today. This is the social matrix in which English exists – and which provides the background for the beliefs people have about it and the reasons it operates as it does in societies around the world.

Demographics and diverse world contexts

Calculating the figures

So far we have asserted that English today is spread widely all around the globe, and that it is in a position unequalled in terms of numbers of overall speakers and range of functions. What in practice does this mean? English is not the language with the most native speakers in the world. Chinese qualifies as that, with over 1.2 billion people having it as their native language. Spanish is also at least on a par with English for numbers of native speakers. But it is when one adds those who speak it as a second language, those who use it as a foreign or international language, and also take into account the range of functions it is used for and the significance of the domains in which it operates, that English's status as the pre-eminent global language of the modern era takes form.

Before we look in detail at the figures it will be helpful to clarify some of the key conceptual categories we will be using. When discussing people's relationship to English, an initial distinction that is traditionally made is that between **native speakers** (NS) and **non-native speakers** (NNS). The precise scope of reference of these two terms, and the way they are or should be used, is, as with so many conceptual categories in World Englishes studies, a source of controversy. We will be returning to some of the arguments around this when we turn to issues of theory in Section C. For the time being I will use 'native speaker' with its common-sense meaning of someone who has spoken English since infancy. This is in contrast to a non-native speaker who has learnt the language later in life. The significance of the distinction is that languages learnt later in life are acquired in a different fashion from those learnt in infancy, which can have implications for the way they are spoken. If one learns an **additional language** as an adult, for example, one is likely to speak it with the trace of one's native language in terms of accent and grammar (a process known as **transfer**).

To complete the terminological picture, alternative terms for native language are **mother tongue** or **first language** (L1), both of which again refer to the language of one's upbringing. It is worth noting, however, that children growing up in multilingual environments may learn more than one language from birth, and so have more than one mother tongue and, somewhat contradictorily, more than one first language. (Further explanation of all these terms and their relative uses and merits will be discussed in Chapter 13.)

An additional point about terminology (and about the clash between conventions and contradictory literal meanings) is that it would be more accurate to talk of 'users' rather than 'speakers' of English. The latter term gives the impression of favouring the spoken language and, as we have previously noted, the spoken and written forms of the language should not be unproblematically equated. It is traditional, however, to use the term 'speakers' for the general category, that is, as a coverall term for all those who have a certain competence in the use of the language, be it in speaking, listening, reading or writing. This results from the fact that everyone learning a first language begins with the spoken variety, and only later learns the written form. For the learning of a second or additional language this sequence need not pertain, and one is very likely to learn the written and spoken forms simultaneously. Some pedagogic approaches in fact, such as the **grammar-translation method**, favour the written language to the exclusion of the spoken. But for ease of reference, and to maintain coherence with terms such as 'native speaker', I will continue with the use of 'speaker' as the superordinate term, though with the implicit caveat that it is being used as a general category, and that when it comes to people's actual language practices things are, as always, far more complex and varied.

These, then, are the categories used to refer to different types of speakers. But identifying exactly how many people around the world do speak English is a far from easy task. The reasons for this are twofold. In the first place, there are, unfortunately, no comprehensive data-gathering procedures designed specifically for recording world language use figures, and so one has to piece together relevant information from sources such as censuses and statistical yearbooks. Given that these will only ever be very inaccurate, they need to be interpreted, and thus the figures one ends up with inevitably have a large margin of error.

A second issue concerns the presuppositions one needs to make in deciding who counts as a speaker of English. Both components of this concept – being a 'speaker' and the entity called 'English' – are open to varying interpretations. Decisions need to be made about what level of proficiency constitutes knowledge of the language (e.g. is an intermediate-level learner a speaker of the language?), and what range of varieties should be included in the category of 'English' (e.g. do contact languages such as Tok Pisin, which are mutually unintelligible with standard British or American English, count as 'English' for this purpose?). The indeterminate nature of both these issues further stretches the margin of error. Having said this, much intensive work has been carried out on compiling indicative statistics, and as long as the results are approached with the above caveats in mind, they are a good starting point for providing the context to the wider discussion of English in the world.

How many people speak English around the world?

David Crystal has, over the last two of decades, collated figures from various international organisations and linguistic surveys, and cross-referenced these with similar studies by other scholars (e.g. Bright, 1992; Graddol, 1997) to give a rough indication of the likely numbers of people using the language around the world (Crystal, 1997, 2003, 2008, 2012). He estimates that at the beginning of the twenty-first century, totals for first language speakers of English are somewhere between the 400 and 500 million mark (Crystal, 2012). There is obviously a vast difference between the top and bottom estimates here (a full hundred million people), and this is likely due to both decisions over whether **pidgins** and Creoles (mixed-languages developed from contact between English and other languages) are included in the reckonings, as well as difficulties approximating the percentage of English-speakers in some populations.

A figure of this sort is predominantly the result of adding together all the native English speakers from the leading English-dominant countries, plus estimates of those who have it as a native language living elsewhere in the globe. In calculating these figures, it has to be remembered that even in the two historically central English-speaking countries – the UK and USA – millions of people do not have the language as their mother tongue. Furthermore, many of the English-dominant countries – Canada, New Zealand, Ireland, Wales and South Africa – are officially bilingual or multilingual (in South Africa's case, English is one of eleven official languages). In all these cases, the national population is not coterminous with the number of English speakers. Taking this into account, the rough totals for English speakers in these countries are as follows:

United States of America	approx. 250m
United Kingdom	approx. 60m
Canada	approx. 24m
Australia and New Zealand	approx. 20m
The Caribbean	approx. 5m
Ireland	approx. 3.7m
South Africa	approx. 3.6m

This gives a base total for mother-tongue speakers in the major English-dominant countries as somewhere between 350 and 380 million.

Estimates of non-native English speakers are even more difficult to determine with anything approaching certainty. This is again partly due to the difficulty of finding source data, but even more to do with issues about who counts as an English speaker. The binary opposition between native and non-native speaker may suggest there is a straightforward distinction between mother-tongue countries and the rest, but the actuality is far more complex than this, and English has a variety of roles in a range of countries and territories around the world. As well as those listed above in which it is a dominant first language, there are many countries where it is used as a **second language** – that is, it has an official status (it is accorded the role of **official language**) alongside one or more local languages. In these countries, it is often used as the primary means of communication in areas such as administration, the law and education, while other languages operate for the remaining aspects of everyday life. There are around 60 countries in this category, including, for example, India, Nigeria and Singapore. However, even in countries where English does have official status, the proportion of the population actually speaking it remains modest – likely to be only 20 per cent to 30 per cent at best. This is because its use is mostly limited to urban areas and to white-collar employment, which excludes the majority of the population (Mufwene, 2010, p. 57). Still, even given this caveat, a total number of speakers in these countries is likely to near 600 million (Schneider, 2011).

And finally, English is often now taught as the primary foreign language in schools in many parts of the world, so the populations of over another hundred countries (McArthur lists a total of 139 places (1998, p. 54)) will come into contact with the language in this context.

The total Crystal settles on, taking account of these various factors, is between one and a half and two billion speakers of English worldwide. This is in comparison to the 1,213 million first language speakers of Chinese, and the 329 million first language speakers and 60 million second language speakers of Spanish. (These statistics for Chinese and Spanish are taken from Ethnologue, a survey of the world's languages published by the Summer Institute of Linguistics in the United States. This collects information on areas such as the status and location of languages, along with their numbers of speakers and different varieties. Ethnologue's own figure for first language English speakers in 2011 is 328 million.) Viewed from this perspective English is currently the most spoken language around the globe.

Before leaving the statistics, it is worth noting how estimates of worldwide English speakers have increased rapidly over recent decades. In 2008, David Crystal reviewed his own writings on this topic, and catalogued a progression in the calculations, beginning at a approximately one billion speakers of English in a 1985 article entitled 'How many millions use English?'; upping this to 1,350 million in the first edition of his *English as a Global Language* (1997, p. 61); then revising it again to 1,500 million in the second edition (2003, p. 69); and by 2008 coming to a total of up to two billion. In great part, this rapid expansion is due to the vast population growth in countries such as India and China. For example, in India, English has long had official status and is thus embedded in the culture; current estimates for number of English speakers there are around 300 million (Schneider, 2011); this is out of population in 2011 of 1.2 billion, and estimates for 2030 are that this figure will have increased to approximately 1.53 billion, making it the largest in the world. It is for these reasons that discussions about the future of English increasingly suggest that development in these two countries will play a significant role in determining what happens to the language in the coming decades (e.g. Graddol, 2010).

Implications of the statistics

The crude but indicative summary is that today close to two billion people – that is, almost a third of the world's population – have a certain competence in English. Even with the necessary vagueness of this figure, we can draw some important implications. The first is that, as has been widely noted in recent years, a significantly larger proportion of English users are now non-native speakers than native speakers – in fact, the ratio at present is along the lines of 4 to 1. Some indication of the scale of this can be given by noting that in China alone up to 350 million people are learning English, which is a similar number to the total of mother-tongue speakers of the language (Gu, 2009, p. 28). An important related point is that for the majority of people around the world today, English is being learnt after infancy, and their knowledge of the language is thus a product of institutional education.

A further important corollary of these figures is that two-thirds of the world's population *do not* speak English. So although it is the pre-eminent global language in today's world when compared to its competitors, it is still far from a universal resource, and twice as many people do not speak it as do. But an associated point is that even if a great many of the world's population have no practical knowledge of the language, it may still influence their lives in so far as it exists as a concept or idea within the culture. For example, people may aspire to learn it, motivated by beliefs about the benefit it could have for their lives, even if they have no experience of, or opportunity for, actually doing so. And as we have noted, beliefs and debates around the language can be as important for its existence in society as the actual use of it. For this reason, its influence is not a matter merely of number of speakers, but also of the roles it plays and the profile it has.

The history of English: the British Isles

A great deal of the diversity in the varieties of English, in people's experience of the language and their attitudes towards it, is a result of its history. The way that English has spread, the circumstances under which it has come in contact with other languages, the roles it has been assigned, and the associations it has attracted, all provide the context for the current state and status of English around the world, and for this reason it is worth reviewing the main events and processes which constitute the history of the language.

As we shall see, English was diverse from the very beginning. The idea of a single English only develops comparatively late in its history and, ironically, does so at much the same time as the language is travelling abroad and being diversified by foreign experience. The history of English is also a history of **language contact** – of the way English has interacted with the languages around it, has influenced and been influenced by them, and is itself, from its very earliest years, a hybrid language. To this we should add that the history of the language is of course, the history of the people who speak the language. It is the history of how different groups of people come into contact, and the political relationships between them. We shall begin in this section by looking at the development and spread of English in the British Isles; and in the next section go on to look at its move overseas and the processes that transformed it into a global language.

The Old English period

Robert McCrum describes the making of English as the result of three invasions and a cultural revolution (McCrum, 2010). It is a consequence of the often violent history of the British people in the second half of the first millennium, which saw the language shaped by the arrival of the Anglo-Saxons, the Vikings, the Normans, and by Christianity. Each of these altered the cultural landscape of Britain, and each brought linguistic influence from abroad to alter local patterns of language use.

English – or rather, what was to develop into English – was first brought to Britain around AD 449 when tribes from the north of Europe – the Angles, Jutes and Saxons, traditionally referred to collectively as the Anglo-Saxons – invaded and began to settle. In the previous decade, the Romans had completed a gradual withdrawal, and although during the Roman period – from their invasion circa 55 BC to the beginning of the fifth century – Latin had been the dominant language of government and culture in the British Isles, it departed with the colonisers. The indigenous languages of Britain were Celtic, similar to present-day Welsh and Cornish, and during the Roman period many communities would have been **bilingual** Celtic and Latin. The English language shows little trace of Celtic influence, however, and the vast majority of **Old English** vocabulary is of Germanic origin, with a provenance in the various dialects spoken by the Anglo-Saxon tribes. Recent scholarship suggests that the Anglo-Saxons and Celtic-speaking Britons lived alongside each other, but with the Anglo-Saxons as the dominant class. From the very beginning, therefore, social politics affected the distribution of languages among communities in society.

In the early centuries of the Old English period there was no notion of a unified 'England' as a political entity. It was not until the time of King Alfred (849–899) that partial unification occurred, although he did not rule over the entire territory of what we now call England. There was also no standard version of the language, either in the spoken or written form, but instead a collection of regionally variable dialects. At this time, therefore, the relationship between a 'nation' and a language was not a fixed one. This notion, which has been so influential for the way that different languages are conceptualised in Western cultures, would not come into full effect for another 800 years.

During the eighth century, following the Anglo-Saxon conversion to Christianity which began with Augustine's mission to Britain in AD 597, English began to borrow a great deal of vocabulary from Latin via the church. There was also influence during this period from the Vikings, who first came to Britain at the end of the eighth century and began to settle, occupying large parts of the country, in the ninth century. In 878, a treaty was signed between Alfred (who still retained power in the south) and the Danish king Guthrum, giving the latter rule over an area north and east of a line drawn from London to Chester, which is known as the Danelaw. The linguistic result of this was the influence of the Norse language on an ever-evolving English.

The Middle English period

The next major influence on English was the Norman Conquest of 1066, which introduced another high-status language to Britain in the form of Norman French. This marks the beginning of what is known as the **Middle English** period. Throughout William the Conqueror's reign, the nobility retained their lands in Normandy, and England was, in effect, a colony. Whereas in the very early days of its history, English had been the prestige language and the Celtic languages were spoken by the subjugated people, now it was English which operated as the **vernacular** with Norman French as the language of status. Society as a whole, though, was decidedly **multilingual**, with English as the vernacular, French the language of the court and of literature, and Latin the language of the church and school. In addition, Danish was spoken in the north, Cornish was still spoken in Cornwall, Welsh was spoken on the border with Wales, and Low German was spoken by immigrant settlers from the continent living in East Anglia.

The picture, then, is of different languages being spoken in different geographical areas and different **domains** – that is, different institutional contexts such as the court, the church, and so on. The co-existence of these languages, and the inevitable contact between them, resulted in a great deal of linguistic cross-fertilisation. Much of this influence was shaped by the politics of the different languages and their relative status and social positioning in different domains. Norman French, for example, left its mark on the vocabulary of English in areas relating to institutional power such as government (which is itself a French loanword), and the court.

It was also during this period that the notion of England as a distinct political entity within Britain began to emerge. It was not until the fourteenth century, however, that the use of French began to decline, and not until the accession of Henry IV in 1399 that England has its first king since the Norman invasion who spoke English as a first language. As we can see, then, for the first one thousand years of its life, English was far from the single, stable language of a unified country. For all its early and middle years it existed alongside other languages, often in a position of social inferiority, and was influenced extensively and repeatedly by the languages of people invading or settling in the country.

The Early Modern period and standardisation

It is in the sixteenth and seventeenth centuries that English first fully begins to resemble the way it is now, and to become a 'singular' entity. This is the beginning of what is known as the **Early modern** period, usually dated from around 1450. After the decline of French, a

London-based variety of English began to emerge as the prestige language, marking the first stage in the process of **standardisation**.

As we have discussed, the notion of the standard is of fundamental importance for how languages are perceived in modern-day society, and for issues such as the relationship between language and national identity. An understanding of how a standard language develops – or how it is constructed – is thus of key contextual importance for debates in World Englishes studies. The process has been analysed by the American linguist Einar Haugen (1966) as consisting of three different phases. Each of these, the result of a complex of specific historical events, has been instrumental in shaping moderns ideas of English.

The first phase in the process is that of **selection** – that is, the choice of a particular variety to act as the central standard. This occurred in incremental stages during the late fourteenth and early fifteenth centuries as a number of key government and administrative decisions were made with respect to the language. For example, in 1348 English replaced Latin as **medium of instruction** in schools; in 1362, it replaced French as the language of law and was first used in parliament. From the 1410s, after the Battle of Agincourt, royal proclamations began to be made in English; and by the 1430s all government documents were written in the language. In order that these documents could be understood across the length of the country, they needed to be in a consistent form of the language. As they were being produced in the Chancery in Westminster, it was the variety used here, which has come to be known as Chancery English, that provided the model.

Another important event for this process occurred in 1476, when William Caxton published the first book in English. He did this in Bruges, but later that year set up a printing press in Westminster, thus introducing the technology to England. The ability to replicate the same text in great numbers – and the decisions he made about which variety to use in print – began a process of 'fixing' the language, which was to have far-reaching consequences for the way that variation was (and is) viewed.

The next important stage in the process of standardisation is the **elaboration** of the variety so that it is capable of being used for different functions. This involves extending its range by expanding its vocabulary and grammatical flexibility. In the sixteenth and seventeenth centuries, a vibrant native literature developed, with writers such as Thomas Wyatt, Henry Howard Earl of Surrey, and Sir Philip Sidney introducing Italian and Classical forms such as the sonnet and blank verse into English literature. The Renaissance and Reformation also saw the translation of classical and religious texts into English so that they would be accessible to a wider, popular readership. The publication in 1611 of the King James Bible (or 'Authorised Version') was one of the pivotal events in this respect, and contributed to the process of elaboration of function by making one of the canonical religious texts available in the vernacular.

Throughout the seventeenth century, Latin was still operating as the language of science both in Britain and internationally, but coinciding with the foundation of the Royal Society in 1660 – many of whose members, such as John Wilkins and Francis Lodwick, had a particular interest in issues of language – English began to be modified and elaborated for use in this domain as well. In 1664, the Society went so far as to appoint a committee to consider ways "to improve the English tongue, Particularly for philosophic purposes" (cited in Baugh and Cable, 1993, p. 260). The coining of new scientific terms, and the development of precise registers, supplied English with the range to tackle analytic concepts, and in the last few decades of the seventeenth century a shift occurred towards English becoming the default language for major scientific texts. This can be neatly illustrated by the fact that Isaac Newton's *Philosophiæ Naturalis Principia Mathematica* of 1667 was published in Latin, but his later *Opticks* of 1704 was in English. Another significant event in this strain of the history is the founding in 1665 of the Royal Society's *Philosophical Transactions*, the first and longest-running scientific journal in the world, which again chose English as its medium of expression.

A further stage in the process of standardisation is the **codification** of the chosen variety by means of its recording in dictionaries or grammar books. This process begins in earnest for English in the eighteenth century. Early grammars of the language, such as William Bullokar's *Pamphlet for Grammar* (1586), and John Wallis's 1653 *Grammatica Linguae Anglicanae* (which, despite its subject, was written in Latin), were meant as educational tools to assist with the teaching of English rather than as guides to correct usage. It was during the eighteenth century, with works such as Robert Lowth's *A Short Introduction to English Grammar* (1762), that guides aiming to outline a standard English grammar began to emerge, and instigated a tradition of prescriptivism over what counted as 'correct' English.

The development of dictionaries followed a similar pattern. Early dictionaries, such as the first extant monolingual English dictionary, Robert Cawdrey's *A Table Alphabeticall*, published in 1604, were intended as guides to 'hard words' – that is, those that had been "borrowed from the Hebrew, Greeke, Latine, or French" as the vocabulary of English was expanded. By the beginning of the following century, there were occasional works which attempted to define the everyday language, such as John Kersey's *Dictionarium Anglo-Britannicum* of 1708, and Nathan Bailey's *An Universal Etymological English Dictionary* of 1721. It was not until the mid-eighteenth century, though, and Samuel Johnson's *Dictionary of the English Language* (1755), that the template for the modern conception of the dictionary was perfected. Johnson's dictionary, by dint of its authority and popularity, proved to be an extremely important milestone for standard English in the way that it mapped the form of the language and made choices between variant spellings which, in most part, are still followed in standard British English today.

Johnson's initial intention had been to definitively document the language to prevent further variation. In 1747, as he began work on the project, he published a *Plan of a Dictionary of the English Language* which outlined his ambition, declaring that the "one great end of this undertaking is to fix the English language" (Johnson, 1747, p. 11). This notion of 'fixing' the language – of regulating the perceived disorder of contemporary usage and producing a stable, uniform and exact code for communication – has been a recurring aspiration in language planning. It was the intention behind the language academies, and the goal of the language engineers who dreamt of constructing a perfected artificial language. But by the time Johnson came to publish his dictionary nine years later, he had concluded that this purpose was impossible:

> Those who have been persuaded to think well of my design, require that it should fix our language, and put a stop to those alterations which time and chance have hitherto been suffered to make in it without opposition. With this consequence I will confess that I flattered myself for a while; but now begin to fear that I have indulged expectation which neither reason nor experience can justify. ... may the lexicographer be derided, who being able to produce no example of a nation that has preserved their words and phrases from mutability, shall imagine that his dictionary can embalm his language, and secure it from corruption and decay, that it is in his power to change sublunary nature, or clear the world at once from folly, vanity, and affectation.
>
> (Johnson, 1755)

Despite its shortcomings in this respect, the *authority* invested in the dictionary as a material record of the language – which began with Johnson, and has continued most noticeably with the *Oxford English Dictionary* (*OED*) – is still a key instrument in establishing what counts as the standard language, particularly in the absence of a language academy. The *OED*, for example, calls itself 'The definitive record of the English language', suggesting that, while it may fall short of fixing the language absolutely, it is still the arbiter of meaning, form and usage.

Along with these various language-specific events, the wider political climate of the eighteenth century also contributed to the idea of a standard language, especially as it operated as a **national language**.

During the eighteenth century, the notion of nationalism was growing in Europe, based around an ideology which associated a people's identity with the territory in which they lived and the culture they practised. Before this, the concept of a single national language had been of relatively little political significance, but with the rise of the idea of a national identity it became politically symbolic (Anderson, 2006). The sentiments of this view are summed up in the German philosopher Johann Herder's assertion that language "expresses the most distinguishing traits of the character of each nationality, and is the mirror of its history, its deeds, joys and sorrows" (cited in Ergang, 1966, p. 149). In the British context, the political rationale for promoting a uniform variety was consolidated by the Act of Union that was passed in 1707, incorporating Scotland into a single political entity now called Great Britain. In 1800, Ireland was then formally incorporated into what had come to be called 'the United Kingdom', and as the British Empire expanded in the nineteenth century, notions of a standard English were further promoted so as to provide a model for Britain's overseas territories.

The story we have, then, is of a single homogenous English being, in effect, 'constructed' by the determinants of its history. It is not a construct orchestrated by an institutional centre, but one which has had several different agents, and been a mixture of the political climate (e.g. the development of nationalism), the influence of technology (e.g. the invention of the printing press), and the enterprise of a number of individuals and social groups. If these historical events had occurred in a different way, so the language itself would in some way be different. In other words, the trajectory of development was not inevitable, but was the product of historical contingency.

It is also worth underlining the fact that the standard language develops both in practice (i.e. in terms of people's use of the language) and as an ideology (i.e. their opinions about the language) (Milroy and Milroy, 1999). That is to say, there developed at this time a standardised form of the language that people actually use, but there is also the *idea* of the standard – the complex of embedded beliefs in the social consciousness – which is itself influential in shaping attitudes, behaviour, and even policy towards English. The two are obviously interrelated, but they are also separate in that the ideology of standard English is not an exact fit with the practice. What people believe about language can and does differ from the way they use it. And it is this that results in many of the 'problems' we shall be looking at.

The history of English: the wider world

The reasons for the current global spread of English can be distilled down to three related major historical factors: it was the language of the British Empire; it was the language of science and the industrial revolution; and it was the language of the United States as it grew into a political and economic superpower in the twentieth century (Crystal, 2003). The first of these processes begins in the Early Modern period when Britain began engaging in overseas commercial ventures, including the acquisition of colonies.

Colonisation

Whereas the story of the development of English in the British Isles is mostly unitary – or at least, while different parts of what is now the United Kingdom experienced different histories of English, the national language ideology that took root in the eighteenth and nineteenth centuries has created a perspective which groups them as part of the same story – the spread of English beyond the British Isles is defiantly varied and multiplex. Colonisation – which was the driver behind most of the initial overseas expansion of English – was not a uniform experience. The history of every colony is distinct and each created a different set of circumstances under which cultural and linguistic influence occurred. It is, however, possible to give a very general outline of the British colonial project, and divide the many colonial experiences into broad categories according to their purpose and consequences.

Colonisation as a process involves the establishment, often by violent means, of communities on foreign soil that are governed by or on behalf of the ruling authorities in the colonisers' home country. These newly formed communities establish a dominant relationship over the indigenous peoples, while at the same time retaining political and cultural associations with the home nation. Among the cultural consequences of this process is that language practices in the settled territory becomes greatly influenced by the colonisers' language practices.

The history of British colonisation begins in earnest in the seventeenth century, when, on 31 December 1600, the East India Company was granted a Royal Charter by Elizabeth I. Many of the earliest colonies are what Salikoko Mufwene (2001) classifies as 'trade colonies', that is, forts or posts established in areas such as the coast of West Africa and various Asian ports for the specific purpose of trade. In these instances, the lack of a common language between the indigenous inhabitants and the colonisers leads to the development of makeshift languages comprising elements from the native languages of all those involved.

A second type of colony is what Mufwene refers to as 'settlement colonies'. In these cases, there is large-scale population relocation from Britain, with the colonisers establishing permanent settlements in the new territories, and as a result, exporting their language with them. In doing so, pre-colonial populations were displaced, and in many instances massacred, or decimated by imported foreign diseases. The reasons for people emigrating from Britain to settle elsewhere included issues such as population growth, a surplus of labour, religious dissent (as in the case of the Pilgrim Fathers who created the Plymouth Colony in 1620), and criminal deportation (as in the case of Australia's 'First Fleet' – the group of ships, carrying among its one and a half thousand passengers about 800 convicts, which sailed from Britain in 1787 to establish the first European colony in Australia). Settlement colonies in America gave rise to a further variant of colonisation when labour was imported from elsewhere to work on the huge rice and cotton plantations that had developed in the south of the country and in the Caribbean. This labour was supplied by slaves who were transported principally from West Africa.

In the eighteenth and nineteenth centuries, in what was the height of the colonial period, a third type, referred to by Mufwene as 'exploitation colonies', was established in places such as India and Nigeria. The intention in these instances was to gain political control over the territories so as to exploit their natural resources. To do this, small administrative communities were set up which kept the indigenous population in subjection. In the case of the British colonies, the strategy was to educate a small elite from the local populace who worked as part of the administration. This was referred to as 'indirect rule', a principle first developed by Lord Lugard, High Commissioner of the Protectorate of Northern Nigeria at the end of the nineteenth century. English was thus introduced through formal education, but restricted to this elite group. It was, in effect, part of the apparatus of control, and subsequently became associated with the Empire's command.

In each of these types of colonisation, different patterns of contact between the colonisers and the indigenous people resulted in different linguistic needs and different forms of language contact. Thus, while within Britain a standard language ideology was developing which was regularising aspects of the language, as English was being spread abroad it necessarily became mixed and diversified. This happened both in terms of the different British dialects that were being exported – the colonial process brought together people from different areas of Britain, and, to an extent, from different social classes – and in the ways the language was adapted to the new contexts in which it was being used.

Pidgins and Creoles

One particularly acute linguistic outcome of the history of colonisation is the development of pidgin and Creole languages. These are **contact languages** which result from the strategies developed by different groups who do not share a common language but need to improvise a means of communication. They appeared in various places around the world, particularly from the seventeenth century onwards, both as trading languages and as a result of the mass transportation of slaves from Africa to the Caribbean.

As makeshift languages developed for ad hoc communicative encounters between different communities, pidgins typically have reduced vocabularies and simplified grammar. Sociolinguists usually identify a pidgin according to its location and to the language which provides the majority of its vocabulary, which is known as the **lexifier**. For example, West African Pidgin English is the broad term for the variety spoken along the west coast of Africa from Gambia to Cameroon. The vocabulary derives mostly from English, but the grammar is a composite of various African languages.

Closely related to pidgins are Creole languages. Traditionally, these are often defined as the result of pidgins being adopted as a first language by a community. That is, whereas as a pidgin lacks native speakers, if it then gets passed on to the children of a community who are raised speaking it as their main language, its structural and functional complexity expands and it comes to be used as a full language within society.

The process of a pidgin becoming a Creole is referred to as **creolisation**. There is, however, some controversy about exactly how this occurs. While some pidgins appear to change into Creoles by being nativised by a community, other contact patterns have also been observed. Mufwene, for example, argues that pidgins and Creoles developed in separate parts of the world as a result of different forms of contact between Europeans and non-Europeans. In the trade colonies, interaction was sporadic, thus giving rise to pidgins; in the settlement colonies, it was more regular and sustained, and this resulted in the development of Creole languages (Mufwene, 2006).

It is also worth stressing that although the two terms suggest distinct phenomena, in practice this is not the case. There are varieties which are referred to as pidgins which not only have native speakers but do in fact operate as official languages. For example, the English-language pidgin Bislama is an official language along with French and English in Vanuatu in the South Pacific. In some cases, the term **expanded pidgin** is used to refer to a variety which has some native speakers and is used in certain domains such as education and administration, yet does not have the full status of a Creole. Nigerian Pidgin English, for example, has over 20 million speakers in the world, and more than one million speak it as their first language, and, as we have seen with the work of Aig-Imoukhuede, it has an emergent native literature.

Traditionally, the social status of these varieties has been very low, in part because for a long time they have not been considered 'proper' or 'real' languages, and also because 'pidgin' is used in non-academic contexts as a synonym for 'broken English'. This issue of status is also of importance for World Englishes studies and, again, is one to which we will return.

Postcolonialism and the era of globalisation

Prior to the nineteenth century, administration of the colonies had mostly been overseen by the trading companies which originally set them up. In the nineteenth century, the British government began to take more direct interest in them, giving rise to the 'British Empire'. Power became centralised and, as a consequence, standard British English was promoted as the dominant model of the language. Yet concurrent with this was the beginnings of nationalist sentiment in many colonies, which would eventually lead to independence. The first colony in which this happened was what became the United States. In 1776, following disputes over taxation and concerns over parliamentary representation, the United States achieved political independence through armed uprising. In order to avoid a similar scenarios elsewhere, the British government negotiated a form of self-governance for Canada in 1867, and later granted what was known as dominion status to other settlement colonies: to Australia in 1901, New Zealand in 1907 and South Africa in 1910. In exploitation colonies, such as India and many of the African colonies, independence was gained through political struggle. In many instances, English was used as the language of the independence movements because of its usefulness as a means of communication for the different ethnic and linguistic groups who made up the populations of these territories. In the decades after the Second World War, colony after colony gained its independence: India, Pakistan and New Zealand in 1947; Ghana and Malaysia in 1957; Nigeria in 1960; and so on. A great many of these, with the exception only of Tanzania and, to an extent, Malaysia, retained English as a central part of their national culture after independence (Schneider, 2011, p. 53).

The history of colonisation and its **postcolonial** aftermath is one of the main reasons for the spread of English; but another important factor has been the complex of cultural, economic and political influences which took hold during the twentieth century – many of which are specifically related to the dominant position of the United States in world politics. As David Crystal writes, "in the 20th century, cultural power manifested itself in virtually every walk of life through spheres of American influence" (Crystal, 2006, p. 427). The centrality of English is evidenced in the following domains: in politics, where it now plays an official or working role in the proceedings of most major international political gatherings, from the United Nations, to NATO, to ASEAN; in economics, with New York and London operating as central players in the financial world; in the press and broadcasting, with global organisations such as Reuters being based in London and the Associated Press being based in New York, and news services such as CNN International, BBC World News, and more recently Al-Jazeera English. It is also a dominant force in forms of popular culture such as the movies, with the continuing global ascendancy of Hollywood (figures suggesting that up to 80 per cent of the feature films that get a theatrical release are in English (Dyja, 2005, cited in Crystal, 2012), and popular music, which again is centred around traditions in the UK and US. It also plays a significant role in global education and academia, both as a medium of instruction in many countries and as the international language of science. In addition, it has many specialised roles, such as its use in the domain of international travel and safety, where it is the basis for the controlled languages used in the aviation and maritime industries (Airspeak and Seaspeak respectively). And finally, it has been the principle language of modern communications technology, especially since the invention of the internet (Crystal, 2003).

Before leaving the history of the language, it is worth bringing the story up to date into the twenty-first century. In doing so, we can see that, while the concentration of political power around the US in the twentieth century was instrumental in creating English's current global dominance, the present century may well lead to different political, and thus linguistic, trends. If we look, for example, at the figures for language use on the internet in recent years we can see how English's global dominance is not without competitors. The internet was begun is the early 1980s, and its initial development was predominantly US based and thus Anglophone. In 2010 (less than two decades after the invention of the world wide web), just under two billion people were estimated to be using the internet (out of a world population of close to seven billion). Of these, 536 million were English users, which is 27 per cent of the total of all users. The next two largest languages on the internet were Chinese, which had 445 million users, comprising 22.6 per cent of the world internet population, and Spanish with 153 million users (7.8 per cent of the world internet population). Thus English was still, by some margin, the most used online language around the world.

But comparing these figures to those of ten years earlier we see that English is not nearly as dominant now as it was then. If we look at the expansion between 2000 and 2010 – a period during which internet use as a whole grew by 444 per cent – we see that the total of English-language users rose by 281.2 per cent – a substantial figure – but that in comparison, the Spanish total rose by 743.2 per cent, and the Chinese total by a staggering 1,277.4 per cent. (Arabic also increased massively in those ten years – by 2,501.2 per cent – so that in 2010 it had 65 million speakers.) In other words, in the year 2000 about two-thirds of internet users were English speakers, but by 2010 this share had decreased to a little over a quarter (Internet World Stats, 2011). In part, these figures represent the social and geographical history of the internet. Development in its formative years was essentially led by US research institutions and companies; it was here that the majority of web content was generated, and for this reason it was mostly Anglophone. As the online world has expanded and more non-English speakers have adopted it, so the internet has become multilingual. These statistics therefore show the other major linguistic groups catching up. But it also apparent that although English continues to dominate online communication at the present moment, if trends do continue along these lines, it will not remain in this position for long. So while the spread of English has been rapid and extensive, and while English does now play a major role in practically all spheres of global society, this should not be seen as an end point. The history of the language is ongoing, and the concepts we are attempting to pin down and the issues we are analysing are dynamic and subject to continuing flux and evolution.

Tasks

In light of what we have discussed in this chapter, consider the following study questions:

- What are the implications of the statistics of English speakers around the world for English's status as a 'global language'?
- How has the history of English shaped modern-day beliefs about the language?
- What different factors lie behind English's current status as a global language?

Feedback for these questions is given in the 'Commentary on tasks' section at the end of the book.

4 Problems for practitioners in World Englishes

The brief history of the language in Chapter 3 illustrates the way that the story of English – or the stories of the many worldwide Englishes – is part of a wider history of English-speaking people. It is part of the history of the contact they have had with other communities, of the beliefs they have associated with the language, and of the practices they have developed to promote or regulate it. Historical linguists traditionally distinguish between the 'internal history' of a language – the changes that occur to its form: to pronunciation, grammar and lexis – and the 'external history' – how events in the wider world have affected or been implicated in the use and status of the language. In Chapter 3 we concentrated predominantly on the external history. Were this a **sociolinguistic** study of World Englishes rather than an applied linguistics one, it would have been worth looking in further detail at the internal history, and at the linguistic trends that led to the current formal variation in English around the world. As our interest is on how issues concerning the language present problems for its use in society, the focus has been on the *social* history of the language, and on the people who have been influenced and affected by its development. It is this aspect of its history which offers the more useful context for our exploration, and which often lies behind the problems the language poses for those who work with or use it as part of their everyday life.

In this chapter, we will consider two broad social mechanisms which play an important role in the social life of the language. At this stage of the exploration the focus is on identifying problems that occur in these contexts and formulating the types of questions they present for language professionals. In Section B, we shall go on to consider how people have attempted to answer these questions, and will examine various case studies in order to evaluate the success of their proposed solutions.

The teaching and testing of World Englishes

The first context to look at is the teaching and learning of English. Why should this be a particularly important issue for the study of

World Englishes? To answer this let us begin by considering what it means to learn a language. Languages can be learnt at different stages and in different circumstances during the life cycle, and each of these involves different patterns of acquisition. For millions of people, English is a first language – it is the language of the community in which they are raised, and they acquire its spoken form as a natural part of their social development and without the need for any formal or structured 'teaching'. In such cases, infants acquire the variety that is spoken around them. For broad sections of society this does not mean a standard English, but rather a local regional or social dialect. When they then enter formal education, they are taught the standard, in both its written and its spoken forms. Even in mother-tongue English countries, therefore, institutional education is instrumental in shaping certain aspects of the linguistic practices and beliefs of members of society. And for this reason, choices that educators make with respect to the language can have important implications for society as a whole.

Institutional education is also crucial for the way the language exists and evolves in non-mother-tongue countries. As we have seen, the majority of English speakers around the world today learn it as a second or additional language. This often means they learn it via formal schooling of some sort. As such, teachers and teaching institutions are key mediators in the way in which English is introduced to people worldwide.

In discussing the influence of education, it is worth underlining the fact that decisions made by teachers and educators are a combination of the practical (e.g. pedagogic strategies for effective language teaching) and the ideological, in that they impact upon how people perceive English, and how beliefs about the language have social consequences for its users and the wider community. The French philosopher Michel Foucault described education as "a ritualisation of the word" (Foucault, 1972, p. 227) in that it controls both the cultural knowledge that society values and passes on from generation to generation and how people are expected to use language as a means of communication and expression. Throughout our discussion in this book, this twofold aspect to the existence of language – as both something people use and something people think about – is of crucial importance. And education has an influence on both.

In this chapter, we will look predominantly at issues relating to English education in non-mother-tongue countries – that is, where it is learnt as a second or additional language. These are commonly known as **TESOL (Teaching English to Speakers of Other Languages)** contexts and, given the demographics of English speakers around the world, they are increasingly important for current debates about the language.

What variety of English should be taught?

What, then, are the specific problems that language educators have to engage with? A key issue – if not *the* key issue – for English education, especially in countries where English is not a mother tongue, is what model of the language should be taught. Given the diversity of worldwide forms of English, which variety is best taught to students? And what are the consequences of this decision for the learning process, for the practices and psychology of students and teachers, and for the politics of the language in the wider society?

There are two broad approaches to this issue. These are the choice between a standard variety of the type spoken in an English-dominant country such as the UK or USA, and a 'local' model of the language. Andy Kirkpatrick (2007) describes this alternative as being between an **exonormative** native speaker model – that is, one which looks to external norms, namely those used in native-speaker countries – or an **endonormative** nativised model – one which uses the norms that have developed as the language has become 'indigenised' by the local community.

In taking a decision about which of these models is likely to be more appropriate, educators need to weigh up a number of factors. These factors will vary considerably depending on the circumstances in which the language is being taught; that is, there is not a straightforward 'right' or 'wrong' answer which will have universal validity for all English language teaching contexts. Instead, teachers needs to take account of:

- issues related to the suitability of the variety as a means of communication;
- issues related to the practice of teaching the variety;
- issues relating to the cultural politics of the variety.

It is possible to divide these various factors into two sets of dichotomies: practical concerns and ideological concerns; and those relating to what happens in the classroom and those relating to the wider society. We can plot these dichotomies on a simple diagram (Figure 4.1). In each quadrant of this diagram (labelled *a* to *d*), different issues pertain depending on the context and purpose of the learning.

Let us look at what these different factors mean for the two broad approaches to the question. First, for the learning of a 'native speaker' variety:

a) From a practical point of view, a key motivating factor for the learning of English is that it has a global reach. One of the chief arguments in favour of using standard UK or US varieties as

	Beyond the classroom	Within the classroom
Practical issues	a	b
Ideological issues	c	d

Figure 4.1 Factors involved in the choice of teaching model

teaching models, therefore, is that they (are thought to) allow for universal intelligibility. This functional ability is based on the present status and spread of these varieties around the world; as global sociolinguistic trends develop and alter, the affordances of these varieties may also change and other varieties may assume the function of pre-eminent international standard. But for the moment, due in part to the fact that native speaker varieties *are* used globally as teaching standards, it is these varieties which come closest to acting as international standards.

b) A related issue is that standard UK or US varieties are extensively codified, which means that reference tools for them already exist (i.e. there are a range of available dictionaries and grammars of standard British and American English). Similarly, teaching resources for these varieties are plentiful, and both the UK and USA have large English Language Teaching (ELT) industries which supply English language education expertise all around the world. In terms of classroom practice, therefore, the availability of these pre-existing materials is both convenient and cost-effective, and provides a ready-made support structure for educators.

c) Moving to ideological issues, the native speaker varieties have prestige and legitimacy in many parts of the world, and this also makes them attractive models for both individual learners, and governments and policy makers.

d) The prestige these varieties have frequently translates into motivation for learning them. Students often identify these varieties with aspirational lifestyles or a range of instrumental benefits, and this provides impetus for the learning process. There is a converse consequence to this as well, however, in that a native-speaker model is unlikely to be something a student will ever fully or perfectly attain, and if acquisition of this type of variety is considered by the student to be the goal, the learning process is likely to be marked by a sense of frustration and possibly even failure (Kirkpatrick, 2007).

In many respects, the issues relating to the teaching of a local variety are the inverse counterpart to those for a native-speaker standard:

a) Whereas US or UK varieties have international currency, many local varieties do not, and one argument against them is lack of international intelligibility. This issue is often over-stated, if not completely unfounded, however, and varietal difference need not be an impediment to international communication. Furthermore, if the language is going to be predominantly used in local contexts – as, for example, it may well be in countries where it operates as an official language – the local variety is likely, in fact, to be the more appropriate form.

b) Whereas standard US or UK varieties are well codified, many local varieties have yet to undergo this process, or are at the very early stages of it. So while teaching resources such as textbooks and assessment instruments are pre-existing and plentiful for US or UK standard varieties, they do not exist for many local varieties. This can have consequences in terms of cost and extra work for educators. However, the adoption of a local variety as a teaching model can be the impetus for further codification, and can assist in enhancing the status of that local variety. From an education policy perspective, therefore, there are long-term advantages to choosing a local variety which may outweigh the short-term inconveniences associated with limited pre-existing resources.

c) In terms of ideological considerations, the advantages and disadvantages of using a local variety depend on the status that variety has in society. Where it is stigmatised, it will obviously not have the same value as a prestige variety. Yet in contexts where it is well established and linked closely to cultural identity, it can have positive associations.

d) The local model is likely to be both attainable and familiar to the students in a way that an exonormative native-speaker model will not be, and this can be a positive consideration for the pedagogic process.

In summary, the choice of which variety to use as a teaching model involves issues that concern the availability and suitability of resources, the cost implications of accessing or generating materials, the purpose for which the language is being learnt, the prestige and status accorded to different varieties in particular contexts, and pedagogic concerns relating to motivation and attainability. The relative balance of these issues will differ depending on the contexts in which English is taught. In countries where English has a long-established history and official status, for example, the advantages of using a local variety may be greater than in those countries where it is still predominantly a foreign language. The 'problem' for educators, therefore, is to make informed decisions which navigate these various factors while taking into account the insights about the use of language in a global context which World Englishes studies provides.

Who should teach English?

The question of which variety to use as a teaching model is not the only problem related to World Englishes which confronts language educators. Another issue concerns the person doing the teaching, and the type of linguistic resource that they constitute. That is, teachers themselves – in that they each speak particular forms of English – are an embodiment of the diversity of the language, and their own linguistic background and profile thus act as a variable in the educational process. This linguistic profile often acts as a determinant in hiring practices in educational institutions, and is promoted as a key element of successful language teaching. The issue is one which leads to a great deal of controversy, and the arguments on either side are a mixture of the practical, the ideological and the ethical.

Again, there are two main categories that can be used to anatomise this issue: teachers who are native speakers of the language, that is, come from one of the English-dominant countries and are therefore from outside the community in which the language is being learnt; and local teachers who have English as a second or additional language. There are also two perspectives from which to view the decision: how it affects learners, and how it affects those doing the teaching.

Many of the factors that have an impact on this issue are counterparts of the question of which model of the language to use. From the students' perspective, a native-speaker teacher can provide what is seen as an authentic model of the language as it is spoken in an Anglophone country. They are also often thought to have an intuitive knowledge about usage norms, and, if English is being learnt as a 'foreign' language (i.e. as a component part of the culture of one of the mother-tongue countries), they can draw on their cultural background as a heuristic. The counter-argument is that non-native speakers act as role models of successful later-life acquisition of the language, they have experience of learning English in similar circumstances to their students (i.e. as an additional language), and are also familiar with local educational and cultural norms. As we can see, therefore, the case for either category will in part depend on the reason that students have for learning the language, and the different requirements these involve.

But decisions of this sort also have implications for the teachers themselves. It has traditionally been the practice in many regions of the world where a standard US or UK model is valorised, for ELT instructors to be hired solely on their status as native speakers, and have no need for professional teaching qualifications. This obviously disadvantages the local teacher population, both in practical (i.e. professional and economic) terms and on a psychological level. It also undermines the professional status of the teaching industry as a whole. The teaching of a local variety, however, can professionally advantage local teachers, and avoid undermining their self-esteem in the way that the promotion of a native-speaker model indirectly casts them as imperfect speakers of the language. Furthermore, the multilingual competence that local teachers are likely to have (i.e. knowledge of local languages in addition to an expertise in English) can be a productive resource in the classroom.

How should English be tested?

An important complement to the teaching of English is the testing of it, and this also is implicated in the pedagogy and politics of World Englishes. Testing is a two-way facing exercise: it can be an important part of the education process itself, in terms of evaluating knowledge and focusing and motivating the act of learning; but it also plays a role beyond education, acting as a determinant in the organisation of society. These two effects are known as **washback** and **impact,** and correspond broadly to the dichotomy discussed above between factors that influence education in relation to what happens in and what happens beyond the classroom. Washback is the effect that a test has on teaching and learning practices. For example, in Japan, English exams traditionally test grammatical structures rather than communicative competence, and thus the washback is that teaching strategies in the classroom focus predominantly on the grammar-translation method (known in Japan as *yakudoku*), and students can often come through several years of school and university education without developing skills for communicating in the language to any great extent.

The outward-facing implication is the impact examinations have in society. For many students, an immediate and practical purpose of learning English is to pass what are known as **high-stakes tests,** that is, those which have important social consequences for the test takers. These are tests of the sort which regulate access to employment or education opportunities, or have consequences for other vitally important life opportunities. As McNamara and Roever write, placing modern practices into a historical context:

One of the most pervasive functions and consequences of language tests throughout history is their use as sorting and gatekeeping instruments. These tests, imposed by a more powerful group on a less powerful one, tend to have severe, life-changing, and not infrequently life-ending consequences for their takers, from the Biblical shibboleth test followed by the immediate slaughter of those failing it to the modern language tests that form a precondition for promotion, employment, immigration, citizenship, or asylum.

(McNamara and Roever, 2006, p. 1)

Examples of these last categories include the way that people wishing to gain permanent residence in or become citizens of the UK need to prove proficiency in English measured at ESOL Entry Level 3, and pass the 'Life in the UK Test' which examines knowledge of everyday cultural and social practices in the UK. (Legally people can also take the test in Welsh and Scots Gaelic, but to date almost no one has done so.) Australia and Canada also have language tests as part of their citizenship procedures, while people applying for New Zealand citizenship have to take the International English Language Test System (IELTS). Tests of this sort, therefore, are not solely part of the educational process, but play a role in the political regulation and organisation of society (Shohamy, 2006) and act as an institutional means of constructing a bond between language practices and national identity.

Many of the issues around the practice of English tests in the era of World Englishes are similar to those relating to its teaching. Most tests are predicated on the idea that the language is composed of a set core of correct usages – traditionally taken to be those of the ideal native speaker – and that the design of the test will 'catch out' lack of proficiency in these usages. Concerns have been voiced that many of the mainstream English language tests are structured around linguistics norms which do not accurately represent the range of varieties that are used around the world (Davidson, 2006). Paralleling the issue of which variety of the language should be used as a teaching model, a key question for testing therefore becomes: whose norms should provide the standard for the test? This, plus the issue of how one measures 'proficiency' in the language, are the central problems for the testing of English in a global context.

As with the issue of the teaching model, there are two traditions of answers to this: those who advocate the use a standard native-speaker variety (where proficiency is the ability to replicate native-speaker usage), or use of a local variety (and the ability to communicate fluently according to local communicative norms). Suresh Canagarajah (2006), however, argues that such a dichotomy over-simplifies the way that the language is actually used around the world today. Because English is now a multiplex language, proficiency in it necessitates being 'multidialectical': "[a] proficient speaker of English in the postmodern world", he contends, "should be able to shuttle between different norms, recognizing the systematic and legitimate status of different varieties of English in this diverse family of languages" (Canagarajah, 2006, p. 234). In other words, in a world in which people move from context to context, they will need access to different types of English. This does not mean they need to be proficient in *all* varieties, but instead that they have communicative strategies which can negotiate the diversity in the way that English is now spoken in the era of globalisation. The issue here is once again striking a balance between the practical realities of testing proficiency in the language, and reflecting the sociolinguistic realities of how people use the language in their everyday life.

$$***$$

In sum, there are a complex of practical and ideological issues relating to the teaching and testing of English, many of which relate to the circumstances in which the language is taught, and the purposes for which it is learnt. The diversity in the language is matched by the diversity of contexts in which and for which it is taught, and educators need to weigh the many implication of this in making decisions about their teaching. In Section B, we will return to this issue, and consider some of the strategies that have been proposed as solutions to these various open questions. Before doing so, however, let us consider the other major context that produces 'problems' with World Englishes, that of language policy.

The World Englishes question in language policy

While the education sector plays a crucial role in determining aspects of English's existence around the world, this existence is also influenced by other forms of social regulation, such as those proposed and enacted by national governments. The general term for this type of regulation is **language policy**, which refers to the directives devised by organisations and institutions for the use of language in society. While much of this occurs at the level of national governments, other bodies, from transnational organisations to individual companies, also devise and enact policies for the use of language. And with the range of roles that it now plays in numerous countries, along with its status as a global *lingua franca* and the language of international commerce, English increasingly features as a subject of such policies in contexts all across the globe.

Language policies for global English are not a recent development. During the colonial period, policies for English were enacted by the governing powers for the purposes of regulating language use in the colonies. One of the most famous of these is 'Macaulay's Minute'. Written in 1835 by the British politician Thomas Macaulay, this lays out a language policy for Indian colonial administration based around the use of English. Macaulay's objective was to form "a class of persons, Indian in blood and colour, but English in taste, in opinions, in morals, and in intellect" and the English language was to be the vehicle for effecting this (Macaulay, 1972 [1835], p. 249). Following independence, policies retaining English as an official language were also enacted by many postcolonial countries. In this instance, one of the rationales was a striving for political stability following the divisions created during the colonial period. In many contexts, English, despite being an ex-colonial language, could act as a common and neutral medium of communication which would help surmount ethnic divisions and build a sense of national unity, as well as maintaining connections with the international community (Rassool, 2007). In instances such as these, therefore, English has been promoted as a means to particular political ends, and it is used in this way because of the cultural associations and social status it has within that particular historical context.

Language policy issues for English today predominantly relate to how governments and other organisations aim to deal with the consequences of the spread of the language. There is a broad dichotomy here between policies which act on the assumption that English brings positive benefits and those which are concerned about its negative consequences, and most forms of regulation attempt to strike a balance between the two that suits their particular contexts and concerns. One issue, for example, becomes how to take advantage of the international communicative affordances of English while maintaining the ethnolinguistic vitality of the local culture. In transnational organisations such as the institutions of the European Union, for instance, should English be promoted as a *lingua franca* which can assist with the inevitable communications challenges of such a diverse group of peoples, and if so, what implications will this have for the cultural identity of non-English speaking nations? Likewise in developing nations, is English-language education likely to assist with personal and community socio-economic advancement, or would mother-tongue education provide firmer and more sustainable foundations for the nation's development?

Another frequently voiced concern about the spread of English relates to the effect it is having on other languages around the world, and specifically 'smaller' languages, that is, those with comparatively few speakers and less prestige or functional flexibility in society. The fear here is that the spread of English is a contributing factor to **language death** – the process whereby a language ceases to exist as a contemporary means of communication, either because those who speak it do not pass it on to their children, or because a process of **language shift** occurs and the community move to the use of another language. This phenomenon occurs most often in multilingual contexts in which a powerful or **majority language** such as English takes over the functions that were previously played in society by a **minority language** (i.e. one spoken by a small or a more politically marginal section of the population) and that, as a result, speakers of the minority language begin to adopt the majority one as their primary means of communication (May, 2006).

The statistics that portray the current patterns of linguistic diversity in the world are stark. It was estimated that, at the turn of the millennium, 96 per cent of the languages in the world were spoken by just 4 per cent of its population (Summer Institute of Linguistics, cited in Crystal, 1999). Statistical predictions further suggest that of these estimated 6,900 languages currently spoken worldwide (Ethnologue, 2011), somewhere between 20 and 50 per cent are likely to die out by the end of this century (Krauss, 1992). Given this picture, the processes governing language loss, and the fact that English is one of the principal majority languages in the world today, it seems a likely hypothesis that the spread of English is in some way related to the demise of smaller languages. For this reason, English has been described in some quarters as a 'killer language' (e.g. Nettle and Romaine, 2000; Skutnabb-Kangas, 2000), and one of the pressing problems for language policy becomes how to combat this effect.

In almost all scenarios with which language policies deal, the issues are far from clear-cut, and gauging how regulation can assist is not straightforward. For example, the picture of English overwhelming minority languages is complicated by the lack of conclusive evidence about the causal relationship between the spread of English and language death, as well as by the strong desire that many communities have for the benefits that a prestige language such as English can bring. Productive policy needs to begin by untangling the issues, evidence and assumptions on which it acts, therefore, and these are questions with which applied linguistics can help.

✳✳✳

In summary, then, policies for global English are a response to the identity and associations that history has produced for the language. Many of the motivating factors behind these policies relate to abstract notions of what English is – its status as 'a global language', 'a language of economic opportunity', 'a killer language' – and these become the basis for acts of social regulation which aim to promote or protect against the language for various particular purposes. How such regulation works out, however, is often a complex matter, and is one we shall return to in Section B, where we will look at a selection of case studies where language policy has been used as an intervention to deal with the effects of the global spread of English.

Tasks

In light of what we have discussed in this chapter, consider the following study questions:

- Why is education an important context for issues relating to World Englishes?
- In what sense will decisions about which variety should act as a teaching model be based on both practical and ideological concerns?
- What different goals do language policies have with regard to English around the world?

Feedback for these questions is given in the 'Commentary on tasks' section at the end of the book.

Section B

Interventions

5 Introduction: regulating and responding to the language

If the issues we looked at in Chapter 4 are some of the problems associated with the spread of English around the globe, what strategies are people taking in order to deal with them? In this second section of the book, we examine the interventions that language professionals have devised and carried out in an attempt to engage with the challenges posed by English and its impact on social and cultural practices around the world. 'Language professionals' in this context refers to all those whose work in some respects revolves around language, and in this case, specifically the English language. This includes those who teach English and who oversee its use in institutions or society. For all these people, decisions about the language – about its form, its roles, its status – are made in the course of their work, and the results of these decisions comprise the interventions that shape the way English exists in society.

Many of these interventions take the form of **language planning**. In its most general sense, language planning refers to deliberate initiatives aimed at influencing the roles, status or nature of a language in a community. Gibson Ferguson describes such initiatives as "conscious, organised interventions" in the way that language is used and perceived in society (Ferguson, 2006, p. 20). Planning of this sort is often associated with government bodies, but can also take place in and via a range of other institutions. The process of standardisation that we examined in Chapter 3 is a form of language planning – it comes under the subheading of **corpus planning** (Kloss, 1969), a type of intervention which involves modifying or developing aspects of the form of the language so that it can serve particular functions in society, such as operating as an official language. Other forms of planning include the decisions an organisation such as the European Parliament takes about its working languages, or the choices made by the education sector about what varieties/languages are taught in schools and universities. In sum, language planning can involve issues of promotion, regulation, and even engineering of a language – and at its heart is the contention that the forms and uses of a language *can* be regulated, and that regulatory interventions on the part of organisations and institutions have an effect on the state and status of a language in society. To what extent this is actually the case is a moot point, and something we shall discuss in the course of our explorations of interventions in World Englishes.

The motivation for these attempts at regulation takes a variety of forms. The two pivotal issues about the state of contemporary English that emerged from the discussions in Section A were its use as a language of wider communication and the part it plays in cultural identity politics. Both these issues are stimuli for language planning initiatives; and for this reason the act of language planning relates both to linguistic concerns (e.g. how to ensure or optimise intelligibility) and to explicit political concerns (e.g. how to promote the use of a language as a symbol of national identity).

Finally, it is worth remembering that at both the institutional and the individual level issues about English in the world are, at their core, issues about English users in the world. Thus interventions about the English language – strategies for promoting it, for regulating it, for fixing or modifying its nature – are ultimately interventions directed at people's behaviour, at their social and cultural practices, and at the linguistic resources they use to express themselves.

6 The global language paradigm

One of the major problems related to English in the world today is how it can best be regulated in order to act as a medium of global communication. In a sense, the discussion around this question is an extension of an antecedent problem to which English itself is seen as the solution. The problem, simply put, is how a global population which is linguistically diverse can best find strategies to communicate amongst itself. There are a few possible solutions to this, such as the use of translation and interpretation, but an enduring and attractive answer has been the idea of a common language: a single tongue to unite the people of the world. Following the political, technological and economic events of the latter part of the twentieth century, English is now of a status that it is regularly promoted as this common language.

But with the promotion of English as a solution to this long-standing problem, further problems arise: problems to do with linguistic hierarchies (i.e. the way different languages are accorded different statuses in society), and with uniformity of form and function. In abstract terms, these are issues that have been part of the debate about global communication for many centuries. To understand the problems and challenges surrounding the candidacy of English for this role, therefore, it is instructive to look at how 'global English' emerges as the most recent stage in a history of linguistic interventions in the search for a language of universal communication – and to see how the interventions that are being proposed or enacted now are embedded in a history of similarly focused ambitions.

Artificial and auxiliary languages

Philosophical languages

The notion of linguistic diversity as a problem for human societies has long had a hold over the cultural imagination. In the Judeo-Christian tradition it is mythologised in Genesis 11 in the story of the Tower of Babel, and of God frustrating the hubristic ambitions of mankind by condemning the postdiluvian world to speak different languages ("the

LORD did there confound the language of all the earth" (Genesis 11:9)). Founded on the idea of an original, God-given language and of pre-Babelian harmony, there have been attempts throughout the history of Western civilization to discover or manufacture a 'perfect' language, and since the European Renaissance this has included the idea of a shared world language (Eco, 1997). With the coming of the Enlightenment in the mid-seventeenth century, two different dynamics emerged which had a bearing on this enterprise. First, there was the development of the idea of an essential relationship between language and nation; and second, the belief that natural languages as they currently existed were in some sense flawed. The conviction was that natural languages were structurally deficient as communicative systems and especially as tools for clear reasoning in what was an era of burgeoning scientific discovery. As the philosopher John Locke wrote:

> For he that shall well consider the errors and obscurity, the mistakes and confusion, that are spread in the world by an ill use of words, will find some reason to doubt whether language, as it has been employed, has contributed more to the improvement or hindrance of knowledge amongst mankind.
>
> (Locke, 1813 [1690], Book III, Chapter XI, p. 47)

Given this dissatisfaction, a number of scholars in the mid to late seventeenth century pursued the creation of **artificial languages** which were specifically designed to be free of the irregularities and ambiguities of natural languages. The ambition was to devise communicative systems which could accurately represent newly established concepts from scientific inquiry and that were thus capable of being used for logical thinking and precise scientific analysis.

Due to the purposes for which they were conceived, these languages are known as philosophical languages. They were not based on pre-existing natural languages such as English, French or Latin, but instead built from the bottom up, with entirely new grammars and vocabulary, and as such are referred to as a priori languages. As well as being intended as a solution to the scientific vagueness of natural languages, some of them were also advanced as universal mediums of communication. For example, Francis Lodwick, who was a member of the Royal Society and, along with John Wilkins and George Dalgarno, one of the pioneers of a priori languages, devised several systems with universalist ambitions. These included his *A Common Writing: Whereby two, although not understanding one the others Language, yet by the helpe thereof, may communicate their minds one to another* (published in 1647), and *The Groundwork of Foundation (or so Intended) for the Framing of a New Perfect Language and a Universal Common Writing* (published in 1652).

In terms of their immediate ambition, none of these many ventures were successful. They have since had an influence elsewhere, however, especially in the field of knowledge classification. For example, John Wilkins's *Essay towards a Real Character, and a Philosophical Language*, published in 1668, was, many years later, to provide inspiration for the English physician Peter Mark Roget when he was devising the structure of his thesaurus. And a similar influence continues to the present day for categorisation systems used by web portals such as *Yahoo!*, as well as library classification systems such as the Dewey Decimal Classification (Brewster and Wilks, 2004). But as solutions to the problem of universal communication, these projects were entirely ineffectual.

The twin rationales behind the philosophical languages – that they would perfect a system of symbolic representation which would allow for precise and accurate expression, and that they would facilitate communication across linguistic borders – are both specific conceptualisations of what a language is and does. It could be argued that the failure of these projects stemmed from the fact that they took these two ideas as the axiomatic starting points for their endeavours, and overlooked the various other complexities that constitute the human use of language. Yet, as we have noted, these same two ideas – albeit in a slightly different formulation – continue to be key to many of the present-day discussions of World Englishes. They also animated the second stage in the quest for a solution to efficient international communication.

Auxiliary languages

In the nineteenth century, a second wave of interest in artificial languages emerged. The ambition in this case was explicitly for a universal language for international communication, and was motivated in great part by the political history of the period – the increasing interconnectedness of the world and the consequences of a nationalist politics leading ultimately to discord and armed conflict between the nations of Europe. The trend was also in part a result of the rise of linguistics as a science. In the nineteenth century, as linguistics first developed as an autonomous area of academic inquiry, the construction of artificial languages was considered part of the work of the discipline. Linguists such as Otto Jespersen, who authored influential books on grammar and the English language, also involved themselves in the invention of new languages. In 1931, at a time when the politics of Europe were again riven with nationalist antagonism, Jespersen wrote of the artificial language movement and its rationale that "there is here a field that can be treated according to scientific methods and which it is of the utmost importance to civilized mankind to see thus treated in order to obtain a satisfactory solution of a really harassing problem" (Shenton et al., 1931, p. 95).

Inventions such as Jespersen's 'Novial' (1928) are referred to as **auxiliary languages** to indicate that they were not intended to replace any of the natural languages, nor did they belong to any one nation. Between 1850 and the Second World War, several hundred of these artificial auxiliary languages were constructed. Unlike the philosophical languages, they were based on existing languages and are therefore known as a posteriori languages. Both their grammar and vocabulary were derived from pre-existing languages, but again the intention was to eradicate the irregularities and redundancies that natural languages invariably develop, and in this way provide a more efficient, and more easily learnable, medium of communication.

The first artificial auxiliary language which succeeded in gathering a community of users was 'Volapük', invented in 1879 by a German priest named Johann Martin Schleyer. A decade later, in 1887, 'Esperanto' was first proposed by Ludvic Lazarus Zamenhof (whose first name, incidentally, was supposedly chosen in honour of the seventeenth-century language designer Francis Lodwick (Eco, 1997, p. 324)). Other notable examples include 'Ido' (1907), which was the attempt at a revised version of Esperanto, and 'Interglossa' (1943), constructed by the British zoologist Lancelot Hogben.

One of the drivers behind the **international auxiliary language** movement was the perceived need for a non-proprietary language. The intention was for them to act as a means of communication which would be culturally (and thus politically) neutral. In practice, the majority were founded upon European languages and so cultural bias was structurally in-built. In addition, Esperanto has grown beyond the remit of a code exclusively for international communication and has developed a small native literature (Sutton, 2008), thus positioning itself as a medium of cultural expression, albeit of rather a unique sort. This ambition to be culturally neutral and non-proprietorial, though, is another recurring theme in the history of the quest for a language of universal communication, and one which again has continued resonance in current debates about World Englishes.

Simplified languages

The field of artificial languages does not ordinarily come under the heading of language planning, although certain scholars have, on occasion, argued that it should. The Estonian linguist Valter Tauli, for example, considered language planning to be the "methodological activity of regulating and improving existing languages or creating new common regional, national or international languages" (Tauli, 1968, p. 27). The reason it does not ordinarily figure prominently in modern institutional language planning, though, is that it has had minimal effect with respect to the ambitions it set itself. As Andrew Large summarises the situation: "The history of artificial languages is one of earnest endeavour with long hours spent in painstaking labour, but also of frustration and failure" (Large, 1985, p. 177). Even the most successful creation, Esperanto, which has approximately two million L2 speakers, is used in over a hundred countries (Ethnologue, 2011), and which does in practice fulfil some of the social functions of a universal language, is not by any means an absolute answer to many of the world's communication problems.

But while the method ultimately lost popularity, the ideals continued, and in the 1920s a next stage in this history emerged, as people began to suggest plans for simplified Englishes which could be used as forms of international communication. The idea here was that an existing natural language – in this case English – could be modified in such a way as to fulfil the needs of a universal language. Specifically this would mean producing a simplified and regularised version of the language – that is, one which repaired the irregularities and redundancies in spelling, grammar and pronunciation with which natural languages are burdened – which would thus be vastly easier both to learn and to use in a proficient manner.

Proposals for simplified languages have been devised for a range of European languages. For example, in the 1910s a linguist in Munich devised a scheme called 'Welt-Deutsch' (WEDE), that consisted of a phonetically spelt and simplified German which, he believed, could be used as a universal language in a post-war world dominated by Germany (Large, 1985). In the Anglophone world, the most notable example of this trend was C. K. Ogden's 'Basic English' (1930). Ogden's intention was to simplify English while simultaneously keeping it natural for the native speaker. He wrote that "[i]t is clear that the problem of a Universal language would have been solved if it were possible to say all that we normally desire to say with no more words than can be easily legible to the naked eye, in column form, on the back of a sheet of notepaper" (Ogden, 1930, p. 9). To this end he distilled English down to a core vocabulary of 850 words (though with supplementary sets of words for specific fields such as science and business), and devised a variety of restrictions on grammar, such as limiting the language to only eighteen verbs. As with the artificial auxiliary languages, the intention was for a universal means of communication which was sensitive to the political desire for cultural 'neutrality'. As Ogden's associate, I. A. Richards, wrote: "Let us be clear about some political essentials from the outset. However desirable a common language for all the world may be, as a means of communication between peoples who in their homes speak different tongues, it neither can nor should be imposed by one nation or group of nations upon others" (Richards, 1943, p. 9).

Although greatly praised and much supported in its day (its advocates included both Winston Churchill and Franklin D. Roosevelt), as with previous interventions Basic English failed to fulfil its own ambitions, and ultimately faded from popular consciousness. There have, however, been occasional similar suggestions since. For example, in the 1980s Randolph Quirk proposed 'Nuclear English', a reduced form of the language with the redundancies of natural English ironed out so as to leave just a communicative 'nucleus' (Quirk, 1982). However, despite the odd continued proposal of this sort, this particular stage in the global language quest seems mostly closed now. And its history seems to have been a testament to John Locke's reflection that: "I am not so vain as to think that any one can pretend to attempt the perfect *reforming* the *languages* of the world, no not so much as of his own country, without rendering himself ridiculous" (Locke, 1813 [1690], Book III, Chapter XI, p. 46). One of the continuing stumbling blocks for such ventures is that at the heart of all natural languages are issues of **creativity**, which involve not only the ability to make ever new utterances out of limited linguistic resources, but also the capacity to adapt and extend those resources to changing social and cultural circumstances. As we discussed in Section A, English – as with all natural languages – is constantly changing and adapting as it moves through time and space. Excessive regulation, however, returns to the aspiration of 'fixing' the language, and this necessarily hampers the generation of new linguistic resources to deal with the dynamism of the social world.

Although an initiative such as Basic English is an example of a failure under its own terms, it has nevertheless had an influence in certain quarters, most notably with the restricted 'report and control languages' of Airspeak and Seaspeak. Furthermore, the principle of simplification does still prevail in practices such as 'Special English', a controlled form of the language used in broadcasting by the Voice of America (the official external broadcast unit of the United States). The simplification process here involves broadcasts being read a third slower than usual, idioms being avoided where possible, and a core vocabulary of only 1,500 words being used as the basis of all reports. But Special English comprises a set of guidelines rather than rules, and as such is more a convention of usage than a language system in its own right. A comparable initiative has been proposed for a wider functional domain by the French businessman Jean Paul Nerrière. He has suggested a similar set of guidelines for the use of a simplified English – what he calls 'Globish' – in international business contexts (Nerrière, 2006). But whereas guidelines may work for specialist purposes such as broadcasting, they are not so efficient in the wider and less regulated communicative contexts of business encounters, and thus Nerrière's Globish is encountering the same problems as the schemes of Ogden and Quirk did before it. This is, however, something of a moot point now, because by the end of the twentieth century the status of 'full' English was such that strategies for a world language once again shifted their approach significantly.

A global *lingua franca*

English as an international language

By the second half of the twentieth century, English without modification or engineering had begun to emerge as a naturally occurring solution to the global language problem ('natural' in so far as it was the result of various historical and political events, that is, rather than the specific result of language planning interventions). Writing in the 1980s, Braj Kachru commented that "[f]or the first time a natural language has attained the status of an international (universal) language, essentially for cross-cultural communication. Whatever the reasons for the earlier spread of English, we should now consider it a positive development in the twentieth-century world context" (Kachru, 1983, pp. 51).

There are two main issues which continue to complicate the picture, however, and which result in the need for forms of intervention. The first is the issue of 'neutrality'. As we have seen, from the time of the auxiliary languages onwards, the desire has been for a language which can operate for international communication without unduly politically advantaging one group over another. The question with respect to English becomes whether the language today has outlived its past – that is, whether the associations of British colonialism, and of American cultural and military imperialism, no longer cling to it – or whether its emergence as the default international language produces or contributes to social inequalities in the world. The second issue is that of intelligibility, and of how a language which has diverse varieties all around the globe can be drawn upon to function efficiently as a stable medium of communication.

For some, such as Randolph Quirk (1985), the answer to these putative problems is to promote a single, standard 'international English', based on native speaker norms. The rationale behind this position is that only a single standard will ensure intelligibility across the board, that native-speaker norms provide a stable and intuitive authority for the form and use of the language, and that the rapid spread of English means that its cultural history is not an impediment to its present-day 'global' identity.

As well as finding a few advocates in the academic community, this position is (or at least, until very recently, has been) default practice in many education systems. But it has also been criticised for not adequately addressing the issue of the cultural politics of English, and of neglecting the significance that English linguistic diversity can have for groups and communities who use the language. Furthermore, people have questioned whether a single centralised standard – and especially one based on UK or US native-speaker norms – *is* necessarily the best solution to universal intelligibility issues. Larry Smith and Cecil Nelson, for example, conducted research into how different varieties of English were understood by speakers from around the world, and found that the US and UK native speakers in their study were *not* the most easily understood. Moreover, the native speakers had greater difficulty than others understanding different varieties. They concluded, therefore, that not only are attempts to teach a native-speaker model in environments where English is a second or foreign language a "losing proposition", but they are also logically flawed given that not even all native-speaker varieties are mutually intelligible (Smith and Nelson, 2006, p. 441).

English as a *lingua franca*

Approaches which advocate an 'international standard English' also contain a further logical perplexity in their foundational argument. They are built on the observation that English is now, in effect, operating as a default language of international communication, and for this reason can be further promoted as an international language. This promotion, however, involves regulation of the language often based on a priori beliefs about the form an international language should take. Yet if English is, to a great extent, already fulfilling the role which this regulation seeks to effect, the question arises as to what such regulation hopes to achieve further, and whether it would not be better to examine how English *is already* currently operating as a global means of communication, and then use this information as the basis for teaching and policy interventions. It is this thinking which lies behind approaches which concentrate on the use of **English as a** *lingua franca* (ELF), and which forego regulative interventions in favour of strategies which aim to align language planning initiatives (such as teaching and testing) with the sociolinguistic realities of how people actually use English as a *lingua franca* and medium of cross-cultural communication around the world.

Lingua francas are another long-standing element in the history of international communication. The term *lingua franca* originally referred to a pidgin used as a trade language in the Levant from the eleventh to the nineteenth century. The lexifier for this was Provençal, which was the shared language of the Crusaders; Muslims in the area often referred to the Crusaders as Franks, regardless of their background, and it was this which led to the term *lingua franca*:

'Frankish tongue'. By the nineteenth century, the term was being employed to refer to any code used as a medium of communication between people speaking different languages. The first citation for this usage in the *OED*, for example, refers to Urdu as a *lingua franca* across much of India in 1872.

What then does it mean for English to be a global *lingua franca* in today's world? As was noted in Chapter 3, the demographics of English use around the world are such that there are now more non-native speakers than native speakers, and thus, in the majority of interactions in which English is used, it is operating as a medium of communication by people who do not share a common language. Some scholars who study this use of the language specifically exclude interactions which involve a native speaker (e.g. Firth, 1996), but to do this is to impose rather awkwardly artificial boundaries around global language use, given the complex patterns of mobility and migration in the world. For example, when English is used as a *lingua franca* in the European Union, communicative encounters are likely to include British and Irish representatives as well as those from other member states, and to communicate all those involved (including the native speakers) will need to draw on a form of the language which is intelligible to all the other participants in the conversation. As such, in scenarios of this sort all participants are using English as a *lingua franca*.

It is probably most useful to think of English as a *lingua franca* as a function rather than a specific variety in its own right. That is, it is not a systematic collection of habitually used features in the way that 'Indian English' or 'Singaporean English' is. There *are* a number of repeated regularities of form in *lingua franca* usage – and we shall look in more detail at these in Chapter 7 – but it is also, importantly, marked by communicative strategies in the way people accommodate to each other's communicative practices and adapt their usage so that it is effective and appropriate for the culturally and linguistically diverse contexts in which it is being employed. An Irish delegate at the European Parliament, for example, if talking to French and Slovenian colleagues, would not use a strong Hiberno-English form of the language, but instead modify her pronunciation and use of vocabulary and idioms in such a way as to ensure maximum clarity of expression.

If overt regulation of the language is anathema to an ELF approach, then (based as it is on surveying the way people actually already use English) what type of interventions are proposed and enacted by language professionals operating in this paradigm? In effect, interventions are predominantly related to the perception of this type of usage both within academia and educational circles, and in wider society – and to countering prevailing attitudes which stigmatise such usage as broken or imperfect English, and drawing upon empirical research for the purposes of legitimating such usage. It is this type of intervention which also underpins approaches which look beyond the idea of an international language and consider the other functions that English fulfils around the world. And it is to these approaches that we turn in the next chapter.

Tasks

In light of what we have discussed in this chapter, consider the following study questions:

- What recurring themes are evident in the history of artificial and auxiliary languages, and how are these relevant to global English?
- Why is the question of whether English has outgrown its past important for its promotion as an international language?
- Why has the history of the search for a suitable universal language been mostly marked by failure, and is there any indication that the use of English as a global *lingua franca* can adequately fulfil this role?

Feedback for these questions is given in the 'Commentary on tasks' section at the end of the book.

7 Codification and legitimation

The Enlightenment philosopher Destutt de Tracy wrote of the problem of a universal language that:

> Even were everybody on earth to agree to speak the same language from today onwards, they would rapidly discover that, under the influence of their own use, the single language had begun to change, to modify itself in thousands of different ways in each different country, until it produced in each a different dialect which gradually grew away from the others.
>
> (*Eléments d'idéologie*, II, 6, 569, cited in Eco, 1997, p. 332)

As we have seen, the fear of plurality and fragmentation has been a recurrent motif in discussions of global English, be it in the context of the future of English repeating the history of Latin, or of diversity being viewed as the enemy of intelligibility. Yet there are also conditions under which distinction is an avowed intention – where the multifarious nature of English is not viewed as a problem, and instead interventions are pursued for the purpose of documenting the diversity in the language, and on occasions for finding ways to enhance patterns of difference.

The reason for these alternative approaches is that the universal language paradigm is not the sole issue for the existence of English in a global context. While the international auxiliary language movement persistently attempted to find ways to ensure their product was politically neutral, the fact of the matter is that languages never truly are. A language is always closely related to the culture in which it is used, and this is as true for English, despite its global status, as for any other language.

In contexts which highlight diversity rather than a unitary ideal, there is often a move to establish ways of reifying the distinct features of the local variety. Practices of this sort include the development of corpora of actual language use, codification projects such as national dictionaries, and the development of context-specific teaching resources (e.g. culture-sensitive textbooks). This chapter will illustrate how such practices act as a means of both providing empirical data about how language is used in diverse world contexts and legitimising these local varieties of English.

Corpora

Much of the history of universal languages was motivated by ideas of what language could or should do, and one of the reasons why such projects almost all failed was that invariably the ideals they had conflicted with the actuality. The attempt to engineer or regulate a communicative system to achieve a set of specific objectives overlooked the holistic complexity that constitutes real linguistic practice. For this reason, determining how people actually use English around the world – understanding the norms and patterns people orient to, the functions and purposes the language is used for, and the ways it is employed in communicative strategies – becomes an important initiative to help inform debate and intervention. One method developed in the last few decades which has assisted this approach to the understanding and planning of languages is **corpus linguistics**. A **corpus** in this context is an electronically stored collection of texts or (transcribed) utterances which is used for the statistical analysis (by means of computer software) of actual language use. These collections are then used to gain a representative picture of a language, and can also act as a reference for the structure and usage of real language. In the last few decades, knowledge about World Englishes has been greatly augmented by the compilation of a number of important corpora.

Resources for comparative analysis

In English studies, the earliest corpus was The Survey of English Usage, set up in 1959 by the Department of English Language and Literature at University College London. By modern standards this had a limited set of samples, consisting of 200 texts, each of 5,000 words, totalling one million words in all. The texts included a variety of printed material, scripted speeches, and news broadcasts, and the aim was to provide an accurate description of the grammar of English as it was used by British speakers.

The next notable English studies project was the Brown Corpus of Standard American English, compiled in the 1960s at Brown University, Rhode Island. This also comprised a million words, with texts drawn from a variety of different categories (e.g. reportage, fiction, humour, religion). This corpus proved to be highly influential, and set a standard for the systematic compilation of English language data. Its layout was copied by a number of other projects, most noticeably four corpora of English from around the world. These were:

- the LOB corpus (Lancaster-Oslo-Bergen Corpus) of written British English, compiled in the 1980s in a collaboration between the universities of Lancaster and Oslo and the Norwegian Computing Centre for the Humanities;
- the Kolhapur Corpus of Indian English, compiled by S. V. Shastri in the 1980s;
- the Australian Corpus of English (ACE) compiled at Macquarie University from 1986 onwards;
- the Wellington Corpus in New Zealand, compiled in the late 1980s and 1990s.

Having these five parallel corpora of similar structure allowed researchers to compare different varieties of the language (Nelson, 2006), and, in the case of the Indian, Australian and New Zealand projects, to differentiate those varieties from the more established British and American Englishes. In other words, they allowed for descriptive comparative analysis of World Englishes, but also acted as codification exercises which highlighted the distinct identity of different national varieties.

A further major development in the use of corpus linguistics was the development of the International Corpus of English (ICE). In 1983, Sidney Greenbaum succeeded Randolph Quirk as director of the Survey of English Usage, and in 1990, initiated the ICE. The aim of this was specifically to collect material for comparative studies of English worldwide. As Gerald Nelson, the current coordinator, explains "Since the project was first mooted by Greenbaum, our long term aim has been to tag the corpora for parts of speech, and to parse each corpus syntactically, so that researchers can compare varieties of English at the level of syntax" (Nelson, 2004, p. 226). At present, the project consists of 20 research teams around the world, each compiling a corpus of their own national or regional variety. Each has the same specifications – one million words of spoken and written English produced since 1989 – and each is following a shared design. The countries and regions involved include: Canada, Jamaica, Hong Kong, East Africa, India, Singapore, the Philippines, Great Britain, New Zealand and Ireland. For many of these, the ICE project is providing the opportunity for the first systematic investigation of the national or regional variety.

Another recently established corpus which provides an alternative perspective on the use of English globally is the Vienna-Oxford International Corpus of English (VOICE; begun in 2001, under the direction of Barbara Seidlhofer). The purpose here is to look not at national or regional varieties, but at how people use the language in *lingua franca* situations. The rationale for this is that, in today's world, the most widespread use of English is as a common means of communication between speakers who have different first languages. To this end, the corpus is composed entirely of spoken interactions in which English is used as a *lingua franca*, and comprises one million words of transcribed spoken conversation from domains such as business, education and leisure.

A similarly focused project is the corpus of English as a Lingua Franca in Academic Settings (ELFA), compiled at the University of Helsinki under the direction of Anna Mauranen (2001–2008), which again contains one million words of transcribed speech, in this case concentrating specifically on English used as a *lingua franca* in academic contexts (e.g. in lectures, presentations, seminars, thesis defences, and conference discussions). It includes data from approximately 650 speakers with over 50 different first languages, though as a rule, excludes any native speakers of English.

Taken together, these projects offer a wealth of empirical data about worldwide English – about its different geographical varieties, and different functions and communicative dynamics – and are providing scholars with the opportunity to analyse the forms and frequencies of usage that actually exist in the way that the language is being spoken and written across the globe.

Consequences of the corpus perspective

As was intimated above, the compilation of these corpora generally has a twofold objective: a descriptive purpose, and a political one. Writing in the introduction to the Kolapur corpus, Shastri contends that:

> [a] systematic and comprehensive description of Indian English is now overdue. Of the major national varieties of English, only the American and the British English have so far been described in some detail though several other varieties have already been indentified among the native speaker varieties. Side by side, some non-native varieties of English have also been tacitly recognized among which Indian English is a major one.
>
> (Shastri, 1986)

An intended aim for Kolapur, therefore, as for other projects such as the Australian Corpus of English, is legitimation through codification. By systematically describing the variety – by detailing its patterns of usage and showing these to be habitual and widely accepted in practice – the corpus is able to act as a cultural artefact marking the existence of the distinct variety.

There are other practical consequences for areas in which the language plays an important role. The VOICE project suggests that:

"[t]he widespread use of ELF [English as a *lingua franca*] in the world and the availability of a description of its linguistic characteristics are likely to have considerable implications for the way objectives of English teaching might be defined" (VOICE, 2011). ELFA likewise contends that "[t]he applications of this theoretical and descriptive work are of considerable practical significance in today's world. We need principled ways of focusing language teaching on aspects which are crucial for smooth communication in the real world, and we need research based ways of assessing learner performance for international use" (ELFA, 2009). In other words, corpus-generated data can be used to inform the sort of decisions about teaching and testing practices that we looked at in Chapter 3, and to assist with solutions based on empirical understandings of how people actually use the language rather than a priori prescriptions about how they should be using it.

Finally, there are a number of other practical consequences for corpus descriptions. For example, a recent project on spoken Australian English lists its objectives as assisting in the development of "Australian speech technology applications, from better telephone-based speech recognition systems ... and computer avatars, to hearing aids and Cochlear Implants improvements, or computer aids for learning-impaired children" (AusTalk, 2011).

Corpus linguistics thus allows for research into the language which has theoretical, political and practical implications. Having a recognised corpus legitimises the notion of a particular variety, and provides it with a tangible identity. From a linguistic point of view, patterns of usage can then be identified and codified, and the empirical evidence thus generated can be used to inform a range of issues in the applied linguistics of World Englishes – from the pedagogic to the development of culturally sensitive technology.

National dictionary projects

Another key mechanism for legitimising a variety is the production of a dictionary. As we saw in Chapter 3, the production of dictionaries played an important role in the development of the idea of the national standard in Britain in the eighteenth century. In the context of World Englishes, the objective is not so much to select and codify a central standard, however, but to circumscribe the distinct usage of a particular language community which can then be promoted as a separate variety of the language. This type of intervention is founded on beliefs about the essential bond between a nation's population and its linguistic practices. As we discussed in Chapter 3, these beliefs are a consequence of the trend in eighteenth- and nineteenth-century European political philosophy to promote the nation state as the principle political unit (Anderson, 2006). As part of this worldview, the language practices of a community were promoted as an essential element of its cultural identity and, given that the principal unit of community was the nation state, so the key unit in which languages were measured was one which was co-extensive with the borders of the nation-state. This led to the ideology of idealised 'national languages', which were identified with a particular standard that was codified in grammar books and dictionaries.

The earliest dictionaries of world English were glossaries produced in the United States at the beginning of the nineteenth century (Bolton, 2006). Working within this context was Noah Webster, who had as his explicit intention the production of a *national* dictionary. In recent years, with the rise of World Englishes scholarship, this same rationale has underpinned similar projects in many regions of the English-speaking world. These include the *Macquarie Dictionary* of Australian English (Delbridge, 1997), Oxford University Press's *Australian National Dictionary* (Ramsom, 1988), *The Dictionary of New Zealand English* (Orsman, 1997), *The Canadian Oxford Dictionary* (Barber 1998), and the *Dictionary of English Usage in South Africa* (Beeton, 1975).

Within the context of World Englishes, the rationale is often explicitly the legitimation of particular usage patterns. Bolton, paraphrasing Quick, suggests that "it is only when a world variety of English is supported by codification (chiefly expressed through national dictionaries) that one can make a strong claim that such a variety is 'institutionalised'" (Bolton, 2006, p. 255). As with the case of corpora, the act of codification is seen to bring legitimacy, and one of the intentions of such dictionary projects is often not simply to make the claim for the recognition of a discrete variety, but to explicitly differentiate this variety from others. As Fredric Dolezal writes, "A dictionary is not a requirement for a people to recognise themselves as part of a distinct set of English language users, but the presence of such a dictionary would undoubtedly seal the argument for the existence of a separate and equal English" (Dolezal, 2006, p. 695).

Noah Webster and the 'band of national union'

As noted, this rationale was explicitly highlighted in Noah Webster's *An American Dictionary of the English Language*, published in 1828. In the appendix to his *Dissertations on the English Language*, Webster states that "a capital advantage of this reform in these states would be, that it would make a difference between the English orthography and the American", and that this would be of "vast political consequence" because "a *national language* is a band of *national union*" (Webster, 1991 [1789], p. 93). He thus argues that by changing spelling conventions one can produce two distinct languages: English and an "American tongue" (p. 92).

Validating the new Englishes

For Webster, therefore, the ambition was to *establish* a national language, chiefly by modifying the orthography of standard British English, and the dictionary was used as a tool for doing this. Subsequent national dictionary projects operate to a similar agenda, but rather than uniquely modifying aspects of the language, they seek to record features that are already distinct to communities within their territories. The *Macquarie Dictionary*, for example, sees itself as a key element in the process of nation-building:

> [T]he *Macquarie Dictionary*, the first comprehensive dictionary of Australian English, is one of the essential parts of Australian nationhood. When new nations were being formed in Europe in the nineteenth century, the preparation of dictionaries was one of the basic parts of nation-building. We were a long time getting a dictionary like this. We should be proud of its service to the people of Australia.
>
> (Horne, 1997, p. x)

The same contention is repeated in the introduction to the dictionary, where the editor-in-chief Arthur Delbridge writes that at the end of the twentieth century, "Australian English is clearly and even officially recognised as the national variety" (Delbridge, 1997, p. xii).

A related intention is that the dictionary should be a means of bringing cohesiveness to the idea of the nation within a particular territory. This is given as an explicit rationale for the *Dictionary of Caribbean English Usage* (*DCEU*): "No different in this regard from other non-British regional dictionaries when they emerged at landmark times in their nation's history – Webster's in the USA in 1828, the *Dictionary of Canadian English* in 1967, the *Australian National Dictionary* in 1988 – the *DCEU* should be an inward and spiritual operator of regional integration even more powerful as a signal of unity than a national flag would be" (Allsopp, 1996, p. xxxi).

A similar purpose of cultural self-promotion is stated in the Canadian context:

> The *Canadian Oxford Dictionary* belongs to the age of the global village, but with a wholesome Canadian bias. This dictionary has dozens of mundane uses – clarifying meanings, settling spellings, suggesting pronunciations, providing synonyms, and all the rest – but the sum of all these uses is much greater than the parts. In the living language there is a reflection of where we have been and where we are likely to go next, and what we have considered important on the way. It is the codification of our common understanding.
>
> (Chambers, 1999, p. x)

One of the ways these projects hope to achieve this aim is by producing a distinct view of the language. For example, the *Dictionary of Bahamian English* states that "[t]his dictionary, the result of four years of fieldwork and research, contains over 5,000 entries for words and expressions used in the Bahamas which are not generally found in the current standard English of Britain or North America" (Holm, 1982, p. iii). And *Macquarie* describes its working method in similar conceptual terms: "This dictionary holds up a mirror to Australian English as it heads for the end of the twentieth century ... [I]t aims to do justice to the distinctiveness of Australian usage, even with common words of world English that have meanings here that they may not have in other national varieties of English" (Delbridge, 1997, p. xiii).

This can, however, prove complicated when the geography of the 'nation' is not clear-cut. This is the problem faced by the *Dictionary of Caribbean English Usage*, which explains that "[w]hereas Canadian English and Australian English, benefiting from the single land-mass of their respective homelands, can each claim general homogeneity, Caribbean English is a collection of sub-varieties of English distributed ... over a large number of non-contiguous territories of which two, Guyana and Belize, are widely distant parts of the South and Central American mainland" (Allsopp, 1996, p. xli). Nevertheless, collecting the diversity under the umbrella term 'Caribbean English' acts to give it the semblance of a cohesive identity, and at the same time distinguish such usage from other varieties of the language.

***

In summary then, dictionaries are seen as effective tools for legitimising the ideological constructs of discrete national varieties. This is a similar process to underpinning 'Ausbau' languages (see Chapter 2), where planning interventions purposefully highlight distinctive features which are different from neighbouring varieties, and in this way promote their individual status and identity.

The process of legitimisation can be a slow one, however. If we take the example of Australian English, we can get a sense of how the history of the perception of worldwide varieties has developed at a very different speed compared to the practice of actually using those varieties. The First Fleet, marking the beginning of European colonialism in Australia and the initial introduction of English into the continent, arrived in New South Wales with its one and a half thousand emigrants in 1788; yet it was not until almost two centuries later that the *Macquarie Dictionary* was published. For the majority of those two centuries, Australian usages of English were denigrated in the global discourse of the language. For example, Manfred Görlach quotes an American linguist writing at the beginning of the twentieth century whose judgement was that "the common speech of the Commonwealth of Australia represents the most brutal maltreatment that has ever been inflicted upon the mother tongue of the great English speaking nations" (Görlach, 1991, p. 147, cited in Kirkpatrick, 2007, p. 70). As Andy Kirkpatrick (2007) records, it was not until the middle of the twentieth century that 'Australian English' began to be promoted as a legitimate entity in its own right. Instrumental in this promotion was Arthur Mitchell, a linguist who had studied in London and returned to Australia in 1940. As chairman of the Australian Broadcasting Commission (ABC) in the 1950s, he was in a position of authority to promote the home-grown variety as a national standard, and from this followed the codification work which resulted in the two Australian English dictionaries discussed above.

There are, then, two strands of the development of English in contexts such as this: first, the way that the language itself develops in terms of the patterns of usage habitually spoken by the local speech community; and second, the way perceptions of the local variety develop and the extent to which people accept it as part of the local culture. Many of the interventions we are looking at in this section of the book involve researching the first of these in order to influence the second. And it is to another highly influential context for the implementation of such interventions that we now turn.

Re-conceptualising English: educational strategies

As we discussed in Chapter 4, an important arena in which language practices are influenced and in which beliefs are shaped is institutional education. For some scholars (e.g. Althusser, 1971), education is *the* main social instrument for the production and reproduction of the mainstream ideologies which affect the way that social power is distributed in a community. The ideas and beliefs taught and learnt in schools and universities both reflect and reinforce the prevailing beliefs in society as a whole. For this reason, the education sector is targeted as the site for a range of interventions relating to World Englishes, where the purpose is not only to find effective ways of teaching the language (and ways which are appropriate for students living and studying in different social and cultural contexts), but also to ensure that these methods and their outcomes are sensitive to the political issues associated with the language.

In Chapter 4, we outlined the choices open to educators about which model of the language to use, and how this relates to both practical and ideological concerns. As we observed then, the decisions that educators make with respect to this issue will depend on the context in which the language is being taught, and the purposes for which it is being learnt. In societies in which English operates as an official language, and in which there are indigenised codified varieties, complete with resources such as a national dictionary and locally produced teaching materials, the local variety is likely to have a great many advantages as a teaching model. In this final section of the chapter, I wish to consider contexts where English does not have any official or special status, and where it has traditionally been treated as a 'foreign' (rather than a second or additional) language. Here also, research in applied linguistics is leading to practice-based interventions which aim to ensure that English language teaching is sensitive to the needs and circumstances of those using the language around the world.

From EFL to ELF

Teaching in contexts where English is – or at least has been – predominantly a foreign language has conventionally used an exonormative native-speaker variety – a standard British or American English – as its model. This is for two reasons. First, the language has often been taught as one part of the culture of the major Anglophone countries, and the expectations students have about when they will actually use it relate to scenarios such as travelling to English-speaking countries or conversing with native speakers. Second, as the societies in which it is taught (e.g. China, Russia, Japan, many European countries) do not have indigenised varieties of their own, they look to models from elsewhere, and British and American standard Englishes are usually chosen on the grounds that they are considered prestige varieties the world over.

As we have noted on several occasions, however, the demographics of world English use nowadays are such that non-native speakers far outnumber native speakers. In terms of its role as an 'international' medium of communication, therefore, it is often the case that people from countries where English does not have official status will nevertheless be learning it for the purpose of communicating with other *non-native* speakers. Given this changed context, the argument in favour of native-speaker linguistic and cultural norms no longer appears so self-evident.

An early articulation of this revised position was made by Larry Smith in his work on the use of **English as an international language** (Smith, 1976). Smith suggests that an international language is best conceptualised as one used by people of different nations to communicate their thoughts and cultures to each other, and that, given this functional remit, learners should not need to internalise native-speaker cultural norms, and that ownership of the language (i.e. the issue of which group assumes the authority for decisions about how the language is regulated) should no longer be limited to specific nations such as the US or UK.

Smith's conceptualisation is very similar to that underpinning the notion of English as a *lingua franca*. The only main difference is that discussion of English as an international language (EIL) has tended to give the impression – either explicitly or implicitly – that a *single* international standard is emerging, whereas the ELF approach is careful to avoid such a suggestion, and instead focuses on the various strategies that people employ when using the language as a medium of cross-cultural communication. For many people studying this aspect of language use, ELF is best not conceptualised as a 'variety' at all, and instead is understood as "a naturally adaptive linguistic development" (JELF, 2011). That is, as people from different linguistic backgrounds engage in communication with each other via English, they adapt their use of the language to the context (the people, the circumstances, etc) in which they are using it.

Research into the use of English as a *lingua franca* has shown that, despite it being influenced by the diverse linguistic and cultural backgrounds of its speakers, there are a number of non-standard features (which Barbara Seidlhofer calls a "significant common core of vocabulary, grammar and pronunciation" (Seidlhofer, 2005, p. 92)) that occur with noticeable regularity but which appear to make no difference to the intelligibility of the discourse. In fact, speakers using English in *lingua franca* situations often use lexical and grammatical constructions which are logically more regular than those used in standard British and American English. In other words, they naturally repair the irregularities and redundancies of standard English, in much the way that the artificial and simplified language movements intended that their schemes would. For example, work from the VOICE corpus has recorded the following features that are regularly found in ELF interactions (Seidlhofer, 2005, p. 92):

- omission of the '–s' from the third-person singular present tense (e.g. "he sing" instead of "he sings");
- omission of the definite and indefinite articles ('the' and 'a') where standard English would include them (e.g. "he is very good person"); or inclusion of these articles where standard English would omit them (e.g. "they have a respect for all");
- interchangeable use of the relative pronouns 'who' and 'which', regardless of whether they are being used to refer to humans or non-humans (e.g. "the person which came to dinner");
- pluralisation of nouns that are uncountable in standard English (e.g. 'informations', 'advices');
- extension of the use of general or common verbs such as 'make', 'do' and 'have' (e.g. "make sport", "make a discussion", "put attention");

- use of an invariant question tag (e.g. "isn't it") instead of the range of question tags used in standard English (so, for example, "he's coming at six o'clock, isn't it?").

Given the habitual use of these 'non-standard' features in naturally occurring conversation, teaching which devotes great energy and time to training students to reproduce the native-speaker norms for these features is seemingly misguided, if the purpose is to provide students with competence in English for communicating in *lingua franca* situations.

For many scholars working in this area, the issue is predominantly one of perception, in terms of both how these 'non-standard' usages are viewed by educators and language professionals and how they are evaluated in society in general. In other words, there is a gap in perception between how people are able to communicate in English in *lingua franca* situations (the practical knowledge they have) and the beliefs people have about the form a language of international communication *should* take (their propositional knowledge of the topic). From the point of view of the teaching profession, issues of perception then influence how the language is taught. For example, if a feature such as the omission of the '–s' from the third-person singular present tense is seen as a legitimate usage in ELF interactions, it does not need to be 'corrected' every time the student uses it.

A key issue for educators, therefore, is how to determine whether a particular usage is an actual error on the part of the student (i.e. a form they have not yet internalised), or whether it is an emergent feature of ELF interaction. As Ayo Bamgboṣe comments, the latter should be "seen as an acceptable variant, while an error is simply a mistake or uneducated usage" (Bamgboṣe, 1998, p. 2). And the teacher will want to correct the former but not the latter.

Bamgboṣe identifies a number of factors which can indicate whether a new feature (or as he calls it, an 'innovation') has become a norm. These are:

- how many people use the innovation?
- how widely is it used in a community?
- who uses it (i.e. what sectors of the community)?
- where is it sanctioned, and has it been codified?
- what attitudes do people hold towards it?

He considers the most important points from this list to be whether or not the feature has been codified, and whether it is widely accepted within society. If it fulfils these two criteria, then it can be considered an established feature of the social practices of the community, and thus a stable part of their language.

Bamgboṣe's original analysis was addressed at indiginesd varieties (i.e. those which have developed in societies where English is a second language). The same criteria can be applied to the use of English as a *lingua franca*, however, especially now that research in this area is providing empirical data on patterns of *lingua franca* usage and is leading to the development of codification tools such as the VOICE and ELFA corpora. Prior to the collection of this type of data, the tendency was to categorise the majority of 'innovations' as instances of failed learning. Studies in **second language acquisition (SLA)** – that is, the processes involved in the learning of a second or additional language – have postulated that prior to fluency, learners produce what Larry Selinker refers to as an **interlanguage** (Selinker, 1972). An interlanguage is the hypothetical 'intermediate' system used by the learner which combines properties of their first language with properties of the target language. Many of the innovations that ELF research is now showing to be habitual and systematic were previously thought to be features of this intermediate stage in the learning process, and for this reason were categorised as elements of a transitional phase on the road to full proficiency. As more research is conducted into how English is actually used in different contexts and situations, however, many of these 'errors' are being reconceptualised as legitimate features of new varieties or strategies of use, and a more accurate and nuanced picture of the various forms the language takes around the world is emerging. Information from this research can then feed into teachers' practices, and help to inform the decisions they make about the norms they use in teaching the language.

ELF and intercultural communication

As we have seen, however, variation of form is not the only issue that can present problems for international communication via English. **Pragmatic** concerns – the way people construct and interpret meaning – as well as issues related to culturally specific language usage are also of fundamental importance for fluent communication. And here again, norms vary from context to context, thus producing further challenges for the teaching of English as an international *lingua franca*.

One example of the difficulties that can arise for **intercultural communication** from the use of culturally specific patterns of usage is idiomatic expressions. The following is a fictional example – taken from Malena Watrous's novel *If you follow me*, about an American woman working as an English teacher in Japan. Despite being a literary representation of the issue rather than real-life data, it clearly illustrates the way that set phrases which are meaningful for one speech community can be obscure or misleading to another, even when all the individual words and grammatical structures are understood. The two speakers in this passage are the American teacher (the novel's narrator) and her Japanese colleague (Watrous, 2010, p. 108):

> "When you drink," he says, "you become red face."
> "You should talk," I say.
> "I should talk about what?"

In this instance, while the Japanese teacher is able to comprehend the individual words in the expression "You should talk", he is unfamiliar with the meaning of them as a set phrase – in Larry Smith's terms, the language is 'comprehensible' to him but he fails to 'interpret' the intended meaning. One could, therefore, attribute the communicative impasse to limitations in his knowledge of the language, and the fact that he is unfamiliar with idiomatic expressions which are in common use in the United States. But one could just as easily approach the issue from the opposite perspective, and see the problem as a result of the native speaker's failure to accommodate her use of the language to the context in which she is using it. The conversation takes place in Japan, after all, so one could argue that there is no expectation that US linguistic norms should be operating as the default here.

Barbara Seidlhofer has referred to this issue as "unilateral idiomaticity" – that is, one party in a conversation makes extensive use of idioms which, because of their cultural-specificity, are unfamiliar to the other party, and this leads to communicative problems (Seidlhofer, 2004, p. 220). The implications that this type of communication difficulty have for the teaching of English in *lingua franca* contexts are twofold. First, it is important simply to note that culturally specific usages are often problematic in such contexts, and are thus best avoided when conversing with people from different cultural and pragmatic backgrounds. The responsibility for attentiveness to this issue needs to lie with *all* parties in a conversation, of course; it is not an issue solely for the second or additional language learner. In fact, this issue can lead to the seemingly paradoxical situation that it is sometimes non-native speakers who are the more fluent ELF communicators, due to the fact that they are aware of such problems and can tailor their use of the language accordingly.

This leads to the second implication for language teaching: that it can be greatly beneficial to teach students not simply the forms and structure of English, but also about language awareness, and about how cross-cultural variation affects communication. To this end, several people have suggested that a move needs to be made from a curriculum centred around teaching the linguistic and pragmatic norms of native-speaker countries, to one which introduces students to the ways in which English exists and is used in contemporary global society (cf. McKay, 2002; Kirkpatrick, 2007). Andy Kirkpatrick, for example, proposes that teachers working in TESOL contexts should of necessity possess a multilingual and multicultural sensibility, as well as having an understanding of the diversity and variation in English, and of how it relates to local cultures (Kirkpatrick, 2007, p. 188). Equipped with this knowledge, teachers will be able to incorporate into their teaching an awareness of the ways in which English operates in the world, and of how it interacts both with the students' own culture and with the cultures of those they are likely to be speaking to.

Language tests and the diversity of English

As we discussed in Chapter 4, language testing is an important complement to the teaching process, both in the influence it has on the content and structure of the curriculum and in the impact it has on social attitudes to the language in general. As such, practical interventions in the wake of research into World Englishes are also being suggested for the revision of language assessment procedures. Given the context outlined above, these interventions have stressed the need for assessment to be 'contextualised', and for proficiency to be understood as the ability to use English for specific purposes in specific places. Suresh Canagarajah, for example, suggests that tests should be aware of and explicit about the type of norms they are testing, and in this way move away from the idea that there is such a thing as universal proficiency in English – especially when that 'universal' proficiency is in fact conceptualised on the basis of a specific native-speaker US or UK standard (Canagarajah, 2006). He argues that there is a need for the development of tests based on local norms and local situations, which would reflect the ways in which the language has developed into indigenised varieties in many areas of the world. The development of such tests will not only allow for the testing of the skills that students are actually likely to need, but will also contribute to the codification of local norms, thus further legitimising the local variety. Washback from the tests (i.e. the need to concentrate the curriculum on what is being tested) will encourage the development of textbooks focusing on local issues, while corpora of real usage will be needed to provide information about the norms that constitute the local variety and which thus provide the basis for the testing exercises. The institution of testing can therefore both reflect local practices and assist in raising the status of these practices.

Canagarajah goes further with his proposals, however, and argues that local tests alone are not enough, because the way that English exists in the world today means that people often need access both to the linguistic resources used in their immediate community and to non-localised forms. That is, in contemporary society – where migration and mobility are so prevalent – the likelihood is that people will be using English for both local and *lingua franca* purposes, and will want to ensure that their ability to communicate internationally is not limited by the context-specific norms they have learnt. As such, he suggests that tests should cover a similar range of knowledge as that proposed for the curriculum by people such as Andy Kirkpatrick. This would include a focus on language awareness, so that learners can adapt their repertoires to the different situations in which they use them and also to the development of 'sociolinguistic sensitivity' towards different cultural communicative competencies.

The rationale behind all these proposals is that the testing of the language, along with its teaching, needs to reflect how people use English in the world both as a local language and as a *lingua franca*. In a world in which English itself is diverse and various, teaching is best advised to encourage students to recognise and develop their own adaptive communicative strategies – to learn not only how to use the language, but also to be aware of how others use it and of the social and cultural issues that inform that usage.

Tasks

In light of what we have discussed in this chapter, consider the following study questions:

- What impact has corpus linguistics had on the status and study of World Englishes?
- Why are dictionaries considered such an important element in the construction of national identity?
- Why is language awareness an important issue for successful international communication in English?

Feedback for these questions is given in the 'Commentary on tasks' section at the end of the book.

8 Policies and cultural practices

The majority of the interventions we have looked at so far, to the extent that they constitute or feed into systematic language planning initiatives, come under the broad heading of corpus planning. They are concerned primarily with issues relating to the form of worldwide English: to how it does or should look, and the shape it takes, from its spelling through to its grammar. In addition to this, there are two other major types of language planning, both of which are relevant to World Englishes studies, especially in the context of decisions made at the level of policy about the role that English should play in particular national and institutional contexts. These are **acquisition planning** and **status planning**.

Acquisition planning involves decisions made about language education (e.g. which language or languages are to be taught in schools and universities), and the influence these decisions have on a community's language practices (Cooper, 1989). As was noted at the end of the previous chapter, the institution of education is an important and influential context for the production and reproduction of a community's beliefs and social practices. For this reason, acquisition planning is a practical means of influencing the standing that a language has within society. As such, it often accompanies what is known as status planning, which involves legislation regulating which languages are to be assigned to which official roles in different institutional or social domains – for example, which language is to be used for proceedings in government, the law, and so forth (Kloss, 1969). Together, status planning and acquisition planning can do a great deal to determine the language practices of a society, especially in multilingual contexts.

As we saw in Chapter 4, the main policy and planning 'problems' with respect to World Englishes relate to how regulation can either promote the use of English so as to take advantage of its globally dominant position, or put in place protective measures to ensure that this dominance does not have adverse effects on local cultures and communities. In this respect, status planning decisions about what role English should be assigned in relation to other languages, and also what type of English should be promoted in society, are central to many of the interventions that tackle the influence of English in the world today. In this chapter, we will examine a number of case studies involving English-related status and acquisition planning in order to see how policies and politics are affecting the use of English around the globe – and how these policies can also be challenged, modified or resisted by the choices that communities themselves make about their language practices.

English and economic value

Singlish and the 'Speak Good English Movement'

In many countries around the world, English is promoted via status or acquisition planning because of the benefits it is seen to have for the economic development and competitiveness of the nation. One could argue that in the era of globalisation, this association is the principal motivator for governments and institutions to decide to adopt English as an important resource for their citizens. One example of a country whose language policy is based on this rationale is Singapore. Here, English's status as the default medium for global economics and international business has been one of the foundational ideas behind a language policy which operates as an integral part of the country's national development initiatives (Wee, 2012). Yet it is not solely the association between English and economic value that influences English's role in Singaporean society; the language also plays an important part in local cultural identity politics. And this twofold role for the language – its global function as the language of international business and its local function as a marker of cultural identity – has led to conflicts between policy and practice as the government's blueprint for English clashes with the way many people in the country use and identify with the language.

Singapore is an ethnically diverse country whose population of approximately three million is three-quarters people of Chinese origin, one-eighth of Malay origin, and a little under a tenth of Indian origin. When Singapore gained its independence in 1965, it embarked on a project of constructing a unified nation out of this ethnically and linguistically diverse population, and of setting itself up as a state that would prove attractive to foreign investment. Its language policy was instrumental in assisting with both these aims. This policy first assigned each of the three main ethnic communities an official 'mother tongue' (Mandarin for the Chinese, Malay for the Malays, and Tamil for the Indians); and second it established English as an official language for the purpose of operating both as a *lingua franca* across the different ethnic communities and as a tool for global economic engagement. This strategy has, for the most part, been very successful, and Singapore has developed into a modern and economically prosperous state. Yet in promoting this policy, the government has encountered a particular problem with respect to the way that local varieties of English – and specifically the colloquial variety known as Singlish – have developed.

Singlish is a 'mixed' variety of English that is used in informal situations. It has borrowings from Malay, Tamil and different Chinese languages, and also has a range of non-standard features such as a lack of inflectional morphology, reduplication, and the use of discourse particles (see Chapter 2 for details and examples). The official language policy of Singapore positions English as a specifically practical language, however – and one which is purposefully not associated with any particular culture. In other words, whereas the three 'mother tongues' are seen as markers of different Asian identities, English is considered ethnically 'neutral'. And to this end, the government promotes a standard English, unmarked by 'innovations' influenced by the mother tongues.

The government's promotion of a standard English is not related solely to its belief in the need for a neutral *lingua franca* for use across the different ethnic communities. It also sees a standard variety as being of central importance to the country's international standing. In this context it has long considered the existence and use of Singlish as detrimental to the position of standard English in Singaporean society, and has therefore vigorously campaigned against its use. The government's contention is that Singlish will have an adverse effect on the ability of the population to acquire a standard English, and that this could lead to the country becoming cut off from the global economy because its citizens will not be able to communicate adequately in the international *lingua franca*.

The concern that the government has often voiced is that people will lose the ability to distinguish between the two varieties – and that standard English as spoken in Singapore will become contaminated by Singlish. For example, former prime minister Goh Chok Tong has described Singlish as "broken, ungrammatical English sprinkled with words and phrases from local dialects and Malay which English speakers outside Singapore have difficulties in understanding" (cited in Wee, 2012). In assertions such as this, the issue of intelligibility is used as a means of justifying the need for regulations to influence how people use the language. Chief amongst such regulative measures has been the 'Speak Good English Movement' (SGEM), a campaign set up by the government in 2000 to "encourage Singaporeans to speak grammatically correct English that is universally understood" (SGEM, 2011). The movement organises workshops, seminars and contests aimed at promoting and teaching standard usage. The 2010/2011 campaign slogan, for example, is "Get It Right!" which is "a call to action for everyone to make the extra effort to ensure they use the English language accurately and correctly".

Yet while the government warns against the corrosive effects of Singlish, other sectors of society take a very different view, and there has been a popular backlash against its demonisation. These opposing voices have suggested that Singlish is, in fact, a positive cultural resource for Singapore and that it operates as a distinctive marker of Singaporean cultural identity (Wee, 2012). They point out that in fact the government, as well as official bodies such as the Singapore Tourism Board, have themselves used both the idea and the examples of Singlish in promotional materials for the country (Wee, 2010). Furthermore, the logic behind the policy is flawed to the extent that people are able to switch between Singlish and standard English and to use different varieties in different domains and for different purposes. In other words, Singlish and standard English are not mutually exclusive but are a part of the multilingual and multidialectical repertoires that Singaporeans daily employ.

In effect, then, there are two levels of intervention in this case. There are the government-directed policies assigning different roles to different languages and promoting a particular variety of English in order to take advantage of its status as a medium of international communication. Yet at the same time there is grass-roots resistance to elements of this policy, and a popular embracing of the way that the global language is indigenised and incorporated into the local culture in the form of Singlish. And, as we have seen, the balance between these two dynamics – the deterritorialised international language (Blommaert, 2010), and the indigenised local variety – is a recurrent theme through the story of World Englishes.

English as a language for international development

The idea of English as an important resource for the improvement of people's economic and employment prospects has also led to its promotion in international development aid programmes. While literacy education has long been an established element of international development provision, recently language education more generally has also been viewed as something which can assist with poverty reduction and individual and national development. Given the status that English currently has across the globe, 'language education' here usually means 'English-language education'. The aim of programmes which promote English in this context is to provide the populations of developing nations with the communicative resources that will allow them both to participate in the global economic systems from which they have previously been excluded (Seargeant and Erling, 2011) and to access information on topics such as health advice which is available through global electronic media and which can benefit their day-to-day welfare (Norton et al., 2012).

Programmes based on this rationale include the British Council's 'Project English' in India and Sri Lanka (launched 2007), which was set up to train millions of English teachers with the intention that this would assist with social development; and in Bangladesh, the 'Language Teaching Improvement Project' (1997–2008) and its successor 'English in Action' (launched 2008), both funded by the UK government's Department for International Development. The rationale for such projects is clearly outlined in the summary of their aims: 'Project English', for example, states that the "impact of globalization and economic development has made English the 'language of opportunity' and a vital means of improving prospects for well-paid employment" (Project English, 2009), while 'English in Action' explains that it is endeavouring "to significantly increase the number of people able to communicate in English to levels that will enable them to participate fully in economic and social activities and opportunities" (EIA, 2009). The conviction in such statements is that English-language education can help provide the sort of skills that will allow for engagement with the political, financial and knowledge economies which, in today's world, are increasingly conducted at a global level and thus rely on means of international communication.

Policies which are based on this understanding beg the question, however, of the extent to which beliefs about the relationship between English ability and economic development match the way that things actually are. In other words, is it indeed the case that knowledge of English is linked to better pay or better job prospects, and what empirical evidence is there to support such suppositions?

A number of research studies have investigated this question, and their results paint a mixed picture. For example, while it is the case that many Anglophone countries have the highest GDPs, it does not follow that there is a necessary correlation between the acquisition of English and economic advancement in development contexts. Research conducted by Jean-Louis Arcand and François Grin into the economics of language found that widespread proficiency in a dominant language such as English throughout populations in countries in postcolonial Sub-Saharan Africa and Asia is *not* in fact associated with higher levels of economic development for those countries. Their summary therefore, based on these findings, is that "In short, English isn't 'special' in terms of economic development or growth" (Arcand and Grin, 2012).

Other studies which focus on specific contexts have, however, identified a more positive correlation. Munshi and Rosenzweig made a comparative study of English-medium education and Marathi-medium education in Bombay, and their findings indicate that students who had had English-medium classes did benefit in terms of higher salaries (Munshi and Rosenzweig, 2006). Another study, focusing on the situation in West Bengal, found that individuals with primary school education in English had better career prospects and earned higher wages than those without it (Chakraborty and Kapur, 2008). Based on these findings, Chakraborty and Kapur argue that English should be reinstated in the elementary school curriculum (it was removed from primary grades in all public schools in 1983) so as to combat the widening social and economic gap between those sections of the population who are able to afford private English lessons and those who are not. Yet other research, however, has concluded that English proficiency alone does not have a bearing on improved income, and that it is only in combination with other social determinants such as a high level of education in an area in which there is a market-led demand for a specific skills set that English can contribute to socio-economic development. Naz Rassool gives the example of call-centre businesses in India, where English ability is both important and necessary but only in association with broader communication and IT skills and within the context of an industry which is a product of the political and economic circumstances of contemporary Indian society (Rassool, 2012).

The result, then, is a complex picture in which English is regularly associated with economic development both in the public imagination and in policy rationales, but where evidence about the precise circumstances and extent of a causal relationship is at present inconclusive, at least in terms of any general precepts. As such, any simplistic formula equating English ability with economic mobility is likely to be misleading. As Syeda Rumnaz Imam argues, "by no means everyone who acquires English will join the local or global elite" (Imam, 2005, p. 480).

Cultural identity and language rights

We saw in the example of Singapore how language policies need to take account of a range of different political and cultural dynamics, and that these can sometimes be at variance with each other, at least in the minds of those drawing up the policy. A conflict of this sort exists for the position of English in the European Union (EU), where the language has both practical affordances as a *lingua franca* across member states and strong symbolic associations with one particular national culture. EU language policy therefore has to deal with issues of both intergroup communication and cultural identity, and has to attempt to find a solution which can be practically efficient and politically sensitive to the context of modern-day Europe.

Multilingual policy in the European Union

The European Union operates with an explicit policy of multilingualism which is inscribed in its founding documents and has been reaffirmed every time new countries have joined. With the creation of the European Communities in 1958, Dutch, French, German and Italian were adopted as the official languages for the participating institutions, these being the national languages of the six founding countries: Belgium, France, Germany, Italy, Luxembourg and the Netherlands. Each subsequent enlargement has added the national or official languages of the new member states: Danish and English in 1973; Greek in 1981; Portuguese and Spanish in 1986, and Finnish and Swedish in 1995. In 2004 a cluster of Eastern European countries acceded, and Czech, Estonian, Hungarian, Latvian, Lithuanian, Maltese, Polish, Slovak and Slovene all became official languages. Since 2007, when Bulgaria and Romania joined and Irish was given official status, the Union has had a total of 23 official languages.

The importance placed in this policy of multilingualism is a direct result of beliefs about the relationship between language and national identity that have shaped the history of modern Europe. Since the eighteenth century when nationalism arose as a dominant ideology in the politics of Europe, the cultural and political identities of the different European nations have been founded in part on their distinct linguistic identities. The nation-state system which developed at that time – and which underpins modern-day Europe – posited the idea of a culturally and linguistically unified group of people (a nation) based in a particular and well-defined territory (see Chapter 3). A standard national language thus came to be an important symbol of independent cultural and political identity, and when the political association that became the European Union developed after the Second World War, this linguistic dimension of national identity was accorded further significance. As Sue Wright notes, while any language will operate as both a medium of communication *and* a marker of group identity, in the case of a union of individual nation-states this latter function becomes more salient and is therefore explicitly promoted (Wright, 2009).

Yet at the same time, a working union of people with different linguistic backgrounds also needs a strategy to facilitate mutual communication. One of the major challenges for language policy in the EU has therefore been to strike a balance between issues of cultural identity and efficient communication. The policy of the Union in this matter is translation and interpretation, but de facto working practices often mean the use of an unofficial *lingua franca*, which is increasingly English.

As such, there is a degree of mismatch between what is laid out in the policy and what people actually do in practice. The policy means that all 23 languages appear on signs, hoardings, and central information boards; that public relations material is published in all 23 languages, and that interpreting and translations provision is available. Yet beyond this 'symbolic' level, people use the language they think will give them the greatest audience or be most effective for the purpose at hand. And more often than not this is English. Members of the European Parliament, for example, relate incidents where speaking in their own national language, especially if it is one of the 'smaller' languages, will result in their speech having practically no impact – and in some instances they have noticed that their audience will not even bother to listen to the simultaneous translation. In other words, English increasingly acts as the de facto though unacknowledged *lingua franca* throughout the institutions of the EU, and this leads to issues of inequality and disadvantage.

There have been a number of critiques of the current policy of multilingualism, in terms of both its practical implications and its theoretical underpinnings (Wright, 2009). There is, for example, the contention that the type of linguistic homogeneity afforded by having an official *lingua franca* alongside the national languages would not only aid communication but could also provide a sense of common ground between the members, much as English does in Singapore. Another criticism is that the policy as it now stands promotes a very specific type of multilingualism – one consisting of an exclusive cluster of national standards – whereas every individual nation is itself extremely linguistically diverse, and millions of citizens across the continent speak regional or 'minority' languages. And although the EU does also protect and promote these languages (through, for example, the 1992 European Charter for Regional or Minority Languages), the central policy of its institutions is a mix of the pragmatic and the political in its use of national standards only.

Another criticism levelled at the policy is that it is both unwieldy and expensive. Working in dozens of different languages is both time consuming and expensive, particularly when documents need to be translated. Michele Gazzola has estimated that in 1999 (when there were 11 official languages) expenditures in the EU institutions for translation and interpretation came to €686 million. In 2006–07, when the EU had enlarged to 20 official languages, this figure was approximately €1045 million (Gazzola, 2006).

Finally, there is the suggestion that having English as a de facto *lingua franca* rather than as part of official policy conceals a range of inequalities, both social and economic. Those who do not speak the language are at an obvious disadvantage, and in the current situation there is no official language education provision to assist with this. Furthermore, for those who are non-native speakers there is the additional financial burden of having to pay to learn the language. One suggestion, therefore, is a type of 'native-speaker tax' whereby those countries who already have the language as a mother tongue contribute financially to provide ELF training to the other member states (Wright, 2009, p. 111; see also Grin, 2004; van Parijs, 2002).

As has been observed on a number of occasions however, native speakers are not necessarily at an advantage in contexts where English is being used as a *lingua franca* (see, for example, the discussion about "unilateral idiomaticity" in Chapter 7). ELF relies on some understanding of intercultural communication, and non-native speakers who are not bilingual can lack these skills simply because they have no experience of operating in a different language and thus cultivating a sense of language awareness. Indeed, the European Federation of National Institutions for Language (EFNIL), which acts as a forum for the exchange of information about language policy in the EU, uses the epigram from Goethe's *Maxims And Reflections* (*Maximen und Reflexionen*) to stress this very point: "Wer fremde Sprachen nicht kennt, weiß nichts von seiner eigenen" ("Those who do not know other languages do not understand their own"). As they state in the Brussels Declaration on language learning:

> In order to maintain and further develop their own languages and to promote a sense of shared European identity among the citizens of the states of the Union, the members of EFNIL support not only the learning and use of their national/official language or languages but also the learning of additional European languages. It is clearly in the interests of all individuals in Europe that they should be plurilingual. The overall aim is a plurilingual citizenry in a multilingual Europe.
>
> (EFNIL, 2006)

The situation at present in Europe is, therefore, like the one in Singapore, a mix between regulated practices directed by language policy, and the pragmatic actions of those working within this context who use English as a convenient solution to international communication. Often these tendencies are pulling in opposite directions, and proposals from scholars and policy advisors have been put forward suggesting further interventions in an attempt to mediate between the two agendas. Yet the fact that the interventions of policy are often at variance with those of individuals is a sign of the different functions that language plays in the life of all societies, and illustrates the difficulties that centralised language policy can have in regulating the way that people actually use English around the world.

Linguistic rights

While the policies we have looked at above are directed at specific regions, nations or institutions, another form of planning initiative attempts to have a broader scope, and regulate a distinct aspect of language use the world over. One of the intentions of language policy in the European Union is to promote and protect the national cultural identity of individual member states, and within this context English (or any single dominant language) is seen as a possible threat. This same concern also exists on a wider scale, with the fear that the spread of English around the world endangers other, 'smaller' languages, and can lead to so-called 'language death' (see discussion in Chapter 4). A prominent strategy for countering this threat is the idea of **linguistic rights**. The idea here is based on the belief that the language of one's birth or home community is an essential part of one's identity, in the same way that race, gender, or religion are. Advocates of this position argue that the opportunity to learn and use one's mother tongue should be considered "a self-evident, fundamental individual linguistic human right" and should therefore be legally protected (Skutnabb-Kangas, 1998, p. 20).

A general statement to this effect is included in the United Nations' 1948 Declaration of Human Rights, which asserts that no one should be discriminated against on the basis of language, just as they should not on the basis of race, colour, sex, politics or religion. In 1996, UNESCO drew up a more specific Universal Declaration of Linguistic Rights, which was intended to guarantee "the respect and full development of all languages and [establish] the principles for a just and equitable linguistic peace throughout the world as a key factor in the maintenance of harmonious social relations" (UNESCO, 1996). Amongst the specific rights included in this policy are access to primary education, provision against enforced language shift, and the right of minority groups to maintain their language (Skutnabb-Kangas, 2000). And although the policy does not refer to specific languages, it is often interpreted in the contemporary context as an intervention aimed at tempering the ruinous effects of the dominance of English around the world – to prevent it from fulfilling its destiny as a 'killer language' – and ensuring that its spread does not become a threat to linguistic diversity across the globe.

Despite its admirable egalitarian intentions, the linguistic rights paradigm has attracted a number of criticisms, including those which dispute the way it conceptualises language practices, and query the extent to which the communities it aims to help do actually benefit from its interventions. A particular point of critique is the way it is based on an idealised notion of the relationship between cultural or ethnic groups, their identities, and specific languages (in much the way that the EU's policy of multilingualism is). As Stephen May puts it, linguistic rights arguments "assume – in their less sophisticated manifestations, explicitly, and even in their most sophisticated forms, implicitly – an almost ineluctable connection between language and (ethnic) identity" (May, 2006, p. 535). In other words, they tie a particular language to a particular people, and in doing so seemingly ignore the dynamic sociolinguistic complexities of multilingual societies, especially in a world where mobility and migration are increasingly common and people are often not rooted to one sole locality. This type of underlying assumption can in turn lead to unintended consequences. For example, Jan Blommaert has argued that, not only does the paradigm misrepresent the way in which in many cases it is dominant local languages rather than English which provide the threat to indigenous languages, but also the target groups of such policies often in fact wish to learn a language such as English because of the opportunities it offers for social mobility and for transcending the circumstances in which they are currently caught (Blommaert, 2010). In this respect, too strong a stress on the ring-fencing of local languages can inhibit the ways in which societies adapt to changing economic and political circumstances, and reinforce rather than alleviate social inequality.

Appropriating English

Another oversight of the linguistics rights paradigm is the way that a global language such as English is often 'indigenised' by local communities, and through adaption and appropriation becomes part of those communities' cultural identity. The concept of the **appropriation** of English is an important one for the recent global history of the language. It refers to the ways in which many communities in diverse world contexts now perceive the language as an element of their own culture, and consider the variety that they speak to be a legitimate form of the language in its own right. In other words, English has become a 'local' language for many societies across the globe, and they no longer feel the need to adversely compare their usage with standard British or American varieties.

The appropriation of English can take a number of forms. In some instances, minority or marginalised groups will align themselves with its global associations as a way of promoting an independent sense of identity within an otherwise restrictive society. For example, Yoko Kobayashi has written of how women in Japan often look to the learning of English (especially via study-abroad programmes) as a means of escaping or circumventing patriarchal strictures within Japanese society, particularly as these impede career prospects (Kobayashi, 2007). Similarly, William Leap has examined the extensive use of English by gay communities in countries such as Indonesia, the Philippines, and Tonga, where the language is used alongside other cultural practices as a marker of resistance to traditional sexual and gender norms (Leap, 2010). In both cases, English has a symbolic role for these groups because of its cosmopolitan associations with certain modern, Western values, and can thus be appropriated for their own sociocultural purposes.

Another form of appropriation occurs in communities where the language has been imposed by historical or political events. In the 1960s, the Nigerian writer Chinua Achebe famously wrote that:

> my answer to the question, Can an African ever learn English well enough to be able to use it effectively in creative writing? is certainly yes. If on the other hand you ask: Can he ever learn to use it like a native speaker? I should say, I hope not. It is neither necessary or desirable from him to be able to do so. The price a world language must be prepared to pay is submission to many different kinds of use.
>
> (Achebe, 1965, p. 29)

In the literature created in Anglophone postcolonial societies, use of English has been a focus for intense debate. Some writers, such as the Kenyan Ngũgĩ wa Thiong'o, have purposefully taken the decision *not* to use English for their creative work because of its pernicious colonial associations. In Ngũgĩ's case this has meant that his later novels have all been written in the Gĩkũyũ language, despite the fact that this severely narrows his potential readership (though his novels are then translated into English). Others, such as Achebe, as well as Frank Aig-Imoukhuede and Nissim Ezekiel who were discussed in Chapter 2, have followed a strategy of appropriation, and of moulding and reworking the English language so that it can express the ideas, emotions and cultural sensibilities of their native speech. As Yamuna Kachru and Larry Smith summarise the situation, "Some writers feel the agony of using a medium for expressing themselves that did not originate from the same source as they did ... On the other hand, there are writers ... who celebrate the medium as it transforms itself by undergoing the processes of acculturation and nativisation under the impact of their creative energies" (Kachru and Smith, 2008, p. 166). Out of the latter tradition developed what are known as the "new literatures": writings by Commonwealth and postcolonial authors using the medium of English, but adapting, expanding and appropriating it for their own creative and cultural purposes. And as the global influence of English continues to spread, so this type of appropriation is evermore commonplace, and practised in a range of genres from the novel to rap music.

The ownership of English

Lying behind discussions and debates about the appropriation of English is an influential ideology about language that is expressed in the metaphor of 'ownership'. There is a common conceptualisation of language that likens it to a 'possession' (you can 'acquire' a language, or 'lose' it, words can be 'borrowed' or 'loaned' from one language to another, and so on), and the corollary of this is that the group who has possession of a particular language in some sense 'owns' it, with all the implications that this involves. In the history of Western ideas, and since the development of nationalism in eighteenth-century Europe, languages have traditionally been understood to belong to the nation state who speak them. French, for example, is associated with France; it is part of its cultural heritage, and is understood to belong to the nation's culture   and is explicitly promoted as such by the *Académie français*.

The global spread of English (or of any language) complicates this formula though. As far back at the late nineteenth century, Mark Twain expressed the opinion that "[t]here is no such thing as the Queen's English. The property has gone into the hands of a joint stock company and we [the United States] own the bulk of the shares" (Twain, 1989 [1897], p. 230). From the latter half of the twentieth century and the point at which there became more non-native than native speakers of English, there is a good argument to the effect that the balance of power has shifted once again. In the last few decades, this point of view has been much debated in academia. An early assertion to this effect was made by Randolph Quirk who, in the 1960s, wrote that "English is not the prerogative or 'possession' of the English" (Quirk, 1962, p. 17). Two decades later, Henry Widdowson gave an influential address at the International Association of Teachers of English as a Foreign Language's (IATEFL) 1993 conference, in which he argued for the need to revise traditional notions of ownership. In doing so he echoes the metaphor that Twain used a century earlier:

How English develops in the world is no business whatever of native speakers in England or anywhere else. They have no say in the matter, no right to intervene or pass judgement ... The very fact that English is an international language means that no nation can have custody over it ... [I]t is only international to the extent that it is not their language. It is not a possession which they lease out to others, while still retaining the freehold. Other people actually own it.

(Widdowson, 1994, p. 385)

For scholars and language professionals who share this view, the association between the English language and the locus of its origin are of little significance in the modern, globalised world. And for this reason, they argue, native speaker norms – that is, the patterns of usage that constitute standard British English – should no longer be unproblematically promoted as the only 'correct' or authoritative variety of the language.

An important point to be noted about discussion over the **ownership of English** is that it operates as an argument rather than an empirical description of the way English exists around the world. In other words, it is about social attitudes to the language as much as it is about communities' actual linguistic practices – and these social attitudes will be context-specific and depend to a degree on the circumstances of the communities in which English is being used. In some cases, for example, the associations the language has with British or American culture may be actively desired, as is the case for the groups discussed in Yoko Kobayashi and William Leap's work above. For Widdowson, however, the intention is to combat what for many years was the default supposition that British or American English should be the touchstones against which other usages were to be evaluated. His argument is, therefore, a form of intervention aimed at recalibrating the debate within academia.

✳✳✳

As we have seen throughout this section of the book, many of the interventions that are enacted or proposed for English in the world are founded on particular beliefs about language and its role in society. To examine the structure and rationale of these beliefs, and the way they exist in wider complexes of thought and behaviour, we need finally to look at the theoretical underpinnings of the discipline – and it is to this we will turn in the third section.

Tasks

In light of what we have discussed in this chapter, consider the following study questions:

- What different elements are there to the discourse of English as a language of economic opportunity?
- Should English be seen as a threat to language diversity around the world?
- Why is the metaphor of ownership a key issue for the existence of English around the world?

Feedback for these questions is given in the 'Commentary on tasks' section at the end of the book.

Part II

World Englishes as an academic discipline

Section C

Theory

9   Introduction: generalising about the specific

As the title of this third section indicates, we now turn our attention to theory. So far in the book we have looked at the phenomenon of English in the world, and at scenarios where this phenomenon constitutes challenges for people using or working with the language. We have looked at the interventions that people have made in response to these challenges – interventions that constitute practical knowledge for dealing with the language. In this final section, we switch our focus to how this practical knowledge – along with other analyses of the global spread of English – has been abstracted into theoretical knowledge; and we consider the value of such theory for our understanding of the state and status of English around the world today.

Before proceeding to the body of World Englishes theory itself, it is worth saying a word about the nature of theory, and about how this relates to the aims of the discipline. After all, 'applied linguistics' (which operates as the general field of academic inquiry in which the approach to World Englishes studies outlined in this book takes place) is, as the name suggests, a determinedly *practical* discipline. It purports to be concerned primarily with *applied* knowledge, targeted, in Christopher Brumfit's often quoted phrase, at the "investigation of real-world problems in which language is a central issue" (Brumfit, 1995, p. 27; see also the Series Editors' Introduction, p.ix). Theory, on the other hand, is, by definition, knowledge which is abstracted and generalised. So theory and practice are, in many ways, contrastive concepts. One might therefore expect there to be an uneasy relationship between the two: applied linguistics aims for practical solutions to real-life problems, theory seeks out generic patterns and law-like regularities.

There are two points worth making in response to this apparent discrepancy. The first is that *all* explanation is, in some sense, theoretical because it relies on finding general precepts to account for the details of particular incidents. For a description of *what* happened in an event to be transformed into an explanation of *how* or *why* the event happened, it is necessary to relate observations about the specific incidents to knowledge about general patterns of activity. And this is in essence what theories do. As Alex Rosenberg writes: "Theories, in short, unify, and they do so almost always by going beyond, beneath and behind the phenomena [that] empirical regularities report to find underlying processes that account for the phenomena we observe" (Rosenberg, 2000, p. 70). In other words, theories in applied linguistics are a means of relating specific linguistic features or incidents to broader trends in the use of language, and formulating these trends in such a way that they can be used to account for any similarly occurring linguistic features or incidents. To turn the contents of this book from a list of unconnected descriptions of language use into a discussion of the nature of English in the world today we therefore need to set these various and diverse descriptions into a theoretical framework which draws them together under a set of general precepts about how language operates in society.

The second point to make is that the type of theoretical explanation that operates in World Englishes studies (WES) is not an exact equivalent of that traditionally found in the hard sciences, and that in applied linguistics, theory and practice have a mutually supportive relationship. In the hard sciences, a canonical formulation of what constitutes a theory is the nomological–deductive method, whereby phenomena are explained by deducing them under universal laws of nature (the word 'nomological' deriving from the Greek *nomos* meaning 'a law'). Advances in science are traditionally understood to be made by first hypothesising that a particular pattern of events constitutes a natural law (e.g. "for every action there is an equal and opposite reaction"), then deducing experimental predictions from this hypothesis, and finally testing the hypothesis to see whether these predictions come true. Established hard sciences (such as physics or chemistry) can thus be characterised as disciplines that contain sets of such laws.

Unlike the hard sciences, however, the discipline of applied linguistics is less concerned with the formulation of universal laws, and instead aims to generate theoretical knowledge which is sensitive to the social contexts in which language is used, and which can be used to inform practices which take place within these or similar social contexts. The notion of theory in this respect is still synonymous with explanation, and has as its aim the development of a descriptive conceptual vocabulary which can explain the nature of the phenomenon under investigation. This still involves the identification of patterns which can be generalised across the phenomenon, as well as the matching of patterns in one domain (linguistic practices) with those in others (social or political practices) and the attempt to establish causal links between the two.

Yet the social aspect of language use means that the formulation of *universal* laws is likely, given the type of phenomena they would need to subsume, to be either impossible or impractical. In other words, the notion of a universal law is either one which simply does not apply to the intricate and extensive complexities of the sort of social behaviour that is evident in everyday social language practices, or one which would result in formulations that would simply be too general to be of any actual use. For example, given the fact that language and language practices are constantly evolving, and that social configurations are likewise in a continual stage of flux, explanations related to the use of language in society will only hold true under the current conditions in which they are observed. When these conditions change, so the phenomenon one is attempting to explain will also change. And this is especially the case when social conditions are undergoing the sort of rapid and profound changes brought about by processes of globalisation. Theories in applied linguistics therefore need to be able to address the developmental flux of a constantly adapting set of communicative strategies and their consequences. And attempting to contain this within universal laws would simply be misguided.

To explore the way theories in applied linguistics address the challenges of grappling with a complex and shifting social reality, let us briefly revisit the question of why theoretical explanation is necessary at all. A concise answer to this question is contained in the famous assertion by the social psychologist Kurt Lewin that "There is nothing so practical as a good theory" (Lewin, 1951, p. 169). In other words, theories are cultural tools which can be used to inform the way in which we tackle practical problems in the world. They are, to return to the terminology of Pragmatism that we discussed in the introduction, rules for action. When confronted with real-world problems in which language is a central issue, we can draw on established theoretical knowledge as a guide for how to address these problems. We can thus use theoretical explanation as the basis for further intervention. That is to say, the patterns (i.e. theory) that we identify by means of the explicit and retrospective rationalisation (i.e. theorisation) of what is involved in or constitutes the phenomenon (i.e. English in the world) can help us mould our actions in order to ensure that continued or future interventions with the phenomenon have a positive outcome. And in this way, the theory of applied linguistics enters into an ongoing dialectic with empirical and practical knowledge, with the one informing the other in an iterative process of knowledge generation.

In summary, then, the theory that will be outlined in this section provides certain explanatory frameworks for the social, cultural and political issues that have been presented so far in the book concerning the spread of English around the world. As cultural tools developed to assist with the solution of real-world problems, these theories often relate to specific issues that the discipline is, at any given time, attempting to address (often prompted by the social or political climate of the time). As such, the theory rarely has the status of entirely abstract or universal knowledge. Instead, it engages directly in debates about the nature of the spread of English around the world, and the implications this has for those using or working with the language. In this way, the theory itself often has a practical purpose, and aims not just to explain, but to be part of the process that influences English's global existence.

10 World Englishes as an academic discipline

Let us begin our discussion of the theoretical frameworks that have developed around the study of World Englishes by looking at how the discipline itself has evolved. It is, after all, the act of investigating and researching the language that gives rise to the development of theoretical approaches. So to look at how WES has developed – at what it has taken as its priorities and how it has gone about investigating its object of study – can provide a useful overview of the theoretical concerns that the discipline is addressing, along with the social, cultural and political issues with which it aims to engage. To this end, this third section of the book is structured around an investigation into how WES operates as a discipline: how it evolved from other English language studies traditions, how it conceives of its object of study, and how it has developed and debated the theories and methods it uses to analyse the nature of English in the world today.

Theories of disciplinarity

The organisation of knowledge within academia is a complex exercise which facilitates both the teaching of that knowledge and its organisation for the purposes of further knowledge-production (i.e. research and theorisation). By compartmentalising scholarship into distinct disciplines, education systems are able to reproduce knowledge in ways which are both effective and manageable; and for this reason disciplines become the building blocks from which educational curricula are built. They are, in Donald Kelley's words, "[w]hat [gives] concreteness, continuity, and intelligibility to the history of Western knowledge" (Kelley, 1997a, p. 1).

The issue of what exactly constitutes an academic discipline though, and what social and epistemological forces influence its development, is neither a simple, nor uncontroversial, matter. In his book on *Postcolonial English*, Edgar Schneider refers to a "new sub-discipline within (English) linguistics, somewhat fuzzily known as the study of 'World Englishes' or English as a world language" (Schneider, 2007, p. 2). As was discussed in the introduction, the name of this field of study has been a contentious issue from the very start. But in recent years the subject has, nonetheless, begun to gain an independent profile in the wider field of applied linguistics, and is now emerging as a distinct discipline in its own right. What, though, does it mean for World Englishes studies to be a distinct discipline? How does it achieve this status? And what can this status tell us about what people working in the field actually do? It is these questions that we will address over the course of this final section, and, in doing so, map out the theoretical ground on which WES is built.

As we have noted a number of times, the study of English around the world is responding in great part to the rapid and momentous changes that have occurred in global language use. In this respect, the discipline is a response to the phenomenon it has as its object of study. Changed circumstances in the use of English in the world (the fact that more people are using it, for more purposes, across more domains, and in more diverse forms, than ever before) 'naturally' give rise to increased academic interest in the nature and consequences of these circumstances. And this interest coalesces over time into a coordinated programme of research study with a number of specific aims.

Yet the discipline of World Englishes studies did not arise out of nowhere, nor, in practice, is its development simply a response to changing trends in the ecology of global linguistic behaviour. A distinction that is often made in discussion of disciplinarity is that between what Richard Whitley (2000) refers to as the *intellectual* and the *social* organisation of the sciences. By this he means that there are commonly two main influences on the evolution and shape of a discipline: 1) how knowledge is organised according to its substantive content – in our case, the fact that English use has emerged as a salient issue for societies across the globe in recent years – and 2) how this organisation comes about as a result of the social practices of those involved in the production or reproduction of that knowledge (i.e. teachers, researchers, policy makers, etc). So the development of WES is in part motivated by the phenomenon it looks at; but it is also the result of a complex of social, historical and political factors, all of which frame the way the subject is presently studied in academic circles. And it is these various social, historical and political processes which have produced a mostly coherent field of study which we can call World Englishes studies, and which provide the theoretical context in which research carried out in this tradition exists.

There are a number of different elements that go towards the establishment of an academic discipline. Historically, the concept in Western thought develops from the type of practical instruction that was given to disciples and students. As the seventeenth-century philosopher Étienne Chauvin writes in his *Lexicon Philosophicum* of 1692: "Discipline is a conception accepted from a master, such that disciples follow the master's example through his teaching" (cited in

Kelley, 1997b, p. 15). As the meaning of the word becomes elaborated and specific senses are refined, particularly during the sixteenth and seventeenth centuries, it comes to be used to refer to "a department of learning or knowledge; a science or art in its educational aspect" (*OED* (second edition, 1989), definition 2). From a historical perspective, therefore, the motivating force behind the classification of knowledge into distinct categories is primarily related to the context of education: a body of universal knowledge is divided into disciplines for the purposes of teaching. Disciplines in this respect are discursive constructions shaped by the communication and practice conventions of pedagogic communities. That is, they are shaped by the way that educators conceive of, organise and articulate the knowledge they are teaching. But while this may be the origin of the disciplinary organisation of knowledge, the nature of modern academic practice is such that it is not solely educational concerns which influence the shape of these discursive constructions. The sociological conditions that govern contemporary academic research and teaching have resulted in a far more complex interplay of historical, cultural and political forces, all of which combine to produce what are understood as disciplines. And an appreciation of the provenance of a discipline, and the different social influences that shape its concerns, can offer insights into why it is the way it is, and what it is trying to achieve.

Definitions of what constitute a discipline include a range of different components. King and Brownell, for example, include: a community, a domain of academic interest, a tradition (including a complex of beliefs and values), a network of communications, a favoured method of inquiry, and a conceptual structure (King and Brownell, 1966). Kelley draws up a similar, though slightly expanded list, composed of "a characteristic method, specialised terminology, a community of practitioners, a canon of authorities, an agenda of problems to be addressed, and perhaps more formal signs of a professional condition, such as journals, textbooks, courses of study, libraries, rituals, and social gatherings" (Kelley, 1997a, p. 1). We can collate these various characteristics into a list of key factors and suggest that a discipline is usually moulded by the following concerns. (I have laid each of these out in mostly abstract terms here; they will be exemplified and discussed in greater detail in later chapters of this book.)

1 The requirements of the *education* system. A discipline is the result of decisions about how a subject is taught and how curricula are constructed. The creation of teaching materials (textbooks, assessment procedures, etc) signals the emergence of a discipline, and establishes a central canon of key theories and empirical studies which constitute its academic content. It is often the appearance of

the named subject (e.g. 'World Englishes') with a relatively standardised content across different universities which marks the status of discipline within this educational context.

2 The influence of *historical precedent* and tradition in the gradual emergence and shaping of a discipline. Viewing their development from this perspective, disciplines can be seen as the result of a series of historically specific events (i.e. the actions of real people at specific points in time) related to the research and teaching of a particular body of knowledge.

3 The nature of the *phenomenon* (or phenomena) under investigation. From one perspective this can be seen as a primarily ontological question, which revolves around the extent to which there are clearly perceivable divisions within the natural or social world which provide ready-made frames for the division of knowledge (e.g. geology, geography). The organisation and articulation of that knowledge will then be discursive, however, in that it will be systemised according to the discourse and practice conventions of the community which construct a research agenda around it. How the parameters are set for the object of study is often a key factor in the identity of a discipline.

4 The existence of a preferred *methodology* or *theoretical framework*. The means by which phenomena are researched – and the theories which underpin this – can act as a distinctive factor in the shaping of specific fields of knowledge. Methods for the validation of evidence and the qualification of what achieves the status of scientific fact are often accompanied by a body of precedent, which acts as a solid foundation upon which arguments can be built.

5 Conventions related to *language* and *discourse*. Different disciplines will often employ differing conventions in the way that they use linguistic (and other semiotic) resources to frame knowledge. Differences between disciplines in terms of discursive practice can range from the use of a subject-specific vocabulary and terminology (e.g. 'acrolect', 'lexifier', 'corpus planning'), through the manipulation of grammatical and discourse structures, to the adoption of a unique system of symbolic notation (e.g. formal logic).

To what extent, then, does work done within the field of World Englishes studies fulfil the various criteria in the above list? Does WES use distinctive discourse practices and adhere to a particular methodological tradition? Does it have established parameters for what it takes as its object of study? And if so, what do these conventions tell us about the practices and concerns of the discipline, and the way in which it conceptualises its research ambitions?

One salient and concrete indication of the emergence of WES as a discipline can be seen in educational contexts with the recent proliferation of textbooks (such as this one!), courses of study, specialist journals, and other teaching and research-related resources that are now available. For example, the existence of named degrees which teach the subject – in recent years several Masters level degrees on 'World Englishes' have appeared in the UK, the USA, Australasia, and Europe; and it also now occurs in some undergraduate modules as well – along with the fact that certain university departments are even adopting the name of the discipline, for example the Graduate School of World Englishes at Chukyo University, Japan (Sakai, 2005), indicate a growing institutional acceptance of the concerns of the field. The influence is also apparent not only in terms of subject-specific textbooks, but also in the recent development of ELT materials which take a pluricentric approach to the language, such as Macmillan's *Global* series, which includes sections which "give students the opportunity to listen to a wide range of native and non-native speakers of English. These are all authentic and unscripted recordings, and expose students to real English as it is being used around the world today" (Global from Macmillan Education, 2010).

In terms of a research community, there are now major international organisations either dedicated wholly to the subject, such as the International Association of World Englishes (IAWE), or which have subsections related to it, such as the International Association of Teachers of English as a Foreign Language's (IATEFL) 'Global Issues' Special Interest Group. There also exist specialist journals publishing research in this area such as *World Englishes, English World-Wide*, the *Journal of English as a Lingua Franca* and *English Today*; while several academic publishers have series dedicated to work on this topic. (See the 'Further reading' section at the end of the book for details of some of the key texts and journals within this category.)

There appears, then, to be an established presence for the discipline in terms both of teaching materials and elements of educational and research structure. But a simple survey of examples of this presence cannot tell us much about the theoretical concerns of the field. For that we need to examine the rationales, the working practices, and the ambitions of the discipline. Over the four chapters of this section, therefore, I will explore the nature of the discipline with reference to the other four criteria from the above list, considering for each of them the ways in which theoretical debate analyses the problems, practices and interventions that we examined earlier in the book, and how this theory also attempts to offer explanatory descriptions of the nature and implications of the worldwide spread of English.

Four stages in the development of the discipline

Commenting on the role that social factors play in the history of ideas, Michel Foucault writes that the "devotion to truth and precision of scientific methods arose from the passion of scholars, their reciprocal hatred, their fanatical and unending discussions, and their spirit of competition – the personal conflicts that slowly forged the weapons of reason" (Foucault, 1991, p. 78). The rhetoric here may be a little sensational, but the point he is making is clear enough: interpersonal politics between actual people have an important influence on the formation of what later comes to be perceived as universal (i.e. anonymous) knowledge. Or to put it another way, disciplines have a history, and this history shapes their agendas, their working methods and their beliefs about what they study and why they study it.

World Englishes studies has developed from a number of traditions both within and beyond linguistics. Kingsley Bolton suggests that there are three broad groupings of approach that have produced the discipline's current profile (Bolton, 2005, pp. 74–5). These are:

- approaches which have primarily *linguistic* objectives (e.g. English studies, and corpus linguistics);
- approaches which have a combination of *linguistic* and *socio-political* concerns (e.g. sociolinguistic approaches, and the 'World Englishes' tradition associated most notably with the work of Braj Kachru); and
- approaches which are of a predominantly *socio-political* or *political* nature (e.g. Marxist-influenced approaches).

To this list we might add a fourth, more recent and still emergent category:

- approaches which explore worldwide English use within its local and translocal *cultural* contexts (e.g. work influenced by linguistic anthropology).

Approaches in the first of these four categories can ultimately trace their ancestry back to the philological description of the English language tradition that developed in the late nineteenth century. Their more immediate forerunner, though, is the work of Randolph Quirk and University College London's Survey of English Usage from the 1960s (which we briefly looked at in Chapter 7). The goal of this project was the description and contrasting of different varieties of (British) English using samples of naturally occurring language. Its focus was particularly on issues of syntactical structure and historical change, and as such it took a primarily linguistic approach, examining the forms of different varieties, rather than their sociolinguistic functions. As we discussed in Chapter 5, it was a precursor to many of the computerised corpus surveys of English varieties around the world.

The second trend that Bolton identifies develops from work in sociolinguistics and the sociology of language. Work in this tradition (e.g. Fishman et al., 1977) was being undertaken at a roughly similar time to the Survey of English Usage, and it also concentrated on the study of variation. Its approach was not focused exclusively on features of linguistic difference however, but also sought to understand how this variation relates to factors in the social environment.

It is from this tradition that the work of Braj Kachru emerges. Kachru – a Kashmirian-born, US-based scholar – has been a foundational figure in the establishment of the approach known as 'World Englishes'. As I mentioned in the general introduction, there is the danger of terminological confusion here, because although this term was originally used to refer predominantly to the approach developed by Kachru and his collaborators, it has since been adopted by some people to refer to the wider field of study, that is, to all research into English worldwide, regardless of its theoretical bent. Kachru's project, however, has had a distinctive theoretical character and rationale, and his great contribution has been to elaborate sociolinguistic approaches so as to include a focus on the socio-political and ideological issues that accompany formal variation of English around the world. In other words, his interest has not simply been on the nature of diverse varieties of English, but on their status and on the socio-political contexts in which they are used.

The birth of the Kachruvian 'World Englishes' approach can be dated to two conferences held in 1978 in Illinois and Hawaii, organised by Larry Smith and Kachru respectively (Kachru, 1992). Discussion at these conferences focused on issues such as the diversity of English worldwide, the use of the language in postcolonial contexts, and the socio-political issues which pertain to the language's presence in countries and regions across the globe.

A further important event in this strand of the development of the discipline was the launch – or rather re-launch – of the journal *World Englishes* in 1985. In that year, Kachru and Smith took over the editorship of a journal that had previously been called *World Language English*, and renamed it *World Englishes: The Journal of English as an International and Intranational Language*. In adopting the plural noun for the name of the language, and setting out their ambitions in their first editorial statement for an expressly inclusive approach to worldwide varieties and usage (Kachru and Smith, 1985), they consolidated the research brief that had begun at the earlier conferences. And many of the issues identified in those early forums and in the introduction to the re-launched journal have formed the core concerns of the discipline as it has developed in the years since.

Kachru was also a participant at another notable conference at the time, this one held in London in 1984 and arranged to mark the fiftieth anniversary of the founding of the British Council (Quirk and Widdowson, 1985). Focusing on the plurality of both English languages and English literatures worldwide, the issues discussed here were similar to those at Illinois and Hawaii, but they also revealed a notable difference of approach between some of the delegates which then led to an important debate that has done much to define the future of the discipline. The culmination of this debate was an exchange of articles in the journal *English Today* written by Randolph Quirk (1990a) and Kachru (1991), which has come to be seen as something of a landmark event in the development of WES.

The English Today debate

At the heart of this debate is a dispute about the status of different varieties of English around the world and whether these should act as models for the teaching of the language. As we have seen, this remains a vexed question for English-language educationalists, and despite the fact that the debate took place over two decades ago now, a similar set of issues are still being explored both by theorists and by practitioners and continue to generate waves of debate and disagreement (Seidlhofer, 2003a).

The rival positions articulated by Quirk and Kachru had, in fact, been expressed and debated prior to this. As early as the 1960s, Michael Halliday, Angus MacIntosh and Peter Strevens had critiqued the dominance of standard British and American varieties as teaching models in postcolonial contexts (Halliday et al., 1964), and this had provoked a response from Clifford Prator who countersued strongly in favour of the use of native-speaker varieties, suggesting that the latter were more stable than **New Englishes** (i.e. those used in countries where English has an established, official role following a history of colonialism), and that their continued promotion would ensure that speakers of English around the globe would remain mutually unintelligible (Prator, 1968). The exchange of views at the 1985 conference and the subsequent clash in the pages of *English Today* acted as a robustly argued précis and expansion of these issues.

At the heart of the Quirk–Kachru debate is the issue of whether English should be viewed as a single, monolithic entity represented by the model of an Anglo-American standard (*the* English language), or whether indigenous forms from around the globe should be considered legitimate varieties in their own right. Quirk asks whether the ways in which English is used in diverse world contexts should be accorded the status of independent and valid linguistic systems, or whether they are "just the result of the increasing failure of the education system" in postcolonial contexts which is incapable of teaching students 'correct' English (Quirk, 1990a, p. 8).

This question sets the parameters for much subsequent debate. On the one hand, there is the notion of a single world standard (by default, a native-speaker variety) which can function as a model for teaching purposes and against which any divergence is seen as the result of imperfect acquisition of the language; and on the other, there is a plurality of different indigenised varieties. The choice is between what Quirk calls a "single monochrome standard" which should be adequate for the "relatively narrow range of purposes for which the non-native needs to use English" (Quirk, 1985, p. 6), and a diffusion of World Englishes, where the pluralised form of the noun is a telling shorthand for the diversity exhibited by the language in the hundreds of different society in which it is used.

Quirk strenuously argues that 'non-native varieties' are imperfectly learnt versions of standard English, and are therefore not suitable for use as teaching models. Kachru's response is that such varieties are in fact sophisticated, rule-bound systems in their own right, and that they often have institutional backing in the societies in which they are spoken. As such, they have a valid and independent status from both a linguistic *and* a socio-political perspective. He concludes his rebuttal by suggesting that Quirk's position is therefore simply out of touch with the 'sociolinguistic realities' in which English is actually used around the world.

When one lays these two positions out side by side, one can see that they are, in fact, arguing for slightly different ends. Quirk's stance stems from the same tradition as those who campaign for a universal language. He explicitly ties his argument to the idea that "the world needs an international language" and, given this contention, concludes that "English is the best candidate at present on offer" (Quirk, 1990a, p. 10). A similar standpoint has been argued by other scholars in recent years. David Crystal, for example, predicts that a variety which he terms **World Standard Spoken English** will emerge to fulfil the role of pre-eminent international language in the modern era, and he considers it likely that this will be based on a standard American variety (Crystal, 1997).

Kachru, on the other hand, does not frame his argument around the need for a universal language, but instead focuses on the way that English is actually being used around the world, and the implications this has for how language professionals – and particularly educators – should view the language. In effect, he is highlighting what he sees as a conceptual gap between the ways in which English is used, especially in postcolonial countries, and the assumptions which underpin teaching practices in these regions. As he writes: "What is actually 'deficit linguistics' in one context [i.e. an approach which considers certain varieties to be less complex – and thus deficient – in comparison to others] may be a matter of 'difference' which is based on vital sociolinguistic realities of identity, creativity and linguistic and cultural contact in another context" (Kachru, 1991, pp. 11–12). As we have seen, these ideas have since threaded through much of the research into the variation in English use across the world.

Although the two men are advocating different approaches and, to an extent, different ends, they are both motivated by similar 'democratic' intentions for the role that English can play in people's lives. Quirk, on the one hand, sees social mobility – and the opportunity for people to "increase their freedom and their career prospects" (Quirk, 1990a, p. 7) – as an important rationale for why they wish to learn the language, and he thinks that this can best be achieved with the aid of a standard variety such as British or American English which already has high status around the world. Kachru, on the other, argues that indigenised varieties are related to issues of political, social and even psychological identity, and thus to downplay their importance in favour of an Anglo-American standard is to alienate people from their own cultural environment. Far from being emancipatory, therefore, he considers Quirk's single world standard to be fundamentally divisive and to assist in the reproduction of social inequalities.

One of the consequences of Kachru's critique of Quirk and his insistence on the importance of paying attention to the 'sociolinguistic realities' of worldwide English speakers has been to instil a political awareness in the discipline. The 'World Englishes' approach associated with his name provides a **pluricentric** model of the English-speaking world in which the varieties used in various diverse contexts are all accorded equal legitimacy. It does this by combining a descriptive sociolinguistics, which records and categorises English variation around the world, with analyses of the cultural and political contexts in which the language is used. This issue of politics, which was mostly absent from earlier approaches, has become increasingly important for the development of the discipline, and is explicitly foregrounded in the next category.

Political approaches and cultural contexts

The third category of approach identified by Bolton has its roots in a mixture of Marxist theory and ideas from the Frankfurt School, and in many ways draws as much on political philosophy as it does on linguistics. The theorists working in this category all adopt a **critical** agenda – that is, they focus on an analysis of the power relations which sustain everyday social practices and institutions, and do so with the intention not merely of describing the way things are but also of engaging with them in such a way as to alter and, ultimately, improve social relations. They do this by locating English-language practices firmly within their historical and cultural contexts, and aiming to reveal the (implicit) political agendas of those involved in the promotion of English. To this end, the approach has critiqued things such as the role played in the global status of English by the international policy ventures of powerful Anglophone countries (Phillipson, 1992; Pennycook, 1994, 1998), and the ethical responsibilities of the ELT and applied linguistics communities (Pennycook, 2001).

We will examine the theoretical traditions which these approaches draw on in fuller detail in Chapter 9 when we consider the methods and theoretical underpinnings of the discipline. Let me here simply mention two of the landmark texts in the development of this branch of the discipline. A first important publication was Robert Phillipson's book *Linguistic Imperialism* (1992), which analysed the role played by English – and particularly the way that institutions and government organisations have promoted English – in maintaining an Anglo-American dominance on the world stage. Another important development in the argument was Alastair Pennycook's *The Cultural Politics of English as an International Language*, which critiqued the idea that the spread of English should be seen as a "natural, neutral, and beneficial" process, and argued that viewing the history of the language in these terms is at best erroneous, and at worst propagandist (Pennycook, 1994, p. 9).

While this approach has been highly influential and has generated a great deal of debate, for some commentators the stress on political philosophy has been a little too intensive, and has dominated to such a degree that sociolinguistic investigation has almost become ignored. For example, Bolton characterises much of Pennycook's work as being "a brand of critical linguistics with little linguistics" and feels that the focus has moved from language data to "activist pedagogical politics" (Bolton, 2005, p. 75). Whether or not one agrees with this evaluation, the legacy of this approach has certainly been to set an agenda which places political awareness at the centre of the discipline.

The fourth and final strand in the development of the discipline is one which draws on a mixture of linguistic anthropology and political philosophy – the former for its close examination of culturally specific language practices as they occur in different communities around the world; and the latter for an application of globalisation theory to worldwide English use (e.g. Blommaert, 2010; Pennycook, 2007a). The focus in this work is often on fine-grained analysis of the ways in which people around the world use English, and how these linguistic practices are influenced by the flows of people, capital and information which constitute the forces of globalisation. Of particular concern for this approach are the ways in which the differential value that English has in different societies, and the uneven access that people have to it as a resource, result in regular patterns of social inequality. Yet unlike earlier work in the Kachruvian tradition, the approach concentrates less on established varieties located in specific places (e.g. the New Englishes used in postcolonial countries), and more on the fluidity of the linguistic environment in a world characterised by increased mobility – in people moving geographically from place to place, and socially from circumstance to circumstance. Even in the few years since the Kachruvian and critical approaches were developed, the world has altered significantly, and this latest category of approach is trying to get to grips with the linguistic implications of these recent rapid social changes which are occurring across a global matrix.

* * *

The consequences of these four different strands can be seen in a variety of features in the aspect of the present-day discipline. They can be seen in the concerns it has chosen to address, the theoretical paradigms it has traditionally adopted, and the conceptual vocabulary it makes use of. This is not to say that the discipline as a whole is limited to these small group of approaches, but rather that these are the traditions from which it has developed, and thus they have an influence on its ethics, its epistemology, and its fundamental research questions. Even though various of these approaches are at times critical of others, they can be seen to share certain concerns, not least the political implications of the spread of English. We shall return to these different strands in Chapter 11 to explore in more detail the theoretical foundations upon which they rest and to examine the way they have been evaluated. Before doing so, however, we need to address a more fundamental question: how does WES conceive of its object of study. This, therefore, will be the topic of the next chapter.

Task

In light of what we have discussed in this chapter, consider the following study question:

- What factors are likely to lie behind the emergence of World Englishes studies as a distinct field of study?

Feedback for this question is given in the 'Commentary on tasks' section at the end of the book.

11 English as an object of study

Setting the parameters for what counts as English

What does World Englishes studies take as its object of study? One would imagine the answer to this should be fairly straightforward. The discipline examines English in the world: its forms, its functions, its status. As we have noted from the very outset, however, determining what counts as 'English' is a complex and sometimes controversial matter, and it is not too much of an exaggeration to say that this simple question animates almost all the research and theorising carried out under the heading. Defining, refining and debating the nature of the phenomenon under investigation is at the absolute heart of the discipline – and in a sense, the stances taken about what counts as its object of study define the very identity of World Englishes studies.

The discursive construction of English

We have seen in the previous chapter how different scholars have had different ideas about what variety of the language should be used as a teaching model and have taken contrasting attitudes about the relative significance of political issues pertaining to the spread and use of the language. Beyond these issues, though, do they all share the same fundamental conception of what English is? And assuming they do, is it possible to pin down the nature of this core conception and use it as a solid foundation from which all investigations into the topic can begin? Or to put it another way, is everyone who researches the language looking at fundamentally the same thing?

In a survey of the many books published in the twentieth century which use the simple title *The English Language*, Tom McArthur notes that, although they all invariably acknowledge that their object of study is and always has been diverse, they nevertheless opt for an all-embracing title which suggests that the language has, in some sense, also remained constant throughout its history. As McArthur puts it, "[t]he authors as it were proceed in apostolic succession, each charged with producing the latest interim report on the same vast on-going project" (McArthur, 1998, p. 56). In a sense, the term 'the English language' here is what in philosophy is known as a 'rigid designator': there is some concept which all scholars of the language begin with – a commonsensical or traditionally understood notion of what English is – and then they explore, investigate and expound upon the phenomenon, hoping to provide ever more nuanced accounts of its nature. In other words, the name acts as an anchor point grounding the discourse about the language (i.e. the set of beliefs a community has and expresses about the language) as it constantly evolves and the process of knowledge generation continues.

I have mentioned a number of times that the object of study is a discursive construction. By this I mean that the 'English' (or 'Englishes') that the discipline researches is in part shaped by the interests and practices of those doing the research. That is to say, it is the product of the choices that researchers working within the disciplinary framework make about what to focus on, how they generalise about patterns of usage, and the conceptual categories and terms they use to represent these choices. The nature of English itself is manifold and immensely complex. We have noted how up to two billion people speak it in some form or other (see Chapter 3); we have also noted that every person's speech is in some ways unique. Likewise each person's life is unlike another's and so the way their own language use is enmeshed in their everyday experience is also unique. In a sense, the English language as a social phenomenon will be the totality of all these experiences, and will continue to evolve as these experiences (and the people generating these experiences) continue to multiply. Yet of course, scholarship on the subject cannot survey this totality in its entirety. Instead it aims to identify patterns and generalities, to highlight and explain areas and practices that it considers to be of significance, and to distil from the manifold flux of experience phenomena which have the value of knowledge for the communities in which this scholarship is being pursued. All of which is to say that however based in objective observation and description research into the English language may be, the act of research itself necessarily shapes the object of inquiry by the processes it uses to carry out its inquiry; and in this sense, the object of inquiry becomes a discursive construct.

There are a number of different factors which can influence the relationship between the way the world is experienced and the way we conceptualise that experience. For certain disciplines, the boundaries between areas of inquiry may, to a greater or lesser degree, be suggested by the structure of phenomenological reality. For example, the dividing line between zoology and botany is provided to a great extent by the difference in physical structure between animals and plants. Other disciplinary boundaries, however, rely more on factors such as historical precedent or a difference in philosophical perspective. For example, in the case of the distinction between psychoanalysis and analytical psychology, historical development has been the more decisive influence in the separation of the two into distinct fields of knowledge. In almost all cases, though, there is some measure of mix between observable phenomena (what is out there in the world) and strategies of categorisation (discursive construction), and this is the case with WES.

At one end of the spectrum there are certain scholars who go so far as to question whether an entity named 'English' exists at all (e.g. Harris, 1990). In making this contention, they are highlighting in bold type the role that processes of discursive construction play in the discipline. Alastair Pennycook, for example, contends that what is commonly understood as 'English' in the discourse of World Englishes studies relies on a circular argument that goes as follows: the language's existence is asserted a priori by those who are studying it, and then linguistic behaviours which do not correspond to this a priori definition are assigned to other linguistic categories or simply disqualified from inclusion in the definition (Pennycook, 2007b). In other words, according to his argument English as a coherent conceptual entity emerges through manipulation of the discourse rather than ever having been a fully distinct and ontologically stable entity that pre-exists the attention of linguistics.

This may sound like an extreme position to take, yet there are practical examples which illustrate the extent to which a variety of factors, including historical and political ones, noticeably shape what is and is not included in the object of study. There is, for example, a lack of consensus as to whether varieties of English that are spoken within England, or indeed within the British Isles, should be included in World Englishes studies. The New Englishes approach, from which WES has evolved, specifically investigated varieties from 'non-mother-tongue' countries, and to an extent WES has inherited this partitioning. Rajend Mesthrie and Rakesh Bhatt in their book *World Englishes*, for example, limit their examination to the second-language varieties that have developed in former British colonies in Africa, Asia and the Caribbean (Mesthrie and Bhatt, 2008). However, handbooks such as those published by Wiley-Blackwell and Routledge both include British English as a part of the discipline's remit (Kachru et al., 2006; Kirkpatrick, 2010).

The status of pidgins and Creoles

A similar disputed boundary occurs with the question of whether pidgins and Creoles should be considered varieties of English, and thus whether they come within the scope of World Englishes studies (McKay, 2002). Again, publications such as the *Handbook of World Englishes* (Kachru et al., 2006) include entries on them, and the three main journals in the field – *World Englishes*, *English World-Wide*, and *English Today* – have all published articles on them. In some cases, ambivalence towards the issue is reflected in the publishing history of a particular work; for example, it was not until the third edition of Trudgill and Hannah's *International English: A Guide to the Varieties of Standard English* (1994) that a section on Creoles was included. Contrary views on the issue also exist however, such as Manfred Görlach's contention that pidgins and Creoles be considered "independent languages on all counts" and thus not part of the study of English (Görlach, 1997, p. 171).

Salikoko Mufwene has suggested that this issue is an explicitly historico-political one. He argues that the very naming strategies used for certain varieties – the fact that they are categorised as 'pidgins' or 'Creoles' (which in the past were traditionally viewed as less complex than 'full' languages) – is politically motivated, and indicates a marginalisation of them and the communities that speak them (Mufwene, 1997). He suggests that pidgins and Creoles, along with those varieties spoken by the descendents of non-European speakers, are viewed by the mainstream as the "illegitimate offspring of English", and for this reason often classified as separate languages.

In each case, then, the issue is not simply a matter of directing the research towards what is actually out there in the world. It is not merely a matter of locating instances of English use and saying: "this is what we shall focus our attention on". Rather, the notion of what counts as English is always constructed to a certain degree; it is a product of what people think English is, what they say it is, and what aspect of it they choose to place at the centre of the discipline's gaze.

The ideologies of authenticity and anonymity

The ways in which people think about language, and the influence their thoughts and beliefs have upon the role that language plays in society, are investigated in a field of study devoted to what are known as 'language ideologies'. In World Englishes studies, there are two influential but opposing ideologies of the language which structure much of the debate about what the discipline should take as its proper object of study, and which also have a significant influence on the planning and policy interventions of language professionals. These are the notions of 'English as an international language' and of 'English as a local or indigenised language'. I will examine these in detail below. Before doing so, however, it will be useful first to say a word or two about the concept of ideology and how it relates to issues of language use.

The concept of ideology

Ideology has long been a contested concept in the political sciences, and the term has been used with a variety of slightly different meanings by different academic traditions. At its most basic, it relates to systems or patterns of entrenched belief which people have about elements of social life. In one tradition, it is an expressly political concept. This is the tradition closely associated with the thought of Karl Marx and Friedrich Engels, where the term is used to refer to a form of illusory thinking – what Engels calls a 'false consciousness' – which leads sections of society to have a distorted view about their life circumstances, and which in turn allows the ruling classes to retain a position of power and exploitative control over the rest of the population. Ideology in this respect is explicitly a false or distorted set of beliefs about social relations, and the job of the theorist is to expose this falsity and, by doing so, assist with the process of emancipation.

In contrast to this, the sociologist Karl Mannheim developed what he termed the 'total concept of ideology', which refers to the collective systems of thought shared by all members of a community (Mannheim, 1936). These are not necessarily distorted views of social reality, but instead constitute the basic principles, beliefs and values by which a society operates. The notion is similar in a sense to a community's cultural values and practices – it is the way things are done in that community, and the beliefs and presuppositions that sustain this way of life. That is not to say that this conception of ideology is a-political; the belief systems that exist within a community will be influenced by and have an influence on the way that relations of power between different groups are organised, and thus ideologies can produce and reproduce patterns of inequality between different sectors of society. But whereas the Marxist conception of ideology is of something which can ultimately be overcome by critique and class struggle, the total concept of ideology is an always present matrix of beliefs which sustain the operation of society. Ideologies can change, shift and be critiqued, but one can never eradicate the basic phenomenon as an element of social existence.

Language ideologies

For a **language ideologies** approach, it is this Mannheimean sense of the term that is the more relevant. In short, language ideologies can be understood as cultural conceptions or representations of the nature of language and how it operates as part of social life. These patterns of belief can be both explicit – that is, people can articulate them overtly – or implicit – that is, they can act as an unconscious influence on language-related behaviour. In either case, they constitute a shared belief system which influences the ways in which people interact both with language in general and with individual languages (Silverstein, 1979; Woolard, 1998; Kroskrity, 2006).

There are three further points worth noting in relation to this. The first is that language ideologies are not static or unchangeable. As we have seen throughout this book, arguments about the nature, value and influence of English around the world are commonplace, and the details of people's beliefs about the language are being constantly disputed and revised. The second point is that ideologies are not solely mentalist – that is, they are not limited to ideas in the mind – but are also practice-based and behavioural. In other words, the beliefs that people have influence the attitudes and actions they take towards language, including the way they habitually use it.

Finally, as Kathryn Woolard stresses, ideologies of language are never simply about language alone. Instead they are about the ties that exist between linguistic practices and a variety of other social factors such as class, gender or nationality (Woolard, 1998). That is to say, the study of language ideologies acts as a link between linguistic and social theories in that it relates the detailed practices of everyday communication to broader frameworks concerning social and political relations. And it is this symbiosis of linguistic and extra-linguistic concerns, and the associations that the concept of English accrues, which is the nucleus of the object of study for WES.

Authenticity and anonymity

Kathryn Woolard identifies two enduring ideologies in the history of Western thought that have had considerable influence on the ways in which languages are perceived, especially by those formulating policy initiatives. She refers to these as the ideologies of 'authenticity' and 'authority' (Woolard, 2005). She argues that debates about languages – about the values they have, the roles they (should) play, the shapes they (should) take – are wont to refer back to a notion of authority to back up their contentions, and this authority very often takes one of two forms. As will become clear as we outline this division, this also provides a structure for much of the discussion about the role of English in the world.

The ideology of 'authenticity' foregrounds the relationship between a language and the community which speaks it. A language, according to this way of thinking, is closely linked to person and place. Its value is located firmly in this particular relationship and in the role it plays as a fundamental marker of cultural identity. This system of belief derives from the development of the nationalist worldview in eighteenth-century European political philosophy and the way that a community's language practices were promoted as an essential element of its cultural and political character (see Chapters 3 and 8). The language is understood to 'belong' to the people who speak it, and its worth derives from its status as an authentic attribute of the community. For this reason, the language's distinctive nature – its accent, dialect, and literary tradition – are celebrated and viewed as authenticating markers of its individual character.

The alternative ideology, that of 'anonymity', is one in which the value of a language (or dialect) resides in its transcendence over any particular faction of society, and instead comes from its status as a neutral system of communication that is available to all. This attitude is closely tied to the development of standard languages and their promotion as the official medium of communication for institutions and administrative purposes in an expanding centralised state. As Woolard explains:

> Ideally, the citizen participating in public discourse as a speaker of disinterested truths speaks in what we could call a 'voice from nowhere'. The citizen-speaker is not only supposed to be an Everyman, he (or with more difficulty, she) is supposed to sound like an Everyman, using a common, unmarked standard public language.
>
> (Woolard, 2005, p. 5)

This public language is spoken without an 'accent' (i.e. without a marked regional bias) and constitutes the 'correct' form of the language. In practice, of course, history shows how an ideology of anonymity can operate as an instrument for the imposition of the values and practices of the dominant class on society at large, in that it is their language that is chosen to be the 'neutral', universal form.

Both these ideologies are operational in debates about English in the world. Viewing the language as the property of all, as no longer tied to the interests of any one nation, draws on the authority of the anonymous language; promoting it as an indigenised resource appropriated by the communities who use it, draws on the authenticity of ethnic and nationalist movements. Indeed, several of the dichotomies we have encountered throughout this book can be mapped onto this divide: a single monolithic English (anonymous) vs. a plurality of Englishes (authentic); English as an international language (anonymous) vs. English as a foreign language (authentic); English as a language for wider-communication (anonymous) vs. English as a language for identification (authentic).

Based on this proliferation of dichotomies, there would appear to be a paradox or conflict at the heart of WES. The ideologies of authenticity and anonymity are defined by their differences. A language is viewed as authentic when there is a close bond between it and a particular community; it is seen as anonymous when there is an absence of any such link. English around the world is variously promoted both for the way it has been indigenised and appropriated and for its universality and relative neutrality (the way it has transcended its colonial history). Arguments, such as those between Randolph Quirk and Braj Kachru, line up on either side of this divide, and attempt to persuade of the advantage of their own approach.

There are two points to be made with respect to this. The first is that these ideologies are often perspectival. That is to say, the same language or variety can be promoted as anonymous in one context, and authentic in another. For example, standard British English is still widely viewed as the unmarked, neutral form of the language within the UK; but it converts to a culturally marked variety when transplanted to the United States.

The second point is that the two roles are not necessarily mutually incompatible if one sees them engaging different types of 'English'. The properties required of an anonymous language are a strategy of communication that allows for mutual intelligibility around the world; an authentic language requires patterns of usage which can be associated with the culture of the local community. If a single, fixed entity named 'English' is burdened with fulfilling both these functions, then it is likely to be conflicted. But, as we saw with the case of Singapore, communities are able to adopt the language for multiple different purposes within society, and adapt it accordingly – that is, they can use a standard Singaporean English for one set of functions, and Singlish for another. The confusion therefore comes from the fact that the name – in association with another overarching ideology which views a language as a set, fixed and monolithic entity – ignores the fact that variation in language is the norm, and that all speakers have a range of different registers, styles and dialects to draw upon for the different communicative encounters they engage in.

It is for this reason that recent trends in the discipline have attempted to pay close empirical attention to the ways in which people use the language around the world, and employ the findings of this empirical data as a means of reconceptualising the categories – and thus the object of study – with which the discipline works. As Jan Blommaert writes, in the era of globalisation "we need to *move from Languages to language varieties and repertoires*. What is globalised is not an abstract Language, but specific speech forms, genres, styles, and forms of literacy practice" (Blommaert, 2003, p. 608). In other words, the object of study is increasingly complex and, in a sense, amorphous, as the language and its influence continues to spread across the globe. The focus of investigation for the discipline needs to be how people actually use the language, and also how they think about it – that is, the ideologies which influence their behaviour. Rather than seeing

English as being either one thing or the other, being either an
'international' or a 'local', 'indigenised' language, it is better to
understand why it is promoted in these two ways, and when and for
what reasons these ideologies are activated. The answer to this is often
due to the social and political contexts in which the language is being
used or promoted. As we noted earlier in the chapter, language
ideologies are never about language alone, but about a complex of
other social dynamics as well. It is the ways in which English relates to
wider social, cultural and political concerns, and the causal factors
which explain its nature and influence around the world, which is the
focus of the theoretical frameworks that we will examine in the next
chapter.

Tasks

In light of what we have discussed in this chapter, consider the
following study questions:

- Why should determining what counts as English be such a
  problematic issue?
- How do the ideologies of 'anonymity' and 'authenticity' structure
  the discussion about the role of English in the world?

Feedback for these questions is given in the 'Commentary on tasks'
section at the end of the book.

12 Models and theoretical frameworks

Along with the influence of historical traditions and decisions that identify and construct the object of study, another key element in the emergence of a discrete discipline is the set of methodologies and theoretical models it sanctions for pursuing its research. World Englishes studies does not employ a single theoretical approach to which all work within the field conforms, however. Although specific concerns do emerge, and appear regularly and with a certain coherence, there is no core theory or methodology by which all investigation into World Englishes operate. Unlike research in the hard sciences, which holds to an idea of 'progression' with findings building incrementally upon each other, WES instead responds to shifting trends in the social world, and the approaches which dominate the discipline at any one time are those which are the 'best fit' for broader concerns in the political climate of the period. As such, academic inquiry into the spread, nature, and status of worldwide English is conducted by means of eclectic methods, and draws upon a range of theoretical traditions. In this chapter, we will review some of the most influential of these theoretical approaches, and consider what they tell us about the core concerns of the discipline.

Models of the spread of English

The Three Circles of English

There have been a number of models proposed for describing the spread of English around the globe and classifying worldwide varieties, but by far the most influential has been Braj Kachru's **Three Circles of English**. The ideas behind this were developed in several articles in the 1980s, and the model was first published in the 1985 book which stemmed from the conference the previous year marking the fiftieth anniversary of the British Council (Kachru, 1985). The influence of this model has been so extensive that the terminology it uses is employed even by those who directly criticise the model itself; and it has been a challenge in this book to describe aspects of the spread of English without having recourse to this terminology until the final 'Theory' section.

The model – which aims to explain the current sociolinguistic profile of English around the world – consists of three concentric circles (an 'Inner Circle', an 'Outer Circle', and an 'Expanding Circle') which "represent the types of spread, the patterns of acquisition, and the functional allocation of English in diverse cultural contexts" (Kachru, 1992b, p. 356). In other words, the model is intended to reflect the following elements: the different factors that have propelled the spread of the language; how the language has been acquired by the populations of different countries; and the purposes for which the language is used in different countries. The three circles are as given below.

The **Inner Circle** consists of those countries where English is the majority first language and is used as the default medium in practically all domains of society. This therefore includes not only the UK, but also those countries in which English displaced the majority indigenous languages during the colonisation process, that is, the USA, Australia, New Zealand and so on (see Chapter 3). Kachru refers to the English of these countries as being 'norm-providing' in that it acts as the model of the language that is taught around the world to those learning it as a foreign language. That is to say, people learning English in countries such as Japan or Brazil are likely to use a standard British or American English as their target, and aspire to its norms of usage.

The **Outer Circle** comprises countries in which English has an official status but is not the majority language. The pattern of spread is again the result of colonisation, but in these cases English did not displace the indigenous languages but was instead used alongside them for certain specific functions. In these countries, English is a second or additional language for most of the population, and has an official role in institutional contexts such as administration and the education system. Examples include India, Singapore, and Nigeria. These are what Kachru calls 'norm-developing' in that the varieties of English spoken here have deep roots in the culture of the regions and have their own communicative norms – in other words, they are **indigenised varieties** – yet they still tend to lack the status of Inner Circle varieties.

The final component of the model is the **Expanding Circle**, which consists of the rest of the countries of the world, that is, places such as China, Japan, Germany, etc. The use of English in these countries is not directly related to colonialism but to the more general influence of globalisation. English predominantly has the status of a foreign language here, and there are no significant numbers of first or second language speakers. Kachru refers to these countries as 'norm-dependent' in that, in the absence of an established local variety, they look to Inner Circle varieties as their model.

The Three Circles model has several advantages, but it also has its shortcomings. One of its great strengths has been the way that it has altered perspectives on English around the world, moving away from a framework which is most appropriate for monolingual societies and instead advocating the need to view the language in terms of several different World Englishes rather than as a single, homogeneous entity. By doing this, the model has focused academic interest on non-native varieties – especially those of the Outer Circle – which had previously often been treated as deficient versions of Inner Circle varieties, as we saw in the discussion of the *English Today* debate. Throughout his career, Kachru has made a case for seeing non-native varieties as legitimate in their own right, and the model, by highlighting the importance of historical and political processes in the distribution of Englishes around the world and by relating variation to these different historical patterns, has been a powerful tool in this quest.

The limitations of the model that have been identified relate mostly to issues or details it fails to incorporate. Like any theoretical model, it works by means of generalisation, and this inevitably involves a certain amount of simplification. As the philosopher J. L. Austin once observed with regard to the practice of theorisation, "we must at all costs avoid over-simplification, which one might be tempted to call the occupational disease of philosophers if it were not their occupation" (Austin, 1962, p. 38). The model therefore necessarily rationalises the phenomena it is dealing with in order to fit them within the broad categories it has identified as salient for an understanding of the spread and current status of worldwide English. As a number of subsequent commentators have pointed out (e.g. Bruthiaux, 2003; Pennycook, 2007a; Park and Wee, 2009), in doing this it overlooks or sidelines various important details.

A chief criticism of the model is that it deals with language exclusively at the level of the nation-state. In other words, it refers only to national varieties, and ignores the extensive variation that occurs within countries in terms of regional and social dialects, and occupation-related registers. Similarly, it does not capture the more mixed and fluid uses of English which occur in many parts of the world, where people draw on elements of the language and combine them, often in *ad hoc*, creative and complex ways, with local languages (Pennycook, 2007a). Given the global status of English today, this type of language practice occurs with ever greater frequency, and disrupts the neat classifications such as 'Indian English' or 'Nigerian English' with which the model works.

Another limitation is the way the model is unable to deal with countries which do not fall neatly within the three-part system. South Africa, for example, which Kachru himself notes has an awkward relationship to his scheme, has 11 official languages at present (although at the time of the initial development of the Three Circles model, and prior to the new post-Apartheid constitution of 1994, it only had two), and English is learnt as a native language by large parts of the population but by no means all of it. The model also cannot fully accommodate the dynamic nature of the continued changing patterns in the use of the language. The Expanding Circle especially is in constant flux at present. Several European countries, for example, especially those in the north of the continent, now have English as such an integral part of everyday life that it practically has the status of a second rather than foreign language for them. In fact McArthur, in his list of EFL countries (which approximate to the Expanding Circle groupings), has a special category for what he calls 'English [as] a virtual second language', in which he includes 17 places, such as the Netherlands, Switzerland, and the United Arab Emirates (McArthur, 1998, p. 54). And finally, since the devising of the model, the concept of 'English as an international language' has been challenging that of 'English as a foreign language', and again, this development is not adequately accommodated in the three-part scheme. To an extent then, aspects of the model are now somewhat dated in relation to the current geopolitical situation.

Despite these stress points, and given the caveat that all models are in a sense convenient fictions designed to help with description and analysis, the Three Circles model provides a very useful theoretical starting point – plus a valuable system of terminology – for an investigation of modern-day English around the world. And for this reason, a quarter of a century after it was first devised, it continues to be of relevance to the discipline and provide an ongoing agenda for research.

The Dynamic Model

Another framework for the analysis of the historical spread of and variation in English around the world is Edgar Schneider's Dynamic Model (Schneider, 2007). This offers a somewhat more detailed model of the development of English worldwide varieties, with a particular focus on the part played in the process by the identity-construction of communities. Rather than dividing the English-speaking world up into three categories as Kachru does, Schneider identifies five broad phases of historical development for postcolonial Englishes. He posits that all the varieties that have resulted from the transplanting of English to overseas territories have gone through these stages, and that comparative differences in the form and status of these varieties relate to how far through the five stages they have moved and the nature of the relationship between variation and identity construction in each instance. In other words, not all varieties progress through all five of the stages, and depending on the historical circumstances different elements of the process will be more salient in different territories.

Schneider's argument is that varieties in postcolonial context – by which he means all instances of English being transported overseas during colonial expansion, including to the United States, Australia, etc – have typically followed a uniform developmental process which is a product of the social dynamics that occur between the two separate factions in the colonial processes: the colonisers and the colonised. Put succinctly, the pattern proceeds as follows: a new group moves into a territory inhabited by people with a different cultural and linguistic background, and, while initially the two groups see themselves as separate communities, over the passage of time the boundaries between them become eroded resulting in an independent cultural and linguistic identity for the territory.

The first stage in the process is what he calls the 'foundation stage'. During this, English is introduced into an area where it was not previously spoken, and the settlers and the indigenous people view themselves as distinct communities with separate identities: the former as representatives of Britain, the latter as owners of the territory. Although some language contact occurs, it is mostly confined to communication between certain members of the communities, such as interpreters or those in positions of status.

The next stage is what he calls 'exonormative stabilisation', during which English begins to be used more regularly across the colony but remains mainly limited to domains such as administration and education. The variety used is modelled on the one the colonisers brought with them (i.e. it is exonormative), and so is associated with Britain and has no independent identity of its own.

Stage three is the process of 'nativisation'. At this point in the history of the contact between the two groups, the political and cultural allegiances that existed pre-colonisation are starting to lose their relevance for the new situation, and the territory is beginning to forge a sense of independent cultural identity. The development of a distinct linguistic identity, in the form of a localised variety of English, is an important part of this. This is then followed by a process of 'endonormative stabilisation' during which the local variety begins to be consciously viewed as part of the territory's cultural identity. This often coincides with or follows political independence from Britain. At this point, the population begins promoting its own norms for the language rather than relying on a British model.

The final phase is that of 'differentiation'. With the local variety securely established, a process of internal linguistic variation occurs across the territory. That is to say, different parts of the population, such as communities in different regional locations, begin to establish their own uses (or dialects) of English, which become a marker of their identity within the wider national culture.

As can be seen, this model again takes a historical view of language development, while also examining the influence of the political and cultural circumstances that constitute this history. Whereas one of the chief purposes (and successful effects) of the Three Circles model was to provide legitimacy for non-native varieties by placing them within the broader framework of worldwide English, the Dynamic Model aims to build on this by offering a more nuanced picture on the sociolinguistic development of postcolonial Englishes. While it is very useful in this regard, again it is primarily varieties-based, and thus does not examine some of the ways in which the language exists in other parts of the world (i.e. the Expanding Circle). We will come back to approaches which explore alternative effects of the global influence of English below; before doing so however, let us look at the important role that political theory has played in the discipline.

Politics and the spread of English

Both the above models are endeavours to account for the way that the spread of English occurred and its sociolinguistic consequences. Political factors are an integral part of this process, due in great part to the fact that much of the history of English has been a story of the execution of cultural, economic and military power, but while both the models do include an awareness of these factors, they are not their overriding focus. As was touched upon in Chapter 10, there are, however, a number of critiques which have focused explicitly (and almost exclusively) on the political aspect of the spread and status of English, and have examined the power relations that underlie the influence that the language has on societies around the world.

Linguistic imperialism

One of the first and most influential studies in this tradition is Robert Phillipson's investigation into **linguistic imperialism** (Phillipson, 1992). Phillipson's argument is that the worldwide spread of English is the result of orchestrated strategies by countries such as the USA and the UK who use the language as a means of extending their own political and economic interests. According to this argument, linguistic imperialism is a subspecies of cultural imperialism, and results in structural inequality between English and other languages, which in turn produces political inequalities between different social groups and different countries. Phillipson draws on the conceptual terminology used by political economists such as Immanuel Wallerstein (1991) to examine ways in which 'centre' nations (i.e. powerful Western countries such as the USA and the UK) exercise power over those in the **periphery** (i.e. the economically poorer, developing countries). Much of Phillipson's focus has been on the way that English has been promoted by the ELT industry. For instance, he looks at the discourses and practices which lead to English being advanced as a tool for social mobility and economic advancement (see Chapter 8), and being regularly favoured in language policies and school curriculums around the world. Examples he cites include the way that institutions such as the World Bank and the International Monetary Fund (IMF) have promoted English education as a means of furthering the aim of national development in poorer 'periphery' countries; and the way that bodies such as the British Council and the United States Information Agency (USIA) have sponsored the teaching of English for international development purposes and have also run extensive teacher-training programmes and subsidised ELT courses and lessons across the world (Phillipson, 1992). His argument, based on such evidence, is that the expansion of English was a "strategic concern of the US and UK governments" (Phillipson, 1998, p. 102), and that processes of this type which boost the presence and status of English around the world also spread the values of the 'centre' Anglophone countries, which allows these countries to maintain a hegemonic position in the world.

The notion of **hegemony** – the power that one group exerts over others – is important here. As developed by the Italian Marxist philosopher and activist Antonio Gramsci, this concept describes the way that the dominant class in society achieves consent from the rest of the populace by making its own belief systems appear as the natural or commonsensical way to look at things (Gramsci, 1971). In other words, domination can be effected not solely by state force (the use of the police, the legal system, etc), but also by ideological means, and by 'manufacturing' the consent of those being dominated. If those in power are able to persuade people, by means of cultural and social practices such as education, religion, and popular culture, to accept that it has a legitimate right to this power, they are able to rule without resistance from the general populace. For Phillipson, English is a means of manufacturing such consent, by making the language of the powerful a desired resource the world over. By orchestrating the spread of English and making its status as a global language appear 'natural' and commonsensical, the 'centre' countries can maintain hegemonic domination over other parts of the world.

A related concept to linguistic imperialism, which has been particularly influential for the linguistic rights paradigm discussed in Chapter 8, is **linguicism**. Coined by analogy with concepts such as sexism and racism, this refers to attitudes which discriminate against people on the basis of language-related issues (Skutnabb-Kangas, 1986). It is used especially to apply to the way that such discrimination occurs due to social and institutionalised practices such as the promotion of certain languages and varieties at the expense – or even the stigmatisation – of others. For example, the use of a prestige variety as a norm by which other languages are evaluated becomes a means of legitimising the one variety at the expense of others. Likewise the promotion of English over minority languages marginalises, sometimes with dire effect, local or minority languages, and by extension the people who speak them.

Various critiques of the linguistic imperialism thesis have been made, in particular about the way it sees the process as being purposely and centrally coordinated by the 'centre' countries, and gives little attention to the actions and agency of communities in the 'periphery'. For example, the argument that there were dedicated policies as part of the colonialist project which aimed to use the spread of English as part of a strategy of political domination is disputed by those who suggest that the evidence actually reveals a different – or at least less cohesive – picture. Janina Brutt-Griffler argues that close scrutiny of British colonialist education policies shows that rather than there being a consistent attempt to promote the language, English was often withheld from the majority of the local population and taught only to an elite who worked for the administration of the colony (Brutt-Griffler, 2002). Another complicating factor for the linguistic imperialism thesis is that the spread of English was also partly a consequence of anti-colonialist struggles in that it was used in many countries as a practical means of uniting ethnically and linguistically diverse communities against colonial rule (Ferguson, 2006). So rather than the global spread of English being simply a matter of the imposition of the language on passive communities, the actions and wishes of local people also played a significant role.

What the linguistic imperialism hypothesis does, however, and one of the reasons it has been so influential, is highlight the importance of critiquing the ways in which the spread of English can produce political inequalities in the global community. If one considers the hegemony of English less as something orchestrated exclusively by an all-powerful 'centre' and instead as the result of a complex of cultural, political and economic factors, one does have a useful framework for exploring the politics of English in the contemporary world. For an understanding of the nature and cause of these cultural, political and economic reasons, theories which analyse the dynamics of 'globalisation' have proved insightful for the discipline in recent years.

Linguistic globalisation

Theories of globalisation

Cultural imperialism, of the sort that Phillipson describes, is often considered to be one of the major effects of the complex of processes that get grouped together under the term **globalisation**. It would not be too much of an overstatement to say that the various social and political processes that constitute globalisation have a bearing on almost all aspects of modern social life, not least language practices. As with several of the other conceptual terms we have looked at during the course of the book, however, this one can also have a range of slightly different meanings. The one used most often in the mainstream media refers to the ways in which companies today are able to take advantage of the opening up of global markets and operate on an international scale. Depending on the political perspective from which one views this, it is either a positive advance in the history of late capitalism or a harmful development that leads to the cultural values of politically and economically dominant countries spreading at the expense of local cultural diversity. This type of globalisation can be seen as a continuation of the desire of the colonial powers to export their own cultural values in the name of the Enlightenment ideal of progress, with the result often being the suppression or destruction of local culture and language.

As we have seen with the critiques of Phillipson, however, this view of the effects of globalisation does not satisfy everyone. There are those who argue that the spread of cultural values driven by globalisation need not lead to homogeneity and the inevitable suppression of local ways of doing things, but can instead result in the emergence of new, hybrid cultural practices. The term **glocalisation** (a blend of 'globalisation' and 'localisation') was coined by Roland Robertson to describe the way in which practices that are exported around the world can be 'indigenised' by local cultures, and come to reflect a mix of global influences and local traditions and identities (Robertson, 1995). Whereas the definition of globalisation outlined above saw cultural influence as flowing in only the one direction – from the politically and economically dominant 'centre' to the less powerful 'periphery'– an approach which stresses hybridity sees influence as multilateral, with ideas, people, technology and finance moving in both directions (Appadurai, 1996). Applied to the recent history of English, this results in the development of new indigenised varieties (along the lines theorised by Kachru and Schneider); and also in the way that new urban Inner Circle varieties are shaped by the language practices of immigrant communities, as, for example, in the development of what is known as "multicultural London English" with its mix of Afro-Caribbean and Southeast Asian linguistic influences (Cheshire et al., 2011).

The two different perspectives on globalisation discussed so far both concentrate on its outcomes – in one case, cultural homogeneity under the hegemony of the 'centre' powers; in the other, the development of hybrid cultural practices. It is perhaps more useful, from an analytic point of view, to take a further step back, however, and, rather than looking solely at effects, examine instead the *processes* that bring these effects about. In other words, we can ask: what are the dynamics at work in the present era of history that create the circumstances which lead to these particular outcomes?

Characterising globalisation in terms of processes rather than effects, a synoptic definition would be that it is the transformation of the world's societies into a vast, interconnected global system (Robertson, 1992). This transformation has been powered by rapid developments in technology. Due to advances in telecommunications, computers and transport, it is now possible to communicate over great distances instantaneously and with ease, and for people, information, commodities, and finance to travel around the globe in very short periods of time. These changed communication and transportation opportunities mean that there are now a whole range of everyday social activities which are taking place in new ways. Given the way that globalisation links together localities all across the world, it is often now the case that people are as affected by distant events as they are by those in their immediate geographical neighbourhood (Giddens, 1999). People therefore interact with the communities in which they live in a noticeably different way from previous generations, and the local environment (with its cultural practices and traditional norms) does not have the same significance it once did for many aspects of their daily lives or senses of identity.

Mobility – the chance to move both geographically and socially – is also much more accessible and fluid when compared to even the recent past, and this again has resulted in fundamental changes in traditional social structures. Not everyone has equal access to the technologies which facilitate globalisation, of course, and the experience of the changes in social organisation are felt in different ways by different people. For example, as was noted in Chapter 6, the motivation to move across the globe in search of enhanced employment opportunities may be a life choice for some but an economically imposed necessity for others. In either case, however, the consequence of increased mobility and the globally interconnected system of social organisation it gives rise to is that it is has a profound effect on the way that people interact and on the cultural practices which mediate this interaction. And it is these changed cultural practices which influence the way language is used and the impact that linguistic globalisation has for English around the world today.

Language and globalisation

We have already noted a number of aspects of the role that language plays in globalisation processes, but to sum it up in broad terms the relationship between the two is one of mutual influence: globalisation processes are greatly affected by language issues, while language practices are extensively influenced by the processes of globalisation. Let us look briefly at both aspects of this influence in the light of the definition of globalisation outlined above.

From one perspective, language facilitates globalisation. The social interaction that increasingly takes place on a global scale necessitates some medium of global communication, and it is in this context that the issue of an international language emerges. As was discussed in Chapter 6, English was already being promoted in this role during the second half of the twentieth-century. The processes of globalisation took advantage of (or were facilitated by) the spread of the language, but are also having the effect of further propelling this spread.

The exact processes by which this has been happening are, however, a matter of dispute. Analysis of the issue moves along a spectrum of criticality, ranging from approaches which in effect celebrate the fact of the global dominance of the language, to those which problematise its political foundations and social consequences. And these differences in approach are informed by different conceptions of linguistic globalisation. At one end of the spectrum are approaches which regard the process as in some sense "natural, neutral and beneficial" (Pennycook, 1994, p. 9; see Chapter 10 above); at the other is linguistic imperialism and its thesis of orchestrated imposition.

The emergence of English as a medium for international communication is not the only issue of consequence related to linguistic globalisation, however. As we have seen, the spread of a language invariably means contact between that language and different contexts, cultures and communities, and this in turn results in different forms, functions and beliefs for the language. As World Englishes studies has explicated from its earliest incarnation, different varieties emerge as the language is moulded by the new communities which adopt it, and in this way a global language such as English becomes polycentric – it no longer has a single centre such as the UK which influences its norms of usage, but instead has multiple different centres around the globe which individually shape its character. One of the chief consequences of this is that it is no longer possible to assume things about the culture of the people to whom one is talking, even when everyone speaks what is superficially the same language. As was discussed in Chapter 5, when English forms change their context and country, in the process, they can also change their meaning.

It is not communicative meaning alone which alters as English travels across the globe, however. When languages move from one location to another, they encounter different cultural practices and norms, and this results in the value and function of the language becoming modified or redistributed according to the needs of the society in which it is being used (Hymes, 1966). For example, while using English in Australia may simply be viewed as commonplace, doing so in China might be seen as a sign of an international outlook or a sense of modernity. In other words, the language has particular associations which are tied to the cultural politics of the place it is being used. Similarly, English spoken with a Ghanaian accent in Accra will have a different value from the use of that same accent in Boston. When used in the latter context, the Ghanaian accent will likely be seen as an indicator of 'foreignness' by the majority of the local population, and people will react to the speaker on the basis of this. Again, the value of the language resource will differ depending on the place, and what might be a prestige variety in one context could become a prompt for discrimination in others (Blommaert, 2005). There is nothing intrinsic in the form of the variety which decides its value; rather, it is determined by the cultural politics of the spaces through which it travels. In this way, patterns of linguistic inequality are far more complex than simply being a case of the dominant 'centre' imposing its values on the 'periphery'. And globalisation, in the way that it at once facilitates the movement of people and resources around the world, and at the same time reshapes cultural relationships by altering patterns of social organisation, provides the key to the way these patterns transpire.

※ ※ ※

The theoretical models we have reviewed in this chapter are among the principal frameworks used to survey and explain the spread of English, and the nature and status of varieties of English and English-influenced language practices around the world. Based on this overview we can suggest that, while it is not the case that World Englishes studies has a fully methodology-based coherence (in that it draws on the range of tools found in social and applied linguistics), a theoretical agenda of sorts nevertheless exists which does give it a general unity of purpose. This is the desire to problematise the notion of a monolithic English and to investigate the social and political implications of the spread of the language around the world. Over the last two or three decades as the discipline has developed, researchers have drawn on a variety of different theoretical models, but threading throughout them is this focus on the way that variation in English is intimately tied to political and cultural identity, and the conviction that studying the subject is able to expose the nature and significance of this relationship.

Tasks

In light of what we have discussed in this chapter, consider the following study questions:

- What shared concerns unite the various approaches to the study of World Englishes?
- What is the nature of the relationship between English and linguistic globalisation?

Feedback for these questions is given in the 'Commentary on tasks' section at the end of the book.

13 Naming and describing the English language

The final category on the list of criteria for a discipline is a specific use of language or discourse. As we discussed when reviewing the history of English in Chapter 3, the language's elaboration in the seventeenth and eighteenth centuries included its enhancement and refinement so that it would be capable of operating as a medium for the pursuit of science. This elaboration ultimately resulted in discipline-specific registers able to deal with the conceptual structure and analysis of a broad range of scientific and academic issues. WES as an emergent discipline has an array of specialised technical usages, such as the terminology relating to the different theoretical frameworks discussed in the previous chapter. In this final chapter, however, I want to consider one particular element of the discipline-specific use of language in WES: the way the object of study is named. This is the issue with which we began the book back in the general introduction. By returning to it here, not only can we review the question with which we first started, but we can also take the opportunity to summarise and reflect upon the many theoretical concerns that have been covered in the chapters since.

The multiple names of English

William James wrote that when he was faced with a paradox about the nature of knowledge, he proceeded by being "[m]indful of the scholastic adage that whenever you meet a contradiction you must make a distinction" (1997 [1907], p. 93). A similar strategy seems to be used extensively in World Englishes studies. Whenever scholars encounter an intractable issue about the nature of English, a first reaction is to make a distinction. And this is usually done by carving up the area of study into subtly different concepts, and assigning each of them a different name. The solution to the debate and disagreement over what exactly is meant by 'English' is often to re-name the language; to identify what is considered its core function or essential nature, and then construct a definition of this revised conception of the language under a modified term of reference. For this reason, in the early twenty-first century the discipline rarely speaks simply of English, but of formulations such as *Indian English*, *English as an International Language*, *English for Specific Purposes* and so on.

The rationale behind these multiple acts of naming relates to the context in which they occur. Whereas in everyday conversation a certain vagueness about the scope of reference for the term 'English' is usually not a problem, the same sort of vagueness will not do for scientific discourse. Applied linguistics as a scientific discipline has as its aim the detailed and rigorous analysis of its object of study, and so it needs a term which precisely delineates the boundaries of that object of study. And although some scholars, such as Randolph Quirk, take the view that:

> A common core or nucleus is present in all the varieties [of the language] so that, however esoteric a variety may be, it has running through it a set of grammatical and other characteristics that are present in all the others ... [and] this fact that justifies the application of the name 'English' to all the varieties.
>
> (Quirk, 1972, p. 14)

for many others this is not a satisfactory tactic. As such, and with the expansion in the use of English around the globe and the concomitant growth in the scholarship that critically examines this expansion, there has been a proliferation of proposals for new technical names to refer to the language and its varieties. And each of these represents a distinct theoretical stance towards the study of English in the world today.

In this final chapter, I will survey this proliferation of names by first drawing up a taxonomy of acts of naming in World Englishes studies, and then analysing the functions performed by the distinctions made in this taxonomy and considering the theoretical motivation behind the different classifications. In this way, we can consider what this multiplicity of names suggests about the state of the discipline and how it views its object of study.

Figure 13.1 gives a list of several of the most common names and classificatory groupings in the current academic discourse on English and its existence around the world. Rather than simply list the names, they have been divided into six categories representing fundamental conceptual distinctions (the left-hand column in Figure 13.1). These six categories are:

1 Varieties marked for *function*: that is, for what purpose is the variety used?
2 Varieties marked according to *community*: that is, who speaks the variety?
3 Varieties marked in terms of their *history*: that is, how did the variety develop?

4 Varieties marked according to their *structure*: that is, what are the structural features of the variety?
5 Varieties marked according to where they fit within an *ecology* of other varieties.
6 English as *multiplex*.

Category	Name
Function	English as a Second Language (ESL) English as a Foreign Language (EFL) English as an Additional language (EAL) English as an International Language (EIL) English as a Lingua Franca (ELF) International English World Standard Spoken English (WSSE)
Community	Metropolitan standards Regional dialects Social dialects Immigrant Englishes Native/non-native varieties Global Global English
History	Language shift Englishes Colonial standards Indigenised Englishes
Structure	Pidgin Englishes Creole Englishes Hybrid Englishes
Ecology	Inner circle varieties Outer circle varieties Expanding circle varieties World Englishes New Englishes
Multiplex	World English English Language Complex (ELC)

Figure 13.1 The multiple names of English

The purpose of dividing the names into these six categories is to help identify the issues that appear most salient for the discipline. Below I will look at each category in turn, and examine how the acts of naming and classification draw on these different distinctions in their conceptualisation of the language.

1 Varieties marked for function

The names grouped together in the first category all stress the purpose for which English is being used. In multilingual environments, the ascription of different functions to different languages is an important means of rationalising the co-existence of multiple languages and of justifying policy decisions about language regulation. Decisions of this sort thus have a bearing on both status planning and acquisition planning, and it is often in the education sector that distinctions about different varieties or usages are reified by acts of naming. For example, schools and universities will run courses on 'English as an additional language' or 'English for academic purposes', thus reinforcing such distinctions by means of a separate curriculum. And although the ascription of function is often a result of the history of the language's introduction into a community – a legacy of colonial education policies, for example – this aspect of the language's identity is relatively downplayed in conceptualisations which foreground function. Elizabeth Erling, in fact, argues that many recent acts of naming purposefully stress function over history and cultural identity so as to efface connotations with a colonialist past and in this way 're-brand' the language (Erling, 2004).

English as a Second Language (ESL)

A long-standing distinction on the basis of function is that between **English as a Second Language** and English as a Foreign Language. This distinction first appears in the 1920s, although it does not become widespread in its modern sense until the 1950s (Howatt, 1984, p. 212). The meaning of ESL is twofold. It can refer to the use of English in countries where the language has some official status, most often as the result of a colonial history. Alternatively, it refers to the use of English in countries in which it is the predominant means of communication and is being learnt by people from non-English speaking backgrounds (Carter and Nunan, 2001). In both cases, this concept of the language assumes bi- or multilingualism with English as an intrinsic part of the daily environment. The exact functions associated with the language will depend on the wider linguistic environment of the country or community in which it is used. It is probable, however, that its use will primarily be in public or institutional domains, and will thus contrast with the language of the home, which is likely to be a community or **heritage language** which is ideologically associated with community identity.

English as a Foreign Language (EFL)

English as a Foreign Language is used contrastively with ESL, and applied to contexts where English is neither widely used as a means of (intranational) communication, nor as a medium of instruction within schools (or in the majority of higher education institutions). Instead, the language is taught as something explicitly associated with the UK, the USA, or other countries traditionally perceived as English-speaking. As such, the name refers both to a teaching standard (based on native-speaker models) and to a function (English learnt as a cultural sampler with no immediate expectation of daily instrumental use, and instead associated with scenarios such as the tourist encounter).

English as an Additional Language (EAL)

English as an Additional Language is a term used when a basic distinction is needed between English as a Native Language (ENL) and other varieties (i.e. ESL and EFL). In many so-called ESL territories, English will be a speaker's third, fourth, fifth etc, language, and thus EAL is thought to be a term which is more sensitive to such multilingual contexts. The adjective 'additional' supposedly removes the ranking of languages implied in English as a *Second* Language, and the name is often chosen to purposefully avoid the perceived discrimination that ESL might unwittingly insinuate.

English as an International Language (EIL)/International English

EIL is another response to the perceived inadequacies of the traditional ESL/EFL dichotomy. It is promoted as a replacement for EFL, and is intended to acknowledge that in countries where English is not used for intranational purposes, the language is increasingly being used specifically for international communication, often by speakers from different countries neither of whom have English as a mother tongue. Due to changes in international communication patterns, English is not limited to the tourist scenarios traditionally associated with EFL, nor does it need to be modelled on native standards or have the cultural associations with ENL countries that are typical of EFL. Exactly how narrow the functional remit of EIL is taken to be depends on the scholar using the term. Henry Widdowson, for example, considers EIL to be a 'register' of English, "associated with particular domains of institutional and professional use" (Widdowson, 2003, p. 55). This is a much narrower conception than that of Tom McArthur (2004) and Mark Modiano (1999), both of whom view EIL as an internationally comprehensible 'variety' (indeed, McArthur suggests that it is close to becoming a standard variety). Some scholars have suggested that the syntactical structure of the two different versions of the name recognises these two different approaches, with 'English as an International Language' highlighting function, and 'International English' suggesting the existence of a discrete (and monolithic) variety (Seidlhofer, 2003b; Erling, 2005). Kachru, for example, suggests that International English misleadingly implies the existence of a codified and globally accepted variety of English (Kachru, 1997). Due to the fact that much work in World Englishes studies in the past two or three decades has had as a primary objective the critique of attitudes which view English as a monolithic entity, EIL is often the preferred term, and International English has a rather more ambiguous status.

English as a Lingua Franca (ELF)

As discussed in Chapter 6, closely related to the concept of EIL, but intended to be more specific about the usage it defines, is ELF. This term has been widely used in research focusing on English in Europe (e.g. Seidlhofer, 2001), and increasingly is also being used for other contexts as well, such as Asia (e.g. Murata and Jenkins, 2009). Although the name specifically highlights a function (English used for *lingua franca* purposes), it is also applied to research programmes that investigate the range of core linguistic features which regularly occur in encounters where the language is used in this way. Scholars who use the term, however, are often quite particular about *not* describing ELF as a variety, preferring instead to refer to it as a strategy for communicative interaction (e.g. Jenkins, 2006).

World Standard Spoken English (WSSE)

In contrast to the sensitivity that definitions of ELF show towards suggestions that there exists a worldwide standard of English, David Crystal's concept of World Standard Spoken English (WSSE) explicitly posits such a variety, and supposes that a converging speech style is emerging within the global community (Crystal, 1997). Adapted from McArthur's identification of a World Standard English (1987), the concept is partly speculative, as it refers to what Crystal believes will emerge in the near future as a spoken standard for international communication rather than something that yet exists. His argument, though, is that, given the current nature of global society, there is a pressing need now for a language to fill the functional role of reliable code for the purposes of global communication, and it is for this reason that such a standard will fully emerge (see Chapter 10 for the similarities of this with Randolph Quirk's view on the same issue). In many respects, this term shares the same conceptual ground as International English, though is perhaps more explicit about the likelihood of a single standard emerging to fulfil this purpose. For this reason, the concept draws a deal of criticism from scholars working in the ELF paradigm who contend that concepts such as WSSE ignore the heterogeneous nature of international communication strategies using English.

2 Varieties marked according to community

As we have discussed on many occasions throughout the book, the association of a language with the community which speaks it is a mainstay of the way languages are conceptualised, with the consequence that beliefs about language play a fundamental role in the politics of identity. This second category consists of a number of subsets. There is community as determined by geographical region, by class or ethnicity, and by supposed psycholinguistically salient factors (concepts such as the native and non-native speaker, which are dependent on distinctions concerning the stage of the life cycle during which the language is acquired). In each case, the name relates a variety to the group who speaks it, and in this way establishes a link between the variety and the communal identity of that group.

Metropolitan standards

Under metropolitan standards are usually grouped standard British English and standard American English, that is, the prestige varieties of the language spoken by the educated classes of influential cities such as London, Washington DC, and Los Angeles, and used as a model in education and broadcasting (Mesthrie and Bhatt, 2008). The term is coined in contrast to 'colonial standards' (see below). Metropolitan standards symbolically represent very broad communities (those of Britain and the USA) and thus come to be identified as national standards, without actually being spoken by large proportions of the populations of these countries.

Regional/social dialects

As was discussed in Chapter 2, varieties distinguished on the basis of regional variation and/or along the lines of class and ethnicity will tend to be conceptualised in relation to a metropolitan or national standard, reflecting the hierarchy of identity markers which places national identity as superordinate to regional or social identity.

(The same hierarchy is found in the relationship between the generic terms 'language' and 'dialect'.)

Immigrant Englishes

These refer to varieties spoken by groups who have migrated to an English-speaking country (Platt et al., 1984), such as Chicano English in the USA (Santa Ana and Bayley, 2004). It is not necessarily the case that people who speak the variety consider themselves a cohesive community, and thus the conception of the variety is imposed upon them rather than adopted by them. As with regional and social dialects, these varieties are often initially conceptualised in relation to the metropolitan or national standard of the country to which the group has emigrated. By distinguishing immigrants from the locally born in this way, this term can create a certain disenfranchising effect.

Native/non-native varieties

The groupings of native or non-native speakers are again not ones which constitute a cohesive community which self-identifies with the category. The distinction is much contested within applied linguistics (see, for example, Paikeday, 1985; Davies, 2003), yet it still plays a pivotal role in beliefs both in linguistics circles and in lay opinion about normative human language behaviour, and therefore continues as an important basic index about a speaker's English language biography. The marked half of the dyad (*non*-native) defines speakers of the variety negatively in contrast with those of metropolitan varieties, and debate over the implications of such a characterisation often forms part of the wider discussion about the legitimising of indigenised varieties (see, for example, the Quirk–Kachru debate discussed in Chapter 10).

Global/Global English

'Global' is a neologism coined by Michael Toolan which is intended to divorce the language from its history and, through this act of re-naming, reflect the fact that the language as spoken in a global context today is no longer under the ownership of the British or Americans. Toolan uses the term to refer specifically to English used as a *lingua franca* between a professional class who communicate in a global context. He explains his rationale as follows:

> Since this international English is not strictly a worldwide language, and since it is becoming increasingly released from a sense of rootedness in one or more ethnic homelands (whether that is

thought of as England, or the Anglo-Saxon world, or the Anglo-American world), we could give it a label which uses neither the misrepresenting term *World* nor the residually-ethnicist one *English*. Hence my suggestion that we call it Global.

(Toolan, 1997, p. 8)

There have been other similar attempts to re-brand the language by an act of alternative baptising. Ryuko Kubota (1998), for instance, cites the example of 'Englic', which was promoted by Takao Suzuki in 1975 as a variety which was to be disconnected from the culture of the dominant Anglo-English-speaking countries, and would "allow the Japanese to communicate with other English speakers without sacrificing their own cultural identity" (Kubota, 1998, p. 302). There is also Jean Paul Nerrière's 'Globish', used to refer to a proposed simplified English for use in international business contexts (Nerrière, 2006). Toolan's neologism is likewise related to a specific community of users, though in this case it is a 'community of practice' (i.e. a group whose identity is based on a shared practice – in this case the world of international business – rather than a shared heritage (Wenger, 1998)) which is geographically dispersed and nationally and regionally diverse.

Also responding to the idea that the current era is one in which new forms of community are resulting from the process of globalisation is the term 'Global English' (e.g. Crystal, 1997). This name often has a less specific sense than 'English as an International Language', and denotes neither a distinct variety nor a particular functional use. Instead, it is used as a companion concept to the more general notion of globalisation.

3 Varieties marked in terms of their history

Although the names of the actual varieties in this category refer to communities (e.g. Irish English, Australian English), their grouping (i.e. the classificatory name used to collect them together) highlights the historical processes which give rise to them. The implication is that the nature of the historical process that produced the variety will be an indication of the way that the variety relates both structurally and ideologically to other varieties and to contact languages.

Language-shift Englishes

These are varieties which develop when a whole community shifts from an indigenous language to English. An example is the case of Irish English, which became a majority language in previously Gaelic-speaking communities (Hickey, 2007). Phonological and grammatical influence from the indigenous language is usually apparent (Thomason and Kaufman, 1988), and the name of the grouping ('language-shift Englishes') highlights the particular historical language contact process which produces this influence.

Colonial standards

Varieties spoken in countries which were settlement colonies, and where English was introduced as a consequence of a 'displacement' colonisation process (Leith, 2007), are increasingly being accorded the status of discrete national standards in the wake of codification projects such as the *Australian National Dictionary* (see discussion in Chapter 7). Here, the highlighting of historical development primarily draws attention to the relationship with metropolitan standards (especially British English) from which these colonial standards now 'diverge'.

Indigenised Englishes

This is a term closely related to the above, and refers to those varieties which have developed in ESL contexts and have become adapted to their cultural environment, resulting in the emergence of stable local norms. The name suggests a completed process (indigenisation), and stresses the cultural appropriation that has occurred as a result.

4 Varieties marked according to their structure

Despite the importance for language **typology** of the structural features of different varieties, names which highlight structure are relatively uncommon in World Englishes studies at present. The names which do foreground structure are mostly applied to varieties which are perceived as being on the outer margins of the family of Englishes. These are the varieties which Mufwene (1997) suggests are viewed as the 'illegitimate offspring' of English, and thus the issue of their genetic make-up is prominent in discussion of their character (Mufwene, 1997).

Pidgin Englishes/Creole Englishes

As was discussed in Chapter 11, there is continuing debate as to whether pidgins and Creoles should properly be included in the English language family at all. Such debate is often framed around the lack of mutual intelligibility between pidgins/Creoles and many other varieties of English, and the close relationship that pidgins and Creoles have with other non-English-based languages – both issues are concerned with structure. There is also a political aspect to the question, though, as has been highlighted by Salikoko Mufwene (see the summary in Chapter 11).

Hybrid Englishes (or Anglo-hybrids)

Hybrid Englishes are bilingual mixed languages, such as Singlish, which occur most often in urban centres as a result of the contact between English and local languages. It is again the close relationship with other languages which results in structure being highlighted in the name of the grouping. Names of this sort are occasionally used as derogatory markers for what is perceived as an amusingly flawed attempt to master a standard variety of English (e.g. Chinglish, from China, and Engrish, from Japan), though these do not usually originate in academic discourse but in the popular media (Seargeant, 2009).

5 Varieties marked with reference to an ecology of other varieties

Although many of the names and classifications listed in categories 1–4 are contrastive or relational (i.e. their meaning depends on their relationship with other classifications), those in this category very specifically conceive of a given variety or grouping of varieties as part of a wider ecology of Englishes. That is to say, they are seen as part of a linguistic environment in which different varieties and languages co-exist in dynamic structural complexes. The ecological metaphor thus draws attention to the ways in which the nature or status of a given variety is conceptualised in part by the role it plays in a world system of Englishes, in addition to its discrete characteristics.

Inner, Outer and Expanding circle varieties

Braj Kachru's highly influential model of English varieties around the world that we looked at in Chapter 12 broadly replicates the ENL/ESL/EFL distinctions, yet also includes the normative nature of the different types of varieties. So Inner Circle varieties are characterised as 'norm-providing', Outer Circle varieties as 'norm-developing', and the Expanding Circle, in which English has traditionally been seen as a 'foreign' language, as having not yet developed local norms and relying instead on the external norms provided by the Inner Circle. This model thus places varieties within a relational matrix, indicating not merely function but also status, on both an overtly political and a sociolinguistic level. The norm-providing varieties of the Inner Circle have a validity in terms of both ideology and linguistic stability. The Outer Circle varieties, however, have a contested validity in ideological terms, and at the same time an emergent stability in linguistic terms (in part dependant on codification projects related to the political struggle for validity). And this scheme of naming aims to foreground all these relational factors.

World Englishes/New Englishes

Likewise associated with Braj Kachru, and with his joint editorship with Larry Smith of the journal of the same name, the term 'World Englishes' is used for the diversity of varieties around the world today. The development in the discipline here was to indicate the multiplex nature of English by adopting a plural noun. Although this term is not used to indicate the structure of the ecological model, it does indicate that any one variety is part of a wider complex of related yet notably different varieties.

The term 'New Englishes' fulfilled a similar function from the early 1980s onwards (e.g. Pride, 1982; Platt et al., 1984), though it has been mostly superseded by World Englishes now. The focus of both terms was initially predominantly on the second-language varieties which developed in former British colonies. As Kachru has pointed out, New Englishes was always a rather misleading term though, as the English spoken in India, for example, is actually older than that spoken in Australia, but the former is included in the category of New Englishes whereas the latter is not (Kachru, 1983). Another term with a similar scope is 'Postcolonial Englishes', which Edgar Schneider uses to cover all those varieties which have their roots in colonial activities, including American and Australian English, as well as English-related Creoles (Schneider, 2007).

6 English as multiplex

There is a certain amount of overlap between this category and the preceding one in the way in which they both stress the plurality of varieties. The extremely broad scope of reference for the terms in category 6 means, however, that they are not used to conceptually divide the field for analytic purposes, but merely to highlight the diversity of the field, and to provide a name which does not imply a monolithic English.

World English

As used by Tom McArthur, World English is meant to imply the diverse nature of the language: "For me, *world English* is both shorthand for *English as a world language* and a superordinate term for *Australian English, British English, Irish English, Nigerian English,* and the like. It embraces all aspects of the language: dialect, pidgin, Creole, variety, standard, speech, writing, paper-based, electronic" (McArthur, 2004, p. 5). Used at an early stage in the academic consciousness of the field, the term served a very wide remit, drawing attention to the spread and diversity of the language. It has mostly been superseded by World Englishes, which includes within its name reference to a belief in the pluralist nature of the language.

Janina Brutt-Griffler also adopts the term World English in her study of the development of the language. She, however, uses it to refer not so much to a variety as to the present phase in the history of the language – a phase in which the majority of the language's speakers belong to bilingual speech communities, and in which the language acts both as an elite *lingua franca* and as a medium of local resistance to cultural imperialism (Brutt-Griffler, 2002).

English Language Complex (ELC)

The term **English Language Complex** was also initially used by McArthur (1998, p. 202), and was then adopted by Mesthrie and Bhatt to refer to "the entire set of Englishes" (Mesthrie and Bhatt, 2008, p. 12). It thus includes everything from metropolitan standards to pidgins and Creoles. The inclusion of the noun 'complex' within the body of the name stresses the plurality in a way in which 'World English' perhaps does not.

Acts of naming: trends and implications

What, then, can this survey of the names used over the past 30 years tell us about the approach the discipline takes to the language? One initial point of note is that all these names take a *descriptive* approach. That is to say, they are based on the principle that the act of naming is the allocation of a term to a particular pre-existing phenomenon (a collection of distinct and systematic patterns of linguistic behaviour), and that the act is not purposefully calling that phenomenon into being. The Englishes listed above are all, according to their advocates, empirically real (they are to be found out there in the real world). They differ therefore from the approaches popular in the first half of the twentieth century which aimed at *re-engineering* the language to better suit the purposes of wide-ranging international communication (projects such as the simplified Englishes discussed in Chapter 4).

As was noted in Chapter 11, however, any act of naming (as part of the broader act of conceptualisation) will highlight certain elements of the phenomenon to the disadvantage of others, and so even the most descriptive approach will still, to an extent, construct the concept of the language. And this is the case with all the names and classifications outlined above. Presuppositions about human society that underlie the research programme lead to the use of these various specific categories by which the language is linked to its social function, to the people who use it and their history, and to the nature of modern global society. As such, each of these categories represents a particular perspective on the status of the language within human society, and provides an index of the state of debate about World Englishes as it is currently being conducted.

Looking at the names from this perspective, what is notable is the extent to which the need to stress diversity and polycentricity is still considered of great importance for the discipline. Beyond the immediate context of World Englishes studies (i.e. beyond this particular academic discipline), the plural form 'Englishes' can still arouse controversy (Jenkins, 2006), and for this reason, names which promote this perspective on the language still fulfil a role several decades after the concept was initially introduced into the discourse.

The other main concerns of the discipline that can be read from this survey are the ways that varieties relate to social, cultural, and political identity, and to the functions to which the language is put in a globalised world. As noted above, both these trends appear to be responding to the debates about the hegemony of English and its associations with a history of imperialism. They do this either by highlighting this history directly in the name, or by shifting focus away from it by positing a functional future for the language which is markedly different from this imperialist past. Given this focus on community identity and function, the traditional concerns of language typology – that is, the structural features of diverse varieties – are less stressed, at least in the naming of varieties. In other words, as the discipline is presently constituted, it is social and political factors which very much take centre stage.

And finally, the great proliferation of acts of naming in World Englishes studies is a testament both to the rapidly evolving nature of English use around the world and to the increased scholarship that records, analyses and, at times, aims to critique and influence this expansion in the forms and functions of the language.

Tasks

In light of what we have discussed in this chapter, consider the following study questions:

- What does the proliferation of names for the language indicate about the scope of World Englishes studies?
- In your opinion, should the language be radically renamed, and what might this achieve?

Feedback for these questions is given in the 'Commentary on tasks' section at the end of the book.

14 Conclusion: The state of the discipline

In conclusion, what does it mean, then, for World Englishes studies to be an academic discipline? From an educational perspective, there is now a substantial and stable body of knowledge that constitutes a subject called World Englishes studies (or some similar formulation), and the status of this is such that it is beginning to be projected onto university curriculums and, occasionally, departmental structures. The pedagogic implications include the fact that there has been a paradigm-shift in the way that the academic mainstream now focuses on the teaching and research of English around the world, and of the attitudinal and ideological disputes which accompany its global spread. This shift affects not only sociolinguistic studies of worldwide English, but also applied linguistics scholarship, and in this way feeds into the training of language professionals, particularly TESOL practitioners and those involved in language planning. Ideally, it is able to inform them of the issues that pertain to the language, and provide frameworks to help with an understanding of how English relates to people's lives, to their experiences and aspirations. The body of theory, in its role as a system of explanation, offers the tools of reflection to assist people working with the language to make informed decisions about their own practices, especially when these involve facilitating or regulating the language use of others.

In this way, there is a direct causal link between the development of WES as an academic discipline (i.e. as a named subject within a curriculum with educational resources and a strong research community), and the legitimisation of diverse varieties and uses of the language in the wider social arena through the mediating influence of the education system. In other words, by being seen as a discipline, the concerns and approaches of World Englishes studies are legitimised within academia, which in turn allows the perspective on English that the discipline is promoting to be disseminated more widely, and to find its way into teacher training courses and language planning initiatives. Or to put it another way, through institutional legitimisation of the discipline comes institutional legitimisation of the concerns of the discipline, as these acquire the authority that comes with a clear institutional identity.

In conclusion then, it is possible to produce a sketch of what World Englishes studies currently consists of. It is an approach to the study of English in the world which is oriented to certain key issues related to the legitimacy of local or translocal varieties and language practices, and the relationship between language and cultural identity. In this it draws on both descriptive sociolinguistics and critical theory-influenced anthropological examinations of situated language in use. Given the history of the discipline, it is often closely related to language education issues (i.e. TESOL concerns), and frequently uses educational contexts as sites of research (examining how English is taught and the perspectives and motivations learners have about the language), while also contributing its own research-based insights to TESOL theory and praxis. And while scholarship in this field may, as Bolton suggests, constitute "a changing disciplinary and discoursal map, marked by a series of paradigm shifts in the last 20 years" (Bolton, 2006, p. 260), it still retains a coherence in terms of shared fundamental concerns and a focus on globally contextualised inquiry into the spread and use of the English language.

As a coda, let me briefly place WES within the wider context of language inquiry. Along with the specific range of concerns that has been outlined immediately above, the study of worldwide English also involves engagement with two fundamental questions about the nature of human languages. On the one hand, the story of global English revolves around an issue that has been a central concern in the philosophy of language: how is it that human speech represents experiential reality, and how does this representational system operate as a means of social expression and communication? This is perhaps the most enduring question in linguistic philosophy, and it is a problem which is usually analysed at the level of language generally rather than specific languages. Attempting to understand how human language is able to represent the world, and how it uses this system of representation for communicating between individuals, has been a starting point for all those dreaming of creating artificial or auxiliary languages, and it lies behind the theoretical history of the search for a plausible and acceptable international language. Approaches to English which position the language in this role, therefore, and suggest planning measures to optimise its effectiveness in this respect, also have to grapple with this question at some level.

Yet while this foundational question may underpin the 'English as an international language' paradigm (and the ideology of an anonymous, deterritorialised language), the phenomenon of worldwide English also necessitates approaches which take account of the relationship between language use and cultural identity, and the complex social, cultural and political effects that result from language variation. Issues of how English is actually spoken, of the patterns of usage which develop and evolve in diverse world contexts and the significance attributed to these patterns, are integral to explorations which examine the social linguistic implications of World Englishes – and these issues have also featured as enduring avenues of inquiry throughout the history of the linguistic sciences.

Throughout the investigations in this book we have been pulled between two poles – indigenised varieties versus international English; territorialised vs. deterritorialised; authentic vs. anonymous, and so on. Behind the specifics of these debates, I want to suggest, are these two fundamental questions in the philosophy and socio-anthropology of language. And for this reason, the study of English in the world today poses a set of problems which go to the very heart of how human language operates, and of the role it plays in lived experience.

Commentary on tasks

The study questions at the end of each chapter are designed to offer an opportunity to reflect on some of the key issues addressed in the text. As I suggested in the general introduction, they can be used either as a reflective strategy for self-study purposes, or as the basis for classroom activities. Below is brief feedback on each of these clusters of questions. This comprises concise summaries of the main concerns covered in each chapter, and of the themes which, taken together, constitute the discipline of World Englishes studies.

2 English in the world today

Questions

- In what ways does the global spread of English complicate the notion of a single standard of the language?
- Why is intelligibility considered such a key issue in debates about English in the world today?
- How does cultural context play a part in communication, and what implications does this have for World Englishes?

Comment

Variation is a fact of life for all languages. Different communities develop different habitual patterns of usage, and this leads to different varieties of the language. A 'standard' variety is one which is promoted in artefacts such as dictionaries and grammar books, as well as in institutions such as the education system. It has social prestige and widespread use, but in terms of everyday usage is just one among many different varieties. With regard to English, the spread of the language has been so extensive that it is used in diverse contexts all across the globe, and inevitably these several different communities develop their own patterns of usage and thus their own individual varieties. In a sense, therefore, the spread of English makes more apparent the intrinsic variation that is a property of all languages, and has resulted in manifold global varieties, each with their own forms and identities.

Given English's global spread it is often used as an international language allowing communication between people from different linguistic backgrounds. To operate for this purpose, it must be intelligible to people from all these different backgrounds, and this often leads to arguments about the need for a single standard of the language. Variation, though, is a product of the language adapting to the cultural contexts in which it is used, and so communication across linguistic and cultural divisions has to take account not only of the possible different forms of the language (different pronunciations, grammatical patterns, spellings and so forth), but also the different cultural meanings and values that are tied up with its use.

3 The context and history of World Englishes

Questions

- What are the implications of the statistics of English speakers around the world for English's status as a 'global language'?
- How has the history of English shaped modern-day beliefs about the language?
- What different factors lie behind English's current status as a global language?

Comment

One of the most striking statistics about the use of English around the world today is that non-native speakers far outnumber native speakers. Current estimates put the ratio at about 4 to 1. This means that a large proportion of people are using the language as a *lingua franca* or additional language in situations where there is no native speaker present. Many scholars argue that because of this, the mindset that sees native-speaker norms as the only correct ones needs to be revised, and that diverse varieties and usages should be viewed as legitimate in their own right.

The bias in perception towards native-speaker norms is in great part due to the history of the language, and the associations it has, first with Britain, and then the United States. Another implication of the history of the language is the way it is perceived in postcolonial countries, where it has played different roles at different stages in the processes of colonisation and independence. In effect, each different place in which English is now used has a distinct historical relationship with the language, and this background influences the way it is perceived there.

The development of English into a global language is also due to historical factors rather than anything intrinsic in the language itself.

By being the language of the British Empire and of the industrial revolution in the eighteenth and nineteenth centuries, and then of the United States as this grew into a political and economic superpower in the twentieth century, the current status of English is a consequence of the cultural and political expansion of the societies who spoke it.

4 Problems for practitioners in World Englishes

Questions

- Why is education an important context for issues relating to World Englishes?
- In what sense will decisions about which variety should act as a teaching model be based on both practical and ideological concerns?
- What different goals do language policies have with regard to English around the world?

Comment

Education is a powerful shaper of social attitudes. For this reason, the way that English is taught – in terms of both the varieties chosen as target models and the ideas associated with it – can have a profound impact on linguistic practices and beliefs in society. For example, to only ever use a native-speaker model in the classroom can lead to the marginalisation of non-native varieties. Both education and language policy often need to find a balance between practical concerns, such as teaching the language for international communication purposes, and taking into account the relation it has to cultural and political identity. Depending on the purpose the language policy is trying to achieve, these different aspects will be stressed in different measures.

6 The global language paradigm

Questions

- What recurring themes are evident in the history of artificial and auxiliary languages, and how are these relevant to global English?
- Why is the question of whether English has outgrown its past important for its promotion as an international language?
- Why has the history of the search for a suitable universal language been mostly marked by failure, and is there any indication that the use of English as a global *lingua franca* can adequately fulfil this role?

Comment

The artificial and auxiliary language movements have had two broad aims: finding a way of 'improving' on natural languages; and engineering a convenient medium of international communication. A recurrent theme in the majority of such projects has been the attempt to produce a language which does not 'belong' to any one group and can therefore act as a 'neutral' means of international communication. This rationale has been one of the reasons why the architects of such projects have favoured invented languages over existing ones. Since English has emerged as a candidate for the role of global language, this question has been reformulated to ask how a language traditionally associated with particular national cultures (i.e. the UK and the USA) can operate as a mostly 'neutral' international language, and to what extent its history (especially as a colonial language) complicates this status.

Arguably, one of the main reasons for the failure of artificial languages is that none of them have been fully embraced by a speech community and thus developed organically to fulfil the range of functions that a natural language can. It is for this reason that a shift has recently occurred from looking at how international communication *should* take place, to how it actually *does*, with the ultimate aim being to use insights from research into English as a *lingua franca* to inform language education and planning initiatives.

7 Codification and legitimation

Questions

- What impact has corpus linguistics had on the status and study of World Englishes?
- Why are dictionaries considered such an important element in the construction of national identity?
- Why is language awareness an important issue for successful international communication in English?

Comment

Corpus linguistics provides a powerful tool for the accurate description of diverse world usages. This, along with the production of dictionaries and other codification projects, gives concrete evidence about the systematic nature of different varieties, which bolsters their status as linguistically and culturally legitimate. Dictionaries especially play an important role in the promotion of the idea of distinct and legitimate national varieties. Given the relationship between language and national identity that exists in many cultures (which is a product of the development of nationalism in eighteenth- and nineteenth-century Europe), national dictionary projects become a practical and symbolic means of promoting a distinct linguistic – and thus cultural – identity.

One of the reasons for the close relationship between language and identity is that different communities develop different patterns of usage which then become associated in public perception with that community. The existence of different patterns of usage can produce problems for intergroup or intercultural communication, however. Being aware of the sort of difficulties that can occur in this respect is a first step to overcoming such difficulties, and for this reason, having a knowledge of how one's first language operates and how it differs from other languages is a good means of producing this awareness.

8 Policies and cultural practices

Questions

- What different elements are there to the discourse of English as a language of economic opportunity?
- Should English be seen as a threat to language diversity around the world?
- Why is the metaphor of ownership a key issue for the existence of English around the world?

Comment

One of the motivating factors behind the promotion of English in many language policies is the perceived relationship it has with economic opportunity. It is often viewed as a key resource for the economic development of both the nation and the individual citizen. This is due to the way it is seen to facilitate social and geographical mobility, to its status as the native language of economically powerful countries such as the USA, and the increasing use of it as the language of international business. The extent to which there is a direct causal relationship between knowledge of English and economic development is not at all clear, however, and several other social factors will also influence the nature of any such relationship.

Another commonly expressed idea about the spread of English is that it is a threat to other languages, especially 'minority' ones. However, here again the picture is complicated by the lack of conclusive evidence about the causal relationship between English's global spread and patterns of language death and agency of local communities in choosing to adopt English. For example, it is often the case that it is other local languages rather than English that are the threat to minority languages; while it also often the case that individuals and communities orient towards English because of the benefits that it can bring due to its status as a prestige, global language.

The close relationship between a community or nation and the language it speaks leads to the notion that that community in a sense 'owns' that language, and therefore has the right and responsibility to prescribe its norms. In the case of English, however, the fact that it is so widely spread across the globe has led people to argue that it can no longer be considered the property of native speakers, and that their norms or beliefs should not be viewed as the only legitimate ones.

10 World Englishes as an academic discipline

Question

- What factors are likely to lie behind the emergence of World Englishes studies as a distinct field of study?

Comment

The development of the discipline of World Englishes studies is partly a response to the changed circumstances over the last few decades in the use of English around the world and the increased academic interest that its emergence as a global force has prompted. But the discipline is also shaped by the history and concerns of the community who teaches and researches the language. It is this community which builds up a conceptual language for accurately describing and analysing the phenomenon of worldwide English, which creates shared aims and ways of working (i.e. methodologies and a canon of theories), and which develops the institutional structures both to pursue this research and to promulgate and teach it.

11 English as an object of study

Questions

- Why should determining what counts as English be such a problematic issue?
- How do the ideologies of 'anonymity' and 'authenticity' structure the discussion about the role of English in the world?

Comment

One of the reasons why determining what counts as English is a problematic issue is the sheer diversity in the language, that is, the variation in form produced by the contact it has had with other languages and cultures as it has spread across the globe. In other words, the multiplex forms the language has, and especially the mixed varieties such as English-language pidgins and Creoles, mean that the process of categorisation will depend on how widely one defines the concept of 'English'. In addition to this, the concept of the language is always in part an ideological construct influenced by the social and political contexts in which it is being used or promoted. Two important ideologies for the language are those of 'anonymity' and 'authenticity' which map on to many of the dichotomies that structure many of the debates about the role and nature of English in the world today. For example, the idea of a single monolithic English reflects the ideology of 'anonymity', while a plurality of Englishes reflects the ideology of 'authenticity'. A similar pattern occurs with the concept of English as an international language (anonymous) versus that of English as a foreign language (authentic). In many ways, these have been the two poles around which the study of English worldwide has been built. It would be a mistake to consider them as necessarily mutually exclusive, however, as speakers are able to use different varieties and registers of English for different purposes depending on their communicative needs.

12 Models and theoretical frameworks

Questions

- What shared concerns unite the various approaches to the study of World Englishes?
- What is the nature of the relationship between English and linguistic globalisation?

Comment

The issue that ties together the majority of work in World Englishes studies is an acknowledgement of the diversity in the language and the way this relates to communities' cultural and political identities. Most approaches share a desire to critique the notion of a monolithic English and to investigate the social and political implications of the global spread of the language. Increasingly, this is done by considering the history and present-day use of English within the context of linguistic globalisation. The relationship between English and globalisation is one of mutual influence: just as globalisation processes are affected by language issues (such as the need, in a rapidly shrinking world, for a means of international communication), so language practices are greatly influenced by the processes of globalisation. In the case of English, the extensive spread of the language first facilitates global communication and then its use for this purpose further propels this spread. At the same time, however, the language becomes influenced by and is adapted to the different social and cultural contexts in which it is used, while also featuring as a factor in the changed social and political conditions generated by globalisation.

13 Naming and describing the English language

Questions

- What does the proliferation of names for the language indicate about the scope of World Englishes studies?
- In your opinion, should the language be radically renamed, and what might this achieve?

Comment

The proliferation of names used to refer to English, and to describe its forms and functions around the globe, reflects both the swiftly changing nature of the use of the language in today's world and the increase in scholarship that examines its current state and status. These various names highlight in particular the relationship between the language and issues of social and cultural identity, as well as the centrality of its perceived function as a means of international communication. Arguments for radically altering the name of the language are based on the contention that the word 'English' no longer reflects the multiplex identities the language fulfils in today's world. Given this multiplicity, however, it is a moot question as to whether any single term would be able to represent the full range of roles and social and cultural interests the language has in contemporary global society.

Glossary

Abstand
Abstand languages, according to a distinction made by the German linguist Heinz Kloss (1967), are those which can be recognised as separate by virtue of being linguistically different from other languages. They are distinguished from **Ausbau** languages, which are linguistically far closer to other languages (to the extent that they are mutually comprehensible), but are promoted as separate entities by language policy, which often augments the ways in which their linguistic features differ from those of their close neighbours.

accent
the features of pronunciation that indicate a person's geographical or social background. The term refers specifically to pronunciation, while **dialect** refers to differences in grammar and vocabulary.

acquisition planning
a form of **language planning** which concerns the way people are taught and learn languages in society, and how language education is used to increase the numbers of speakers of a variety/language. The term was introduced by Robert Cooper (1989).

acrolect
a prestige variety of a Creole. Used in contrast to **basilect** and **mesolect**.

additional language
(see **English as an Additional Language**).

appropriation
the process whereby people in one speech community take up the language traditionally associated with another community.

artificial language
a language purposefully created by an individual or group, often with the intention of producing a 'perfect language' which is free of the ambiguities and redundancies that exist in natural languages. Esperanto, invented in 1887 by Ludvic Lazarus Zamenhof, is a notable example.

Ausbau
(see **Abstand**).

auxiliary language
a language used for communication intranationally or internationally between people who do not have a shared first language. When used in the latter context it is also referred to as an **international auxiliary language**.

basilect
the variety of a Creole which is the furthest removed from its language of derivation. The structures of the basilect and its **lexifier** (the language from which it gets its vocabulary) are markedly different, and thus the two are not mutually intelligible. Varieties of a Creole at different removes from the language of derivation are the **mesolect** and **acrolect**.

bilingualism
the use of two separate languages by an individual or community. Use of more than two languages by a society is usually called **multilingualism** (and by an individual, plurilingualism), though occasionally this is also referred to as bilingualism. Individuals or communities who speak only one language are referred to as monolingual. Although some societies have a very dominant primary language, no modern society is completely monolingual as there will always be some members who speak other languages, while international languages such as English are also increasingly being used globally in domains such as business and the media.

borrowing
the process of adopting a word from one language into another. The term can also be used to refer to the adopted word itself, though **loanword** is an alternative term for this.

codeswitching
the process by which speakers in bilingual or multilingual situations alternate between languages in the course of a conversation. A distinction is sometimes made between codeswitching and codemixing, where the latter is used to refer to the switching between languages that occurs within sentences rather than between them.

codification
the process of establishing a systematic account of a language or language variety. This is achieved through activities such as the compilation of dictionaries, grammar books, and other manuals which provide prescriptive norms for the language.

communicative competence
a concept introduced by the linguistic anthropologist Dell Hymes (1974) to refer to the knowledge necessary for a speaker to successfully communicate in a language by using it appropriately in given social situations.

comprehensibility
(see **intelligibility**).

computer-mediated discourse (CMD)
linguistic communication that takes place via networked computers or other information technologies (such as SMS).

contact language
a language which develops when two or more languages come into contact. A **pidgin** is a paradigmatic example.

context
the environment or circumstances in which an utterance occurs, which has a bearing on the way the utterance is interpreted.

corpus (plural: **corpora**)
a collection of language data (usually electronically stored) which has been assembled either from written texts or from **transcripts** of recorded speech. It is used for the testing of hypotheses and the statistical analysis of actual language use.

corpus linguistics
the theories and methods for using corpora in the study of language.

corpus planning
a type of **language planning** which focuses on regulation of the form of a given language, including such things as its spelling, grammar and vocabulary. Heinz Kloss (1969) introduced the distinction between corpus and **status planning**.

creativity
a speaker's ability to construct an infinitely large number of unique, meaningful sentences. The term is also used to refer to the process of stylistic innovation.

Creole
traditionally defined as a stable language that has originated from a **pidgin** and has come to be spoken as a first language by the children of a community. Some scholars suggest, however, that this process does not account for the origin of all Creoles, and that some are the result of different historical patterns of interaction between Europeans and non-Europeans (Mufwene, 2006).

creolisation
the process by which a **pidgin** becomes a **Creole**. There is controversy in the discipline about how exactly this takes place. Some pidgins change into creoles when the children of a community are raised speaking it as their first language. Others appear to develop more abruptly. Some scholars argue that the distinction is actually that the two developed in separate places in which the pattern of interaction between Europeans and non-Europeans was different (Mufwene, 2006).

critical
analysis which examines cultural, social, and political factors in language and its use in order to uncover (implicit) political agendas.

descriptive
an approach within linguistics which involves observing and describing how a language is actually used by those who speak/write it. This is contrasted with a 'prescriptive' approach, which involves stipulating how a language should be used and what constitutes correct or incorrect usage.

dialect
a language variety in which elements of the vocabulary and **grammar** indicate a person's geographical or social background. It is contrasted with **accent** which refers to differences in pronunciation (though some scholars also include pronunciation in their definition of dialect).

discourse
a term with a variety of meanings related to language studies. Its core definition refers to sequences of connected speech or writing, usually made up of more than one sentence. It can also be used to refer to the use of language in its social context, and the social meanings generated by such context-specific language use.

discourse particle
a word or short phrase which is used in conversation to make discourse more coherent and to indicate something about how the meaning is to be interpreted. Discourse particles mostly appear at the beginning or end of utterances, and are frequently found in spoken conversation. Examples in English include "ah", "well" and "you know".

domain
specific fields of activity or institutional contexts, such as the school, workplace, or home, which have an influence over choices of language use. In multilingual communities, for instance, it is often the case that different languages may be used in different domains; for example, English at school and Gujarati at home.

Early Modern English
the historical stage in the development of English which ran from the mid-fifteenth to the mid-eighteenth centuries (c.1450–c.1750). This period includes the early stages of colonial expansion.

elaboration
part of the process of **standardisation** whereby the social functions of a language are extended (so that it comes to be used, for example, as an academic language, or in domains such as the law and school system), and also that its form (e.g. its vocabulary, stylistic range) is developed to match the requirements of modern life (e.g. to express technological innovations or social changes).

endonormative
being based on local norms, that is, those that have developed as the language has become indigenised by the local community.

English as a Foreign Language (EFL)
the use or variety of English in contexts where it neither has an official status nor is widely used as a means of intranational communication. Instead, the language is taught as being explicitly associated with countries traditionally perceived as English-speaking (e.g. the UK, the USA).

English as a *Lingua Franca* (ELF)
the use of English as a means of communication between people who do not share a common language. Research into ELF investigates the range of core linguistic features and communicative strategies which regularly occur in encounters in which the language is used in this way.

English as a Second Language (ESL)
a term used to refer either to the use of English in countries where it has some official status (mostly due to the legacy of colonialism), or in which it is the predominant means of communication and is being learnt by people (often immigrants) from non-English speaking backgrounds.

English as an Additional Language (EAL)
an alternative term for **ESL** (though sometimes also incorporating **EFL**) which is used when a basic distinction is needed between English as a native language and other varieties or usages. The adjective 'additional' is intended to circumvent the ranking of languages implied in English as a 'Second' Language.

English as an International Language (EIL)
the use of English for general communication across national borders.

English Language Complex (ELC)
a term initially used by Tom McArthur (1998) to refer to the entire set of English varieties. It therefore includes everything from national standards to pidgins and Creoles.

English Language Teaching (ELT)
(see **TESOL**).

exonormative
being based on external norms, specifically those used in native-speaker countries.

expanded pidgin
a term applied to a contact variety which is used in various different domains (e.g. for education and administration) and has some native speakers, but is not considered to have the full status of a Creole.

Expanding Circle
(see **Three Circles of English**).

first language (L1)
the initial language an individual acquires, or the language in which he or she is most competent.

globalisation
the processes by which rapid technological development are producing globally interconnected systems of social organisation which are having profound effects both on the ways in which people interact and on the cultural practices which mediate this interaction.

glocalisation
the process by which global influences are adapted to local practices.

grammar
the way that a language is structured. The term is often used to refer in particular to the way in which words and their component parts (e.g. word endings which denote tense) combine to form sentences. Grammar includes **syntax** and **morphology**.

grammar-translation method
a form of language teaching which focuses on memorising grammar rules and lists of vocabulary. Learners practice their knowledge of these rules by translating example sentences.

hegemony
the power exerted by one group over another. With respect to culture, the term refers to the way that one group or class can achieve domination over others by cultural-ideological means (rather than by state force), and by winning the consent of those being dominated.

heritage language
the ancestral language of a community living in a society in which there is a different majority language.

high-stakes test
a type of assessment tool which has important social consequences for those taking it. Key factors associated with such tests are **impact** and **washback**.

hybrid Englishes
bilingual mixed languages which most often occur in urban centres as a result of the contact between English and a local language or languages.

ideology
systems of entrenched beliefs that people/communities have about aspects of social life.

idiom
a set expression whose meaning cannot be deduced from the sense of the individual words. For example: 'be tickled pink'. Because this use of language is often culturally specific, idiomaticity can cause difficulties for **intercultural communication**.

impact
The effect that a high-stakes test has on general society.

indigenised varieties of English
varieties that have developed in countries where English has been introduced, usually as a result of colonisation, and where the language has been adapted in response to the linguistic norms of the new environment. This adaptation can include the borrowing of new, culture-specific vocabulary, as well as the influence of the phonetic and grammatical patterns of local languages.

inflection
an affix which signals the grammatical function of a word.

Inner Circle
(see **Three Circles of English**).

intelligibility
in its broadest sense, this term refers to the extent to which an utterance is understood. Larry Smith (1992) distinguishes between three levels of intelligibility: 1)

intelligibility: the ability to recognise a word or utterance as being in a particular language; 2) **comprehensibility**: the ability to understand the meaning of a word or utterance; and 3) **interpretability**: the ability to understand the functional intention of an utterance.

intercultural communication
acts of communication that take place between members of different cultural groups. The teaching of intercultural communication skills focuses on an understanding of the cultural norms and expectations which form the context in which all language use takes place, and on how these expectations differ from community to community and the bearing they have on communication.

interlanguage
a term coined by Larry Selinker (1972) to refer to the version of a language produced by someone who is in the process of learning it as a second or foreign language. An interlanguage is an intermediate system in which properties of the learner's first language combine with properties of the target language.

international auxiliary language
(see **auxiliary language**).

interpretability
(see **intelligibility**).

language contact
situations in which regular interaction occurs between speakers of different languages.

language death
the process by which a language stops being spoken, either because its speakers die out or because they shift to the use of another language.

language ideology
the entrenched social beliefs about the nature and function of language which act as a framework against which people make sense of the role and value of language in society.

language planning
the specific measures people employ to regulate the role that language plays in society. Different forms of language planning include **acquisition planning**, **corpus planning** and **status planning**.

language policy
the strategies drawn up by a state or organisation to determine how language is to be used in institutions or society.

language shift
the process by which a speech community moves from the use of one language to another language, usually one which is more socially dominant.

language variation
the way in which the forms and structures of a language vary according to its users and to the circumstances in which it is used.

lexifier
the language from which the majority of the vocabulary of a pidgin or Creole is originally taken.

lexis
the vocabulary system of a language.

lingua franca
a language used as a means of communication by people who do not share a mother tongue or common language.

linguicism
a term coined by Tove Skutnabb-Kangas (1986) in analogy with concepts such as 'sexism' and 'racism' to describe acts of discrimination based on language-related issues. These include the stigmatisation of non-standard or minority languages.

linguistic imperialism
the idea that the spread of English has been orchestrated by the powerful English-speaking countries for their own political and economic advancement. The term is most closely associated with the work of Robert Phillipson (1992).

linguistic rights
the principle that people have rights in relation to their use of language, especially with regards to their **mother tongue** or **heritage language**.

loanword
a word or language feature that has been adopted from one language into another. The English word itself is a loan translation from the German 'lehnwort'. The process is also called **borrowing**.

majority language
a language such as English which has high political and social status. The term can also refer to the language spoken by the majority of a population.

medium of instruction
the language used for teaching in school or university.

mesolect
a Creole variety which is intermediate between a **basilect** and **acrolect**.

Middle English
the stage in the historical development of English from approximately the Norman Conquest of 1066 to the fifteenth century (*c*.1100–*c*.1450).

minority language
a language spoken by a relatively small group within a population, or one which has limited political influence.

morphology
the structure of words.

mother tongue
the language that one acquires from birth. Alternatively referred to as one's native or **first language**.

multilingualism
(see **bilingualism**).

national language
a language operating as a symbol of national identity for a country.

native speaker (NS)
a term which has been much problematised in the last few decades, but which is traditionally used to refer to a person who has acquired a particular language from birth and is fully proficient in it. A **non-native speaker** is someone who has acquired the language later in life, after first learning another language.

New Englishes
a term predominantly used to refer to the newly developed second language varieties of English in postcolonial countries.

non-native speaker (NNS)
(see **native speaker**).

official language
a language which has a special legal status in a country or region, and is used in domains such as administration and education.

Old English
the stage in the historical development of English from the time of the Anglo-Saxon invasions in AD 449 to the Norman Conquest (*c*.450–*c*.1100). Also known as Anglo-Saxon.

orthography
the writing system of a language.

Outer Circle
(see **Three Circles of English**).

ownership of English
the notion that the language is the cultural property of a particular community, and that they thus have the right to specify its norms of forms and usage.

periphery
a term used to describe developing countries in contrast to the 'centre', which consists of the politically and economically powerful Western nations. The term derives from the work of the social theorist Immanuel Wallerstein (1991).

phonology
the study of the sound systems of languages.

pidgin
a new language which initially comes into being through a particular type of language contact which occurs between speakers who need to develop a sustained means of communication (often for trading purposes) but do not share a common language. Pidgins are (with a few exceptions – see **expanded pidgin**) languages without native speakers.

pluricentric
a system is pluricentric when it contains multiple centres to which people orient themselves.

postcolonialism
the theoretical analysis of the cultural legacy and political impact of colonialism.

pragmatics
the study of language from the perspective of its users, focusing on how it is used to accomplish functions in the real world.

prestige variety
a social dialect or accent which has a high status within society. An example of a prestige variety of English is **Received Pronunciation**.

Received Pronunciation (RP)
a social accent of English which was traditionally associated with the educated middle and upper classes in the UK. As a social accent, it is not restricted to any one geographical region. It is also popularly known as the Queen's English, or BBC English.

register
a variety that is defined according to its use in particular social contexts. It is often characterised by the use of specialist vocabulary or jargon. The concept of the register can be distinguished from **dialect** in that the former is a variety defined by its *uses* (i.e. what one is talking about), while the latter is a variety defined by its *users* (i.e. who is doing the talking). For example, an academic register is the type of language use that is appropriate in academic contexts (e.g. writing essays, journal articles, etc).

second language
(see **English as a Second Language**).

second language acquisition (SLA)
the learning process leading to proficiency in a second or additional language.

selection
the choice of a particular variety to act as the central standard. One of the phases of **standardisation**.

semiotics
the study of signs and sign systems. 'Sign system' here means any systematic and conventionalised organisation of meaning-making resources that is used for communication. Central to all semiotic systems is the concept of the sign itself, which can be defined as an entity that communicates a meaning. Signs can include words, images, sounds and gestures, any of which are understood to have a particular meaning when used in a particular context.

sociolinguistics
the study of language use in society. It is contrasted with general or theoretical linguistics which predominantly views language as an abstract system and concentrates particularly on the structure of this system. Sociolinguistics, on the other hand, examines the relationship between language and social life.

speech community
a group of people who have a shared and habitual use of language.

standardisation
the process by which standard norms of a language are established. Einar Haugen (1966) divides the process into different phases which include **selection**, **elaboration** and **codification**.

standard language
the variety of a language which is predominantly used in domains such as education and broadcasting. A standard language does not exhibit regional variation, and is often used as the official variety within a society. It is considered to be a **prestige variety**.

status planning
a form of **language planning** which regulates the roles played by particular languages within society. It includes the allocation of languages to official roles in society; for example, being promoted as a 'national language' or as the medium of instruction in the education system. Heinz Kloss (1969) introduced a distinction between this and **corpus planning**.

style
the distinctive ways in which individuals speak or write, and the choices they make about their use of language, especially in terms of how this varies according to the context (e.g. the nature of the relationships between participants).

syntax
the rules governing the way words combine to create phrases, clauses and sentences.

Teaching English to Speakers of Other Languages (TESOL)
a general term for the teaching of English to people who do not have it as a first language. Traditionally, this term has been more common in North America, though it is now gaining wider popularity. In the British context, a distinction has conventionally been made between Teaching English as a Second Language (TESL) for contexts where the language has some form of official status, and Teaching English as a Foreign Language (TEFL) for contexts where it does not.

English Language Teaching (ELT) is another more general term that is sometimes used.

Three Circles of English
Braj Kachru's highly influential model of English varieties around the world. It comprises the **Inner Circle** of countries where English is a first language (e.g. the UK, the USA), the **Outer Circle** where English is an official additional language (e.g. India, Nigeria), and the **Expanding Circle** where English has been traditionally viewed as a foreign language (e.g. Japan, Finland).

transcript
the written representation of a piece of spoken discourse.

transfer
the influence that a person's first language has on languages he or she learns later.

turn
a single contribution (or utterance) by a participant in a conversation.

typology
the classification of languages made on the basis of structural features and their distribution.

utterance
a complete unit of speech used by someone when speaking.

variation
(see **language variation**).

variety
a linguistic system that is used by a speech community or in a particular social context. Variety is used as a general term to refer to both **dialects** and **registers**.

vernacular
The native language of a country or state. The term is usually used to describe local, non-standard varieties as opposed to official standards or *lingua francas*.

washback
the effect that a test has on teaching and learning practices.

World Englishes
an umbrella term for varieties of English used around the globe, and foregrounding the multiplex nature of the language in the modern world. The term is also used to refer specifically to the approach to the study of worldwide English most closely associated with Braj Kachru.

World Standard Spoken English (WSSE)
a term used by David Crystal (1997) to refer to what he sees as an emerging worldwide spoken standard of English for international communication.

Further reading

As was mentioned in the general introduction, this book focuses predominantly on *issues* and *debates* around world Englishes, and in this sense is very much an 'applied linguistics' perspective on the topic. Books which take more of a sociolinguistics approach, and describe and analyse varieties of English around the world, include Rajend Mesthrie and Rakesh Bhatt's *World Englishes: the study of new linguistic varieties* (Cambridge University Press, 2008), Edgar Schneider's *Postcolonial English: varieties around the world* (Cambridge University Press, 2007) and *English around the world: an introduction* (Cambridge University Press, 2011). Other books which have examined worldwide English variation include Peter Trudgill and Jean Hannah's *International English: A guide to the varieties of standard English* (Edward Arnold, 2008), now in its fifth edition, and Gunnel Melchers and Philip Shaw's *World Englishes: an introduction* (Arnold, 2003).

Two books which provide an introductory exploration of English in a global context are Tom McArthur's *The English languages* (1998, Cambridge University Press), and David Crystal's *English as a global language* (second edition, Cambridge University Press, 2003). Also influential in mapping the terrain for the subject has been David Graddol's work on the spread of English and its likely future influence, which can be found in his books *The future of English?* (British Council, 1997) and *English next* (British Council, 2006).

Two books which have a specific focus on the implications of the spread of English for the teaching of the language are Andy Kirkpatrick's *World Englishes: implications for international communication and English language teaching* (Cambridge University Press, 2007), and Sandra McKay's *Teaching English as an international language: rethinking goals and approaches* (Oxford University Press, 2002). Barbara Seidlhofer's *Understanding English as a lingua franca* (Oxford University Press, 2011) gives a good overview of the issues and debates relating to the use of the language as an international *lingua franca*.

Detailed investigations of the history of English can be found in two edited collections: Richard Hogg and David Denison's *A history of the English language* (Cambridge University Press, 2006), and Lynda

Mugglestone's *Oxford history of English* (Oxford University Press, 2008). *English in the world today: history, diversity, change*, edited by Philip Seargeant and Joan Swann (Routledge, 2012), is a textbook which examines the history of English from a specifically global perspective, while David Crystal's *The stories of English* (Penguin, 2005) provides a good introductory examination of the language's history.

Influential books dealing with cultural and political issues relating to World Englishes include the work of Braj Kachru, especially the foundational *The alchemy of English: the spread, functions and models of non-native Englishes* (University of Illinois Press, 1990), and the edited volume *The other tongue: English across cultures* (second edition, University of Illinois Press, 1992b). Other important books dealing with politico-cultural issues are Robert Phillipson's *Linguistic imperialism* (Oxford University Press, 1992), Alastair Pennycook's *The cultural politics of English as an international language* (Longman, 1994) and *Global Englishes and transcultural flows* (Routledge, 2007a), and Jan Blommaert's *The sociolinguistics of globalization* (Cambridge University Press, 2009).

There are also several books which make in-depth investigations into the nature and role of English in Expanding Circle countries. These include Kingsley Bolton's *Chinese Englishes: a sociolinguistic history* (Cambridge University Press, 2006b), Philip Seargeant's *The idea of English in Japan: ideology and the evolution of a global language* (Multilingual Matters, 2009) and the edited collection *English in Japan in the era of globalization* (Palgrave Macmillan, 2011), and Joseph Sung-Yul Park's *The local construction of a global language: ideologies of English in South Korea* (Mouton de Gruyter, 2009).

Among the notable journals which deal with the topic are the following: *English Today* (published by Cambridge University Press), which offers accessible investigations into all aspects of English language studies; *World Englishes* (published by Wiley-Blackwell), which presents theoretical and empirical research studies of English in global contexts, with a strong focus on social, cultural and political issues; *English World-Wide* (published by John Benjamins), which presents research on modern varieties of English, focusing particularly on work on the dialectology and sociolinguistics of English-speaking communities; and the *Journal of English as a Lingua Franca* (published by De Gruyter Mouton), which examines the nature and sociolinguistic significance of the use of English as a *lingua franca*, and its theoretical implications for work in language policy and education.

Finally, there are now a number of handbooks of essays covering a range of topics on the subject. These include *The Routledge Handbook of World Englishes*, edited by Andy Kirkpatrick (2010), and the Blackwell *Handbook of World Englishes*, edited by Braj Kachru, Yamuna Kachru and Cecil Nelson (Wiley-Blackwell, 2006).

References

Achebe, C. (1965) English and the African writer. *Transition: A Journal of the Arts, Culture and Society*. 4: 18, pp. 27–30.

Aig-Imoukhuede, F. (1982) *Pidgin stew and sufferhead*. Ibadan: Heinemann Educational Books.

Allsopp, R. (1996) *Dictionary of Caribbean English usage*. Oxford: Oxford University Press.

Althusser, L. (1971) Ideology and ideological state apparatuses. In *Lenin and philosophy, and other essays*. Trans. B. Brewster. London: NLB, pp. 121–73.

Anderson, B. (2006) *Imagined communities: reflections on the origin and spread of nationalism*. London: Verso.

Appadurai, A. (1996) *Modernity at large: cultural dimensions of globalization*. Minneapolis: University of Minnesota Press.

Arcand, J.-L. and Grin, F. (2012) Language in economic development: is English special and is linguistic fragmentation bad? In E. J. Erling and P. Seargeant (eds) *English and international development*. Bristol: Multilingual Matters.

AusTalk (2011) https://austalk.edu.au/

Austin, J. L. (1962) *How to do things with words*. Oxford: Oxford University Press.

Bakhtin, M. M. (1986) *Speech genres and other late essays*. Trans. V. W. McGee. Austin, TX: University of Texas Press.

Bamgboṣe, A. (1998) Torn between the norms: innovations in World Englishes. *World Englishes*. 17: 1, pp. 1–14.

Barber, K. (ed.) (1998) *The Canadian Oxford dictionary*. Toronto: Oxford University Press.

Baugh, A. C. and Cable, T. (1993) *A history of the English language*. London: Routledge.

Beeton, D. R. (1975) *Dictionary of English usage in South Africa*. Cape Town: Oxford University Press.

Bickerton, D. (1975) *Dynamics of a creole system*. Cambridge: Cambridge University Press.

Blommaert, J. (2003) Commentary: a sociolinguistics of globalization. *Journal of Sociolinguistics*. 7, pp. 607–23.

Blommaert, J. (2005) *Discourse: a critical introduction*. Cambridge: Cambridge University Press.

Blommaert, J. (2010) *The sociolinguistics of globalization*. Cambridge: Cambridge University Press.

Bolton, K. (2005) Where WE stands: approaches, issues, and debate in world Englishes. *World Englishes*. 24: 1, pp. 69–83.

Bolton, K. (2006a) World Englishes today. In B. Kachru, Y. Kachru and C. Nelson (eds) *The handbook of world Englishes*. Oxford: Blackwell, pp. 240–69.

Bolton, K. (2006b) *Chinese Englishes: A Sociolinguistic History*. Cambridge: Cambridge University Press.

Brewster, C. and Wilks, Y. (2004) Onologies, taxonomies, thesauri: learning from texts. In M. Deegan (ed.) *The Keyword Project: unlocking content through computational linguistics*. Proceedings from the Use of Computational Linguistics in the Extraction of Keyword Information from Digital Library Content workshop, King's College London.

Bright, W. (ed.) (1992) *International encyclopedia of linguistics*. Oxford: Oxford University Press.

Brumfit, C. (1995) Teacher professionalism and research. In G. Cook and B. Seidlhofer (eds) *Principle and practice in applied linguistics*. Oxford: Oxford University Press, pp. 27–42.

Bruthiaux, P. (2003) Squaring the circles: issues in modeling English worldwide. *International Journal of Applied Linguistics*. 13: 2, pp. 159–78.

Brutt-Griffler, J. (2002) *World English: a study of its development*. Clevedon: Multilingual Matters.

Canagarajah, S. (2006) Changing communicative needs, revised assessment objectives: testing English as an international language. *Language Assessment Quarterly*. 3: 3, pp. 229–42.

Carter, R. and Nunan, D. (2001) Introduction. In R. Carter and D. Nunan (eds), *The Cambridge guide to teaching English to speakers of other languages*. Cambridge: Cambridge University Press, pp. 1–6.

Chakraborty, T. and Kapur, S. (2008) English language premium: evidence from a policy experiment in India. Washington University St. Louis. www.isid.ac.in/~pu/conference/dec_08_conf/Papers/ShilpiKapur.pdf.

Chambers, J. K. (1999) Canadian English: 250 years in the making. In K. Barber (ed.) *The Canadian Oxford dictionary*. Toronto: Oxford University Press, pp. ix-x.

Cheshire, J., Kerswill, P., Fox, S. and Torgersen, E. (2011) Contact, the feature pool and the speech community: the emergence of Multicultural London English. *Journal of Sociolinguistics*. 15: 2, pp. 151–96.

Chomsky, N. (1965) *Aspects of the theory of syntax*. Cambridge, MA: MIT Press.

Cooper, R. L. (1989) *Language planning and social change*. Cambridge: Cambridge University Press.

Crystal, D. (1997) *English as a global language*. First edition. Cambridge: Cambridge University Press.

Crystal, D. (1999) The death of language. *Prospect*, November, pp. 56–9.

Crystal, D. (2003) *English as a global language*. Second edition. Cambridge: Cambridge University Press.

Crystal, D. (2006) English worldwide. In F. Hogg and D. Denison (eds) *A history of the English language*. Cambridge: Cambridge University Press, pp. 420–44.

Crystal, D. (2008) Two thousand million? *English Today*. 93, pp. 3–6.

Crystal, D. (2012) A global language. In P. Seargeant and J. Swann (eds) *English in the world: history, diversity, change.* Abingdon: Routledge.

Davidson, F. (2006) World Englishes and text construction. In B. Kachru, Y. Kachru and C. Nelson (eds) *The handbook of world Englishes.* Oxford: Blackwell, pp. 709–17.

Davies, A. (2003) *The native speaker: myth and reality.* Clevedon: Multilingual Matters.

Delbridge, A. (ed.) (1997) *The Macquarie dictionary.* Third edition. Sydney: Macquarie Library.

Dolezal, F. (2006) World Englishes and lexicography. In B. Kachru, Y. Kachru and C. Nelson (eds) *The handbook of world Englishes.* Oxford: Blackwell, pp. 694–708.

Dyja, E. (ed.) (2005) *BFI film handbook.* London: British Film Institute.

Eco, U. (1997) *The search for the perfect language.* London: Fontana Press.

EFNIL (European Federation of National Institutions for Language (2006) www.efnil.org/documents/brussels-declaration-on-language-learning.

ELFA (English as a Lingua Franca in Academic Settings) (2009) www.helsinki.fi/englanti/elfa/elfacorpus.

English in Action (EIA) (2009) Changing learning, changing lives. Brochure.

Ergang, R. (1996) *Herder and the foundations of German nationalism.* New York: Octagon Books.

Erling, E. J. (2004) *Globalization, English and the German university classroom: a sociolinguistic profile of students of English at the Freie Universität Berlin.* Unpublished Ph.D. thesis. University of Edinburgh.

Erling, E. J. (2005) The many names of English. *English Today.* 81, pp. 40–4.

Ethnologue (2011) www.ethnologue.com.

Ezekiel, N. (1989) *Collected poems 1952–1988.* Delhi: Oxford University Press.

Ferguson, G. (2006) *Language planning and education.* Edinburgh: Edinburgh University Press.

Firth, A. (1996) The discursive accomplishment of normality: on 'lingua franca' English and conversation analysis. *Journal of Pragmatics.* 26: 2, pp. 237–59.

Fishman, J. A., Cooper, R. L., and Conrad, A. W. (1977) *The spread of English: the sociology of English as an additional language.* Rowley, MA: Newbury House.

Foucault, M. (1972) *The archaeology of knowledge and the discourse on language.* Trans. A. M. Sheridan Smith. New York: Pantheon.

Foucault, M. (1991) *The Foucault reader.* London: Penguin.

García, O. (2009) *Bilingual education in the 21st Century: a global perspective.* West Sussex: Wiley-Blackwell.

Gargesh, R. (2006) On nativizing the Indian English poetic medium. *World Englishes.* 25: 3/4, pp. 359–71.

Gazzola, M. (2006) Managing multilingualism in the European Union: language policy evaluation for the European Parliament. *Language Policy.* 5, pp. 393–417.

Giddens, A. (1999) *Runaway world: how globalization is reshaping our lives.* London: Profile.

Global from Macmillan Education (2010) www.macmillanglobal.com/about/the-course.

Görlach, M. (1997) And is it English? *English World-Wide*. 17: 2, pp. 153–74.

Görlach, M. (ed.) (1991) *Varieties of English around the world*. Amsterdam: John Benjamins.

Graddol, D. (1997) *The future of English?* London: British Council.

Graddol, D. (2010) *English next India*. London: British Council.

Gramsci, A. (1971) *Selections from the prison notebooks of Antonio Gramsci*. Ed. and trans. Q. Hoare and G. N. Smith. London: Lawrence & Wishart.

Grin, F. (2004) L'anglais comme lingua franca: questions de coût et d'équité. Commentaire such l'article de Philippe Van Parijs. *Economie publique*. 15: 2, pp. 3–11.

Gu, M. (2009) *The discursive construction of second language learners' motivation*. Bern: Peter Lang.

Halliday, M. A. K., MacIntosh, A. and Strevens, P. (1964) *The linguistic sciences and language teaching*. London: Longman.

Harris, R. (1990) On redefining linguistics. In H. G. Davis and T. J. Taylor (eds), *Redefining linguistics*. London: Routledge, pp. 18–52.

Haugen, E. (1966) Dialect, language, nation. *American Anthropologist*. 68: 4, pp. 922–35.

Hickey, R. (2007) *Irish English: history and present-day forms*. Cambridge: Cambridge University Press.

Holm, J. A. (1982) *Dictionary of Bahamian English*. New York: Lexik House.

Horne, D. (1997) Foreword. In A. Delbridge (ed.), *The Macquarie dictionary*. Third edition. Sydney: Macquarie Library, pp. x–xi.

Howatt, A. (1984) *A history of English language teaching*. Oxford: Oxford University Press.

Hymes, D. (1966) Two types of linguistic relativity (with examples from Amerindian ethnography). In W. Bright (ed.) *Sociolinguistics: proceedings of the UCLA sociolinguistics conference, 1964*. The Hague: Mouton, pp. 114–67.

Hymes, D. (1974) *Foundations in sociolinguistics: an ethnographic approach*. Philadelphia: University of Pennsylvania Press.

Imam, S. R. (2005) English as a global language and the question of nation building education in Bangladesh. *Comparative Education*. 41: 4, pp. 471–86.

Internet World Stats (2011) www.internetworldstats.com/stats7.htm.

James, W. (1997 [1907]) What Pragmatism means. In L. Menard (ed.) *Pragmatism: a reader*. New York: Vintage, pp. 93–111

Jenkins, J. (2006) Current perspectives on teaching World Englishes and English as a Lingua Franca. *TESOL Quarterly*. 40, pp. 157–81.

Johnson, S. (1747) *The plan of a dictionary of the English language*. London: J. and P. Knapton.

Johnson, S. (1755) *A dictionary of the English Language*. London: J. and P. Knapton.

Journal of English as a Lingua Franca [JELF] (2011) http://www.degruyter.de/journals/jelf/detailEn.cfm

Kachru, B. B. (1983) *The Indianization of English*. New Dehli: Oxford University Press.

Kachru, B. B. (1985) Standards, codification and sociolinguistic realism: the English language in the Outer Circle. In R. Quirk and H. G. Widdowson (eds) *English in the world: teaching and learning the language and literatures*. Cambridge: Cambridge University Press, pp. 11–30.

Kachru, B. B. (1991) Liberation linguistics and the Quirk concern. *English Today*. 7, pp. 3–13.

Kachru, B. B. (1992) Preface to the first edition, in Kachru, B. B. (ed.) *The other tongue: English across cultures*. Second edition. Urbana and Chicago: University of Illinois Press, pp. xxiii–xxv.

Kachru, B. B. (1992b) Teaching world Englishes. In B. B. Kachru (ed.) *The other tongue: English across cultures*. Second edition. Urbana and Chicago: University of Illinois Press, pp. 355–65.

Kachru, B. B. (1997) World Englishes 2000: Resources for research and teaching. In Larry Smith and Michael Forman (eds), *World Englishes 2000*. Honolulu: University of Hawaii Press, pp. 209–51.

Kachru, B. B. and Smith, L. (1985) Editorial. *World Englishes*. 4: 2, pp. 209–12.

Kachru, B. B., Kachru, Y. and Nelson, C. (eds) (2006) *The handbook of World Englishes*. Oxford: Blackwell.

Kachru, Y. and Smith, L. E. (2008) *Cultures, contexts, and World Englishes*. Abingdon: Routledge.

Kecskes, I. (2010) Situation-bound utterances as pragmatic acts, *Journal of Pragmatics*. 42: 11, pp. 2889–97.

Kelley, D. (1997a) Introduction. In D. Kelley (ed.) *History and the disciplines: the reclassification of knowledge in Early Modern Europe*. New York: University of Rochester Press, pp. 1–9.

Kelley, D. (1997b) The problem of knowledge and the concept of discipline. In D. Kelley (ed.), *History and the disciplines: the reclassification of knowledge in Early Modern Europe*. New York: University of Rochester Press, pp. 13–28.

King, A. and J. Brownell (1966) *The curriculum and the disciplines of knowledge*. New York: John Wiley.

Kirkpatrick, A. (2007) *World Englishes: implications for international communication and English language teaching*. Cambridge: Cambridge University Press.

Kirkpatrick, A. (ed.) (2010) *The Routledge handbook of World Englishes*. Abingdon: Routledge.

Kirkpatrick, A. (2011) English as an Asian lingua franca and the multilingual model of ELT. *Language Teaching*. 44: 2, pp. 212–24.

Kloss, H. (1967) Abstand languages and Ausbau languages. *Anthropological Linguistics*. 9, pp. 29–41.

Kloss, H. (1969) *Research possibilities on group bilingualism: a report*. Quebec: International Center for Research on Bilingualism.

Kobayashi, Y. (2007) Japanese working women and English study abroad. *World Englishes*. 26: 1, pp. 62–71.

Krauss, M. (1992) The world's languages in crisis. *Language*. 68, pp. 4–10.

Kroskrity, P. (2006) Language ideologies. In A. Duranti (ed.) *A companion to linguistic anthropology*. Malden, MA: Blackwell, pp. 496–517.

Kubota, R. (1998) Ideologies of English in Japan. *World Englishes*. 17, pp. 295–306.

Large, A. (1985) *The artificial language movement*. Oxford: Blackwell.

Leap, W. (2010) Globalization and gay language. In N. Coupland (ed.) *The handbook of language and globalization*. Oxford: Wiley-Blackwell, pp. 555–74.

Leith, D. (2007) English – colonial to postcolonial. In D. Graddol, D. Leith, J. Swann, M. Rhys and J. Gillen (eds) *Changing English*. London: Routledge/The Open University, pp. 117–48.

Lewin, K. (1951) *Field theory in social science; selected theoretical papers*. New York: Harper & Row.

Li, D. C. S. (2000) Hong Kong English: new variety of English or interlanguage? *English Australia Journal*. 18: 1, pp. 50–9.

Lippi-Green, R. (1997) *English with an accent*. London: Routledge.

Locke, J. (1813 [1690]) *An essay concerning human understanding, volume 2*. Boston: Cummings & Hilliard and J. T. Buckingham.

Macaulay, T. B. (1972 [1835]) Minute on Indian education. In J. Clive and T. Pinney (eds) *Thomas Babington Macaulay. Selected writings*. Chicago: University of Chicago Press.

Mannheim, K. (1936) *Ideology and utopia: an introduction to the sociology of knowledge*. London: Routledge & Kegan Paul.

May, S. (2006) Language rights. In B. B. Kachru, Y. Kachru and C. Nelson (eds) *The handbook of world Englishes*. Oxford: Blackwell, pp. 526–40.

McArthur, T. (1987) The English languages? *English Today*. 11, pp. 9–11.

McArthur, T. (1998) *The English languages*. Cambridge: Cambridge University Press.

McArthur, T. (2004) Is it *world* or *international* or *global* English, and does it matter? *English Today*. 79, pp. 3–15.

McCrum, R. (2010) *Globish: how the English language became the world's language*. New York: Viking.

McKay, S. (2002) *Teaching English as an international language: rethinking goals and approaches*. Oxford: Oxford University Press.

McNamara, T. and Roever, C. (2006) *Language testing: the social dimension*. Oxford: Blackwell.

Mesthrie, R. and Bhatt, R. (2008) *World Englishes: the study of new linguistic varieties*. Cambridge: Cambridge University Press.

Milroy, J. and Milroy, L. (1999) *Authority in language: investigating standard English*. London: Routledge.

Modiano, M. (1999) International English in the global village. *English Today*. 58, pp. 22–8.

Moore, B. (2011) *What's their story? A history of Australian words*. Melbourne: Oxford University Press.

Mufwene, S. (1997) The legitimate and illegitimate offspring of English. In L. Smith and M. Forman (eds) *World Englishes 2000*. Honolulu, HW: University of Hawaii Press, pp. 182–203.

Mufwene, S. (2001) *The ecology of language evolution*. Cambridge: Cambridge University Press.

Mufwene, S. (2006) Pidgins and creoles. In B. B. Kachru, Y. Kachru and C. Nelson (eds) *The handbook of world Englishes*. Oxford: Blackwell, pp. 313–27.

Mufwene, S. (2010) Globalization and the spread of English: what does it mean to be Anglophone? *English Today*. 101, pp. 57–9.

Mühlhäusler, P., Dutton, T. E. and Romaine, S. (2003) *Tok Pisin texts: from the beginning to the present*. Amsterdam: John Benjamins.

Munshi, K. and Rosenzweig, M. (2006) Traditional institutions meet the Modern world: caste, gender and schooling choice in a globalizing economy. *American Economic Review*. 96: 4, pp. 1225–52.

Murata, K. and Jenkins, J. (eds) (2009) *Global Englishes in Asian contexts: current and future debates*. Basingstoke: Palgrave Macmillan.

Nagel, T. (1986) *The view from nowhere*. Oxford: Oxford University Press.

Naija Lingo (2011) http://naijalingo.com.

Nelson, G. (2004) Introduction: special issue on the International Corpus of English. *World Englishes*. 23: 2, pp. 225–6.

Nelson, G. (2006) World Englishes and corpora studies. In B. Kachru, Y. Kachru and C. Nelson (eds) *The handbook of world Englishes*. Oxford: Blackwell, pp. 733–50.

Nerrière, J-P. (2006) *Parlez Globish! Don't speak English*. Paris: Eyrolles.

Nettle, D. and Romaine, S. (2000). *Vanishing voices: the extinction of the world's languages*. Oxford: Oxford University Press.

Norton, B., Jones, S. and Ahimbisibwe, D. (2012) Digital literacy, HIV/AIDS information, and English language learners in Uganda. In E. J. Erling and P. Seargeant (eds) *English and international development*. Bristol: Multilingual Matters.

Ogden, C. K. (1930) *Basic English: a general introduction with rules and grammar*. London: Paul Treber.

Orsman, H. W. (ed.) (1997) *Dictionary of New Zealand English: a dictionary of New Zealandisms on historical principles*. Auckland: Oxford University Press.

Paikeday, T. (1985) *The native speaker is dead!* Toronto and New York: Paikeday.

Park, J. S.-Y. and Wee, L. (2009) The three circles redux: A market–theoretic perspective on World Englishes. *Applied Linguistics*. 30, pp. 389–406.

Parthasarathy, R. (ed.) (1976) *Ten twentieth-century Indian poets*. Oxford: Oxford University Press.

Patke, R. S. (2009) Poetry since Independence. In A. K. Mehrota (ed.) *A concise history of Indian literature in English*. Basingstoke: Palgrave Macmillan, pp. 275–310.

Peeradina, S. (1972) *Contemporary Indian poetry in English: an assessment and selection*. Bombay: Macmillan.

Pennycook, A. (1994) *The cultural politics of English as an international language*. London: Longman.

Pennycook, A. (1998) *English and the discourses of colonialism*. London: Routledge.

Pennycook, A. (2001) *Critical applied linguistics: a critical introduction*. Mahwah, NJ: Lawrence Erlbaum.

Pennycook, A. (2007a) *Global Englishes and transcultural flows*. Abingdon: Routledge.

Pennycook, A. (2007b) The myth of English as an international language. In S. Makoni and A. Pennycook (eds) *Disinventing and reconstituting languages*. Clevedon: Multilingual Matters, pp. 90–115

Phillipson, R. (1992) *Linguistic imperialism*. Oxford: Oxford University Press.

Platt, J. and Weber, H. (1980) *English in Singapore and Malaysia: status, features, functions*. Kuala Lumpa: Oxford University Press.

Platt, J. T., Weber, H. and Ho, M. L. (1984) *The New Englishes*. London: Routledge.

Prator, C. (1968) The British heresy in TESL. In J. Fishman, C. Ferguson, and J. Das Gupta (eds) *Language problems of developing nations*. New York: John Wiley, pp. 459–76.

Pride, J. (ed.) (1982) *New Englishes*. Rowley, MA: Newbury House.

Project English (2009) www.britishcouncil.org/india-connecting-project-english.htm.

Quine, W. V. O. (1969) *Ontological relativity and other essays*. New York: Columbia University Press.

Quirk, R. (1962) *The use of English*. London: Longman.

Quirk, R. (1982) *Style and communication in the English language*. London: Arnold.

Quirk, R. (1985) The English language in a global context. In R. Quirk and H. G. Widdowson (eds) *English in the world: teaching and learning the language and literatures*. Cambridge: Cambridge University Press, pp. 1–6.

Quirk, R. (1990a) Language varieties and standard language. *English Today*. 6, pp. 3–10.

Quirk, R. (1990b) What is standard English? In R. Quirk and G. Stein (eds) *English in use*. London: Longman, pp. 112–25.

Quirk, R. and Widdowson, H. G. (eds) (1985) *English in the world: teaching and learning the language and literatures*. Cambridge: Cambridge University Press.

Quirk, R. Greenbaum, S., Leech, G. and Svartvik, J. (1972) *A grammar of contemporary English*. London: Longman.

Ramson, W. S. (ed.) (1988) *The Australian national dictionary: a dictionary of Australianisms on historical principles*. Melbourne: Oxford University Press.

Rassool, N. (2007) *Global issues in language, education and development: perspectives from postcolonial societies*. Clevedon: Multilingual Matters.

Rassool, N. (2012) The political economy of English language and development: English vs. national and local languages in developing countries. In E. J. Erling and P. Seargeant (eds) *English and international development*. Bristol: Multilingual Matters.

Richards, I. A. (1943) *Basic English and its uses*. London: Kegan Paul, Trench, Trubner.

Richards, J. C. and Tay, M. W. J. (1977) The *la* particle in Singapore English. In W. Crewe (ed.) *The English language in Singapore*. Singapore: Eastern University Press, pp. 141–56.

Ricks, D. A. (1999) *Blunders in international business*. Oxford: Blackwell.

Roberts, P. (2005) *Spoken English as a world language: international and intranational settings*. Unpublished doctoral dissertation, University of Nottingham.

Robertson, R. (1992) *Globalization: social theory and global culture*. London: Sage.

Robertson, R. (1995) Glocalization: time-space and homogeneity-heterogeneity. In M. Featherstone, S. Lash and R. Robertson (eds) *Global modernities*. London: Sage, pp. 25–44.

Roscoe, A. A. (1971) *Mother is gold: a study in West African literature*. Cambridge: Cambridge University Press.

Rosenberg, A. (2000) *Philosophy of science: a contemporary introduction*. London: Routledge.

Sakai, S. (2005) Symposium on world Englishes in the Japanese context: introduction. *World Englishes*. 24: 3, pp. 321–2.

Santa Ana, O. and Bayley, R. (2004) Chicano English: phonology. In B. Kortmann and E. W. Schneider (eds) *A handbook of varieties of English: a multimedia reference tool*. Berlin: Mouton de Gruyter, pp. 417–34.

Schneider, E. W. (2007) *Postcolonial English: varieties around the world*. Cambridge: Cambridge University Press.

Schneider, E. W. (2011) *English around the world: an introduction*. Cambridge: Cambridge University Press.

Seargeant, P. (2009) *The idea of English in Japan: ideology and the evolution of a global language*. Bristol: Multilingual Matters.

Seargeant, P. and Erling, E. J. (2011) The discourse of 'English as a language for international development': policy assumptions and practical challenges. In H. Coleman (ed.) *Dreams and realities: developing countries and the English language*. London: British Council, pp. 248–67.

Seargeant, P. and Tagg, C. (2011) English on the internet and a 'post-varieties' approach to language. *World Englishes*. 30: 4, pp. 496–514.

Sebba, M. (2009) World Englishes. In J. Culpeper, F. Katamba, P. Kerswill, R. Wodak and T. McEnery (eds) *English Language: description, variation and context*. Hounslow: Palgrave Macmillan, pp. 404–21

Seidlhofer, B. (2001) Closing a conceptual gap: the case for a description of English as a Lingua Franca. *International Journal of Applied Linguistics*. 11: 2, pp. 133–58.

Seidlhofer, B. (ed.) (2003a) *Controversies in applied linguistics*. Oxford: Oxford University Press.

Seidlhofer, B. (2003b) A concept of international English and related issues: From 'real English' to 'realistic English'? *Language Policy Division*. Strasbourg: Council of Europe. www.coe.int/t/dg4/linguistic/Source/SeidlhoferEN.pdf.

Seidlhofer, B. (2004) Research perspectives on teaching English as a lingua franca. *Annual Review of Applied Linguistics*, 24, 209–39.

Seidlhofer, B. (2005) English as a lingua franca. In A. S. Hornby (ed.) *Oxford advanced learner's dictionary of current English*. Oxford: Oxford University Press, p. 92.

Seidlhofer, B. (2009) Accommodation and the idiom principle in English as a Lingua Franca. *Intercultural Pragmatics*. 6: 2, pp. 195–215.

Selinker, L. (1972) Interlanguage. *International Review of Applied Linguistics*. 10, pp. 209–31.

Shastri, S. V. (1986) Manual of information to accompany the Kolhapur Corpus of Indian English, for use with digital computers. http://khnt.hit.uib.no/icame/manuals/kolhapur/index.htm.

Shenton, H. N., Sapir, E. and Jespersen, O. (1931) *International communication: a symposium on the language problem*. London: K. Paul, Trench, Trubner & Co.

Shohamy, E. (2006) *Language policy: hidden agendas and new approaches*. New York: Routledge.

Siegel, J. (2010) *Second dialect acquisition*. Cambridge: Cambridge University Press.

Silverstein, M. (1979) Language structure and linguistic ideology. In P. Clyne, W. Hanks and C. Hofbauer (eds) *The elements of a parasession on linguistic units and levels*. Chicago: Chicago University Press, pp. 193–247.

Simpson, J. (2010) Tribute to Robert Burchfield. www.oed.com/public/editors/dictionary-editors.

Skutnabb-Kangas, T. (1986) Multilingualism and the education of minority children. In R. Phillipson and T. Skutnabb-Kangas (eds) *Linguicism rules in education*. Roskilde: Roskilde University Centre, Institute VI, pp. 42–72.

Skutnabb-Kangas, T. (1998) Human rights and language wrongs – a future for diversity? *Language Sciences*. 20: 1, pp. 5–28.

Skutnabb-Kangas, T. (2000) *Linguistic genocide in education – or world-wide diversity and human rights?* Mahwah, NJ: Lawrence Erlbaum.

Smith, L. E. (1976) English as an international auxiliary language. *RELC Journal*. 7: 2, pp. 38–43.

Smith, L. E. (1992) Spread of English and issues of intelligibility. In B. Kachru (ed.) *The other tongue: English across cultures*. Urbana and Chicago: University of Illinois Press, pp. 75–90.

Smith, L. E. and Nelson, C. L. (2006) World Englishes and issues of intelligibility. In B. Kachru, Y. Kachru and C. Nelson (eds) *The handbook of world Englishes*. Oxford: Blackwell, pp. 428–45.

Smyth, D. (2002) *Thai: an essential grammar*. London: Routledge.

Speak Good English Movement [SGEM] (2011) www.goodenglish.org.sg/category/about/about-us/

Sutton, G. (2008) *Concise encyclopedia of the original literature of Esperanto, 1887–2007*. New York: Mondial.

Suzuki, T. (1975) *Tozasareta gengo: nihongo no sekai [A closed language: the world of the Japanese language]*. Tokyo: Shincho Sensho.

Swallow, D. (2011) www.deborahswallow.com/category/cross-cultural-communication/page/4.

Tauli, V. (1968) *Introduction to a theory of language planning*. Uppsala: Almquist & Wiksells.

Thomason, S. and Kaufman, T. (1988) *Language contact, creolization, and genetic linguistics*. Berkeley, LA: University of California Press.

Toolan, M. (1997) Recentering English: New English and Global. *English Today 52*, pp. 3–10.

Trudgill, P. and Hannah, J. (1994) *International English: a guide to the varieties of standard English*. Third edition. New York: Edward Arnold.

Trudgill, P. and Hannah, J. (2008) *International English: a guide to the varieties of standard English*. Fifth edition. London: Hodder Education.

Twain, M. (1989 [1897]) *Following the equator: a journey around the world*, Vol. 1. New York: Dover.

UNESCO (1996) *Universal Declaration of Linguistic Rights*. Paris: UNESCO, www.unesco.org/cpp/uk/declarations/linguistic.pdf.

van Parijs, P. (2002) Linguistic justice. *Politics, philosophy and economics*. 1: 1, pp. 59–74.

VOICE (Vienna-Oxford International Corpus of English) (2011) www.univie. ac.at/voice/

Wallerstein, I. (1991) *Geopolitics and geoculture*. Cambridge: Cambridge University Press.

Watrous, M. (2010) *If you follow me*. New York: Harper Perennial.

Webster, N., 1991 [1789]. An essay on the necessity, advantages and practicability of reforming the mode of spelling, and of rendering the orthography of words correspondent to the pronunciation. In T. Crowley, (ed.) *Proper English? Readings in language, history, and cultural identity*. London: Routledge, pp. 81–93.

Wee, L. (2012) Language policy in Singapore: Singlish, national development and globalization. In E. J. Erling and P. Seargeant (eds) *English and international development*. Bristol: Multilingual Matters.

Wenger, E. (1998) *Communities of practice: learning, meaning, and identity*. Cambridge: Cambridge University Press.

Whitley, R. (2000) *The intellectual and social organisation of the sciences*. Oxford: Oxford University Press.

Widdowson, H. (1994) The ownership of English. *TESOL Quarterly*. 28: 2, pp. 377–389.

Widdowson, H. (2003) *Defining issues in English Language Teaching*. Oxford: Oxford University Press.

Woolard, K. (1998) Introduction: language ideology as a field of inquiry. In B. Schieffelin, K. Woolard and P. Kroskrity (eds) *Language ideologies*. Oxford: Oxford University Press, pp. 3–47.

Woolard, K. (2005) Language and identity choice in Catalonia: the interplay of contrasting ideologies of linguistic authority. Paper presented at *International Colloquium on Regulations of Societal Multilingualism in Linguistic Policies*. Berlin, June 2005.

Wright, S. (2009) The elephant in the room: language issues in the European Union. *European Journal of Language Policy*. 1: 2, pp. 93–120.

Xu Bing (2004) To frighten heaven and earth and make the spirits cry. *Visual Communication*. 3: 3, pp. 337–43.

index

(Terms in bold are listed in the Glossary)